DAMN FEW

DAMN FEW

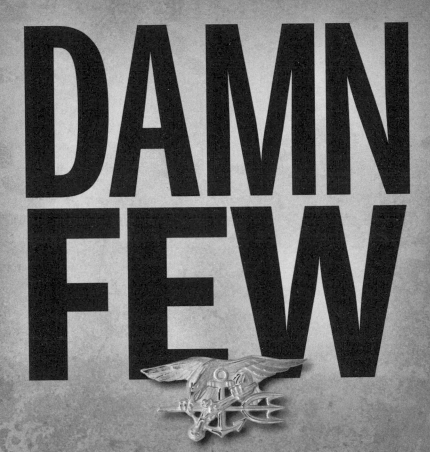

MAKING THE MODERN
SEAL WARRIOR

RORKE DENVER

and ELLIS HENICAN

HYPERION

NEW YORK

Title page photograph is by Rob Greer.
All other photographs are courtesy of the author.

Copyright © 2013 Rorke Denver

Library of Congress Cataloging-in-Publication Data has been applied for.

ISBN: 978-1-4013-2479-7

Hyperion books are available for special promotions and premiums. For details contact the HarperCollins Special Markets Department in the New York office at 212-207-7528, fax 212-207-7222, or email spsales@harpercollins.com.

FIRST EDITION

Book design by Renato Stanisic

10   9   8   7   6   5   4   3   2   1

SUSTAINABLE FORESTRY INITIATIVE   Certified Sourcing
www.sfiprogram.org
SFI-00993

THIS LABEL APPLIES TO TEXT STOCK

We try to produce the most beautiful books possible, and we are also extremely concerned about the impact of our manufacturing process on the forests of the world and the environment as a whole. Accordingly, we've made sure that all of the paper we use has been certified as coming from forests that are managed, to ensure the protection of the people and wildlife dependent upon them.

FOR MY WIFE, MY HEARTBEAT.

FOR MY MOM, MY CHAMPION.

FOR MY DAD, MY COMPASS.

FOR MY BROTHER, MY ARCHETYPE.

FOR MY GIRLS, MY FUEL.

And for my warrior brothers, my deepest respect.

Here's tae us.
Wha's like us?
Damn few,
And they're a' deid.

—Early Scottish toast

CONTENTS

INTRODUCTION:
SEAL TIME

The Sunni fighters had learned to mount three-prong mortar tubes on the beds of Toyota Hilux pickups. These little trucks were scooting around western Iraq like homicidal go-karts. They would pull up to a spot, and—*thoomp, thoomp, thoomp*—the mortar operator would launch three fast rounds, powerful enough to flip a Humvee or dispatch half a dozen U.S. Marines to the hospital or the morgue. Then the driver would slam on the gas and, pedal to the metal, they'd screech right out of there. Once they got proficient, no amount of reconnaissance or technology could pinpoint where these roving thugs would turn up next. By the time my SEAL teammates and I arrived in Anbar Province in the spring of 2006, the mortar boys were certified pros. My first night at Combat Outpost COWBOY outside Habbaniyah, a mortar round came flying over the concertina wire and landed thirty feet from me while I was in the head.

Message received.

"How can we help impact the battle space?" I asked the Marine lieutenant colonel who was in charge of the outpost. "How can we protect the base and help the Marines get after the enemy?"

He didn't have an immediate answer, but I could tell he hated how things stood. "We could definitely use some help here," he said.

These were the dark days before the Sunni Awakening, when the major tribal leaders finally got sick of the senseless violence of Al Qaeda in Iraq and turned noticeably more sympathetic to the U.S. cause. Back then, the area around Habbaniyah was one of the bloodiest in Iraq, truly one of the most lawless places on earth. Improvised explosive devices, rocket-propelled grenades, random sniper fire from hidden alleys and rooftops—the dangers seemed to lurk everywhere. The way the insurgents saw it, the Americans had invaded their country and so deserved to die. These people we were fighting wore no uniforms, answered to no central command, and displayed a maddening ingenuity at threatening the lives of U.S. troops. Conceiving an effective counterstrategy wasn't proving any easier than tracking down Saddam Hussein's weapons program.

The SEAL platoon we were replacing had been training Iraqi Scouts, the Iraqi version of our special forces, though the comparison was almost laughable. The Iraqis were mostly willing soldiers. Mostly willing. But I'm pretty sure Iraq had Boy Scouts with more field experience. Thanks to the efforts of SEAL Team One, the Iraqis had made some progress on the combat basics—how to plan a mission, how to communicate, how to shoot more effectively, and, if at all possible, how not to get themselves or their American trainers killed. Still, these budding special operators hadn't seen much action at all. They'd been going out on night patrols with our guys, which was standard procedure and would have kept them busy in some other war zone. But western Iraq's tribal region was almost entirely dead at night.

The camel spiders and the feral dogs never seemed to sleep. Everyone else was in bed by 8:30, including the pickup-truck mortar boys and their many violent cohorts. Then, as soon as the sun came up, the truck tires were squealing again and the mortar shells were raining down.

I knew we had to find a way to get the SEALs into the middle of the fight and somehow shift the balance in this lopsided battle zone.

First thing the next morning, I sat down with my senior guys from SEAL Team Three. "We gotta get outside in the daytime," I told them. "We have to make ourselves visible to the enemy. We'll beg them to fire on us. We'll be like human bait. But our snipers will be waiting in the palm groves. Our heavy gunners will be out there, too. We'll have to show some nerve here. We might have to dodge some sniper fire and some mortar shells. We'll just have to outshoot 'em, I guess. Anyone up for that?"

It wasn't really a question. I had been with these guys for more than two years already. I'd gone through SEAL training with some of them. It didn't matter that they'd barely had time to unpack the gear yet. These were real-deal, ready-for-action American warriors, as impatient as I was to find some action, just itching to test their training and preparation in a hot battle zone. I knew what those evil grins meant.

"This will get us fighting?" one of our heavy gunners asked.

"No doubt," I told him.

"Then, yeah," he said, as the others nodded and smiled. "We're good to go."

Three hours later, all sixteen of us—snipers Rolex and Ro, heavy gunners Big D and Bakes, communicators Lope and Cams, assistant officers Nick and John, and the rest of the platoon—backed by sixteen Iraqi Scouts, were on our feet, taking a late-morning stroll beyond the perimeter wire of Combat Outpost COWBOY and into the pockmarked outskirts of Habbaniyah. This was a banged-up neighborhood of high-walled houses, open sewers, and potholed streets. Cars and trucks zoomed past us. When bullets are flying, no one likes to drive slowly. Garbage burned in piles on the corners. One whiff of that could sap your appetite for the rest of the day. Most of the local people tried to stay inside. The blocks were eerily quiet until they were ferociously loud. Every block or two had another mosque, some modest, some grand, all of them sending out calls for prayer five times a day. In full kit and body armor in the 110-degree heat—long pants, long shirts, boots, gloves, battle helmet, weapons, ammo and water, probably sixty pounds of gear per man—we did not exactly blend in.

We might as well have carried a giant banner as we walked along: "Go ahead. Take your shot. The SEALs are here."

With the desert sun directly overhead, I took an overwatch position on a rooftop with our snipers. My assistant officers were positioned in a nearby palm grove with our heavy-weapon gunners, a perfect L-shaped ambush layout, when the first Toyota rolled up.

I don't think the Iraqi mortar team had a clue what was coming next. Given the free-fire zone Habbaniyah had become, they had no reason to expect anything at all. Standing on the truck bed, the mortar operator wasn't even looking our way. He was staring at what must have seemed like another easy target for an over-the-wire mortar attack. Maybe he'd hit the next American taking a bathroom break.

But he never got a chance to launch.

On the rooftop, Rolex and Ro put their scopes to their eyes. They tucked their chins tight and squeezed off round after round after round. Their weapons erupted like tightly held jackhammers—*pop-pop-pop-pop-pop*—the shots were flying that fast.

At almost exactly the same moment, Big D fired his ferocious Mk 48 from the grove. That let off more of a low bass rumble. The instant D fired, Nick and John directed the rest of the line to fire, too. All of them erupted immediately. Fast rounds and big rounds, loud and hard, caught the mortar gunner from several different angles, milliseconds apart. His body spun around like a jacket in a clothes drier—one, two, almost three full spins, before he tumbled from the bed of the pickup and onto the ragged concrete below.

Plunk.

From where I stood, I had a straight-on view of the driver. He looked frozen in terror, almost white. His eyes made bull's-eye circles and his hands jumped three inches off the steering wheel. Without glancing one way or another or once touching the brake, he dove out the side window with the truck still rolling forward. As the driver's body was still in the air, one of my snipers swung around and nailed him squarely in the side of his head. The driver's body splattered to the concrete just as the truck careened into a ditch on the left and finally came to a stop.

Our platoon had been on the ground less than a day by then. The guys were bleary from travel and smacked by the heat. But already we were doing what we had come for. We had begun our historic campaign to redefine the battle space and shift the momentum of a frustrating and long-running war.

"I like working the day shift," I told Ro and Rolex as they put their sniper rifles down and we climbed off the roof.

"Any shift," Ro said.

It didn't take long for word to spread across Anbar. A new group of predators were in town now, and they were working around the clock.

HERE IN THE second decade of America's War on Terror, conventional military methods just aren't getting it done anymore. Massive invasions, long occupations, extended nation-building campaigns—they still have their place in the U.S. military arsenal. But some of their legendary effectiveness has definitely begun to fade. Those old approaches are hugely expensive, in blood and in money. The commitments just go on and on. And far too often—Korea, Vietnam, Afghanistan, Iraq—the long-term results don't quite match the hopes going in.

None of this should come as a big surprise. Those old ways of fighting were designed in a very different era for a very different set of threats. We'll never defeat our twenty-first-century enemies with World War II battle plans.

Today's brewing conflicts are mobile and unpredictable. They pop up quickly and almost anywhere. Iran. Syria. North Korea. Somalia. Venezuela. Take your pick of pugnacious countries and nagging trouble spots. The Pak-Afghan border. The Palestinian territories. The Hindu Kush. The fighters are armed and itchy and impervious to calm diplomacy. How much longer until drones and tactical nukes are up for sale on eBay? Just log on to PayPal and type in the dollar amount.

War isn't just nation against nation anymore. It's tribal warlords crazed with ancient hatreds. It's thugs in the Horn of Africa grabbing Westerners for profit and fun. It's a fugitive al Qaeda mastermind holed up in a compound in Pakistan with two or three wives and a secret cache of porn. It's a quiet village in western Iraq that may or may not be housing a makeshift bomb factory, depending on whose intel you believe.

Over the past decade, America's top leaders kept asking what works, what doesn't, and why. More and more often, their answer is the same.

"Send in the SEALs."

And we keep performing spectacularly.

Small, nimble units of highly trained warriors, we are experts at missions that traditional armies were never built for. Lightning-quick commando raids. Highly orchestrated assaults. Discreet operations in challenging environments. Extractions, recoveries, and other bold maneuvers that don't even have names yet. It's an amazing run we've been on since 9/11, and I don't see it slowing down soon. Osama bin Laden. The *Maersk Alabama*. That aid-worker rescue in Somalia. Momentum-shifting operations in Afghanistan and Iraq.

The Army, Big Navy, the Marines—they're great at what they do. They are huge and potent and necessary. But those guys are linear, and we aren't. We're designed for speed and creativity. There's a reason to take the 3/2 Marines and say, "You start here. Get to there and destroy everything in between." They get it done. But if you're saying, "Start here, get to there, kill two guys, capture three, then come out without anybody knowing you were there"—our phone should be ringing off the hook. And it is.

There are barely 2,500 SEALs. We didn't even exist as an organization before Vietnam, when President Kennedy reconstituted the Navy's leftover World War II–era dive teams into a naval counterterror force capable of operating on sea, air, and land. We are a tiny organization compared to the big boys. But we keep achieving things no one else seems able to. Pound for pound, man for man, our success is hard to argue with. We keep proving ourselves over and over again. We are the most resourceful problem solvers on the modern battlefield, ideal warriors for the kinds of wars America is fighting now.

So where do we find the men for these high-risk missions? What combination of talent, training, and instinct do they bring to the fight? Are warriors like these born or made? How can we get more of them?

For the past four years, it has been my job to answer those questions and help create the next generation of SEALs. After completing the SEALs' brutal training program and leading more than two hundred combat missions overseas, I have been the officer in charge of every phase of training, basic and advanced, for these extraordinary assault teams. It is a profound and awesome duty at an urgent and dangerous time.

With all the SEALs' recent successes, we have been getting a level of attention and acclaim we are not used to. It's been very flattering and certainly well deserved. It's produced some stresses as well. But something important has been missing from the discussion. People keep describing what we do, but no one has even scratched the surface of how and why. The unique psychology behind it. What really makes it work. The extraordinary character of those involved. The carefully crafted motivation and training techniques. The many lessons for the future of America's relationship with the world.

This is my account of how we create these special warriors and how they are changing the modern battlefield. The story features a cast of lethal and aggressive warriors, who turn out to be amazingly dedicated and patriotic men. It's not just a tale of heart-pounding gunfights, though we have plenty of those. It's not just a recap of our withering training regime, though that's how we got here. It's the up-close-and-personal revelation of who we are and how we got here. Much of this story has never been fully told before. Secrecy remains an important part of what we do, and there are some details that must remain secret. You will not find them here. But as I have learned as a SEAL leader, openness and honesty can be powerful weapons as well. In that spirit, we have been explaining ourselves and our vital mission as we never have before. With the Navy's full support, a group of us helped to make a uniquely realistic movie called *Act of Valor*, sharing key SEALs lessons with the world. Ours is a story that really needs to be told—loyally, truthfully, and well.

I tell it the only way I know how, through my own experiences and insights as a proud SEAL officer, informed by the experiences and insights of my closest brothers and friends. To them and to my family, I owe nearly everything.

My own SEAL dream was launched by a book I found inspiring. My hope is that this one teaches lessons that go far beyond my life and my journey, past the battlefields I have fought on, inspiring a whole new generation of warriors to carry on this special dream that all of us share.

PART ONE

Learning It

1

TRAIN TOUGH

We should remember that one man is much the same as another and that he is best who is trained in the severest school.
—Thucydides

The M4 is a loud rifle. The Mk 48 machine gun is even louder. And the boom from a .50-cal comes on so strong, it can rattle nearby buildings and shake large hills.

On a gun range, we all wear ear protection. We have to, those weapons are deafening. But when the battle was raging and I was squeezing off rounds, I swear I never heard the sound of my own weapon, barely an inch from my right ear. I felt the recoil. I smelled the smoke. I saw the brass fly out of the ejection port. I knew I was getting rounds in on my target. But it was like someone had reached a giant hand onto the battlefield and turned down the volume on the shooting soundtrack.

There's actual science behind this. When a lion roars, the sound is so loud—114 decibels or so, the rough equivalent of a jackhammer on a midtown Manhattan sidewalk—the lion should suffer serious hearing damage. But that doesn't happen. When the lion is in full battle cry, something in his genetic coding knows to protect him from the earsplitting volume of his own ferocious roar.

Human predators have that mechanism, too, as I discovered immediately on the battlefield.

War is just a more extreme version of the hunt. The reality of a living target changes everything. The experience of warfare—not just psychological but physical as well—sent me all the way back to a basic predatory-survival mode. It eliminated everything that wasn't needed in the struggle between life and death. And it heightened all those things that were. My concentration. My intensity. My single-mindedness. It made me better just when I needed it most. Then, when the fight was over or I'd gotten behind a wall or a vehicle and that moment of absolute urgency had passed, the volume exploded back on again.

"Good shot," I could hear my teammate say.

We looked like a couple of novice bus drivers who'd gotten separated from their routes. Two baby ensigns, my buddy Jason and I, walking across the parking lot in our pressed dress blues without any medals at all. We hadn't earned any yet. But as we made our way to the Grinder that morning, both of us could just feel it. Something momentous was about to occur.

"Man, this is it," Jason said to me.

"We're here," I agreed.

We'd completed the thirteen-week course at Officer Candidate School in Pensacola, Florida, and earned the Navy's entry-level officer rank. We'd driven out to California in my creaky Jeep, stopping in Colorado to spend a few days with my mom. Orders in hand, Jason and I made our way across the magnificent Coronado Bridge, high enough for any Navy ship to go under, except for an aircraft carrier, arriving at the SEALs' beachfront compound across the bay from downtown San Diego. We knew we were following in the footsteps of the SEALs who'd come before us. This is where it began for all of them. Now, finally, it was our turn.

I felt like a young Spartan just starting the *agoge*, fully aware of the warrior tradition I was entering, still in awe at the rigorous training I was about to receive. There was no doubt in my mind that morning. I had come to one of the most exhilarating and intimidating moments of my life.

Anyone expecting some high-tech, James Bond facility would be taken aback by how basic the Naval Special Warfare Center is. No retina scans, no laser guns—just a complex of low-slung cinder-block buildings behind a high razor-ribbon fence, some classrooms, barracks, a mess hall, a very large obstacle course, and a gym, all of it jammed so close to the Pacific Ocean you can hear the surf from almost anywhere. *Functional* would be a good word for the architecture, though the views are out of this world.

At the center of it all is the Grinder. For SEALs, the Grinder is sacred ground. It's our crossroads and our town square, a big, open, asphalt rectangle with administrative and training offices along all four sides. SEALs are always coming and going from the Grinder. A lot of SEAL physical training happens on the Grinder. In summer months, the concrete gets so blisteringly hot, instructors have to hose it down so the recruits won't singe their hands doing push-ups. The Grinder is where SEAL graduations are held and where, like a constant taunt, the SEAL exit bell hangs. A famous sign is also there: THE ONLY EASY DAY WAS YESTERDAY.

There wasn't much of a welcome when Jason and I arrived. A

woman in the Student Control Office gave us our room assignments in the barracks. A Navy petty officer I figured must be an instructor looked up from a file just long enough to say matter-of-factly: "After you drop off your bags, you two get into PT gear. Go out to the beach. The class is working out right now. Join them." We did what we were told. We threw on shorts and white T-shirts and ran out to the beach, where about sixty young men in identical shorts and shirts were on their backs in the sun. They looked like human scissors, frantically kicking their feet up and down.

"Oh, a couple of new ensigns," one of the instructors called out as Jason and I trotted up. "You just gonna stand there, *sirs*?"

It was the first of many sarcastic "sirs" I would hear from an enlisted instructor, who had to understand that even the freshest officer candidate could someday become his platoon commander or future team commanding officer. But a "sir" from him couldn't remotely be taken as a sign of deference or respect. The enlisted instructors made perfectly clear who they thought was in charge, and it wasn't some rosy-cheeked officer. That was a lesson that would stick with me for years: Rank is nice, but it isn't the only gauge of power or importance. In training or at war, the bigger question is who has the influence, the knowledge, and the personal authority—who has the balls—to make things happen. On the beach that day, I was in that instructor's world.

"You guys will PT right in front of everybody," he said. Jason and I went to the front of the group and got busy.

After all my years playing sports, I thought I was in pretty good condition. But I had never worked out like this before. Set after set of push-ups and sit-ups were challenging enough—fast and hard. But this particular instructor was some kind of fiend for these up-and-down flutter kicks. He made us do hundreds of them. I noticed he was kicking right along.

As the fresh recruits struggled and groaned, five or six other instructors were swimming like sharks through the class, looking for people to destroy. It didn't take long for one of these instructor-enforcers to stand menacingly over Jason, who looked like he was hurting even worse than I was.

"Ensign!" he said sternly. "You don't think you can do this?"

As Jason tried to answer, for some reason my mind wandered off to an old hunting joke I'd heard from my dad. Two hunters are being chased by a bear in the woods when one of them stops to put on a pair of running shoes.

"What are you doing?" the first hunter asks. "You'll never outrun that bear."

"I know," his friend answers. "But all I have to do is outrun you." That must have been my brain's way of telling me: As long as the instructor is yelling at Jason, he isn't worrying about me.

Jason kept it going through the pain. So did I. As the hard-nosed instructor moved along to someone else, all I could think was, Wow! This is day one, huh?

Not even.

It was pretraining. The instructors were still waiting for a full class to assemble. Some kind of storm was clearly gathering. No one could guess what devastation it might deliver. But I was getting my first real taste of BUD/S.

BUD/S, or Basic Underwater Demolition/SEAL, is the toughest military entry program anywhere. I've been through Army Ranger School. I've studied all the other elite basic training programs including Army Special Forces, Air Force Pararescue Jumpers, British SAS, and Dutch KCT, four tough ones—and had friends in all of them. None of those schools is as difficult to survive as BUD/S. It's a three-phase, six-month onslaught of physical and mental challenges that push prospective SEALs to the absolute limit of their endurance—and then beyond. No one is supposed to die during BUD/S. Steps are taken to avoid that. For their safety, the recruits are constantly hydrated and the instructors carefully time how long anyone stays in ice-cold water. But the demands really are superhuman, meaning they go far past what any sane person would expect to endure anywhere, ever.

Every SEAL must graduate from BUD/S. You're not a SEAL unless you do. BUD/S is what distinguishes our community from all those other fine special-operations forces. When a SEAL encounters another SEAL he has never met before, the first question will almost always be: "What BUD/S class were you in?" And then they'll start to argue about whose BUD/S class was tougher, each totally certain that his class was the toughest ever in the whole history of BUD/S.

Toughness really is the standard at BUD/S.

Or as one of the instructors told Class 223 when we had finally all arrived: "BUD/S is tough because tough makes better SEALs." Then the instructors got busy proving it.

Our days were packed with boat races, heavy-log drills, and open-ocean swims. We did calisthenics with medieval ferocity—bursts of 3,000 sit-ups, 7,000 lunges, God-only-knows-how-many flutter kicks. And then there was SEALs' famous twenty-station obstacle course. Laid out on the sand in a giant square, the O-course tested stamina, balance, coordination, and upper-body strength with rope climbs, balance logs, tire jumps, monkey bars, and a barbed-wire sand crawl. The stations had appropriately twisted names: the Weaver, the Spider Wall, the Slide for Life, and the Dirty Name, so called because of all the expletives shouted in exhaustion there. The cargo net climb was frighteningly high. All I'll say about that is good luck if you have a problem with heights.

We ran almost everywhere we went. The running started at 5 a.m. with a bleary-eyed four-mile sprint in boots and camouflage pants. We didn't stop running until we hit the barracks mattresses at night.

"Drop!" the instructors ordered, seemingly at random. Immediately everyone had to hit the dirt or the concrete or the sand or the classroom floor. Our heads had to face the nearest body of water—the ocean, the bay, or a swimming pool—acknowledging the SEALs' historic connection to water. Then we had to bang out 20, 30, or 50 fast push-ups. When the instructors weren't yelling "Drop," they were often calling "Hit the surf!" Wherever we were, whatever we were doing, and whatever we had on, we went running for the ocean and dove in.

A word about water temperature: There is no way to fully explain how painfully cold San Diego Bay and the open Pacific Ocean can be, even in the fall. The temperature goes from colder to coldest. It never feels just cold. The very first time I heard "Hit the surf," I still had a smile on my face, thinking, We're gonna run over the hill and hit the surf. This is exactly what I've been waiting for. Coming from northern California, I figured the Pacific off San Diego, not ten miles from the Mexican border, had to be balmy and inviting. Wrong! We all went charging over the berm, then fifty yards down to the water, and dove in. The water was freezing, freezing cold. I couldn't believe how cold it was. As I came running out, all I could think was, Wow, swimming is fun. Leaping into the glacial chill is definitely not.

To get a sense of how cold that water feels, try a little experiment On a cold winter day, stand outside with a hose and drench yourself from head to toe. Then stand in front of a fan for ten or fifteen minutes. If it's hot outside, fill a bathtub with cold water and ice. Twenty minutes of that will give you a good idea. Wet cold just feels colder than dry cold. I have seen BUD/S students jackhammer-shivering so violently they pulled a muscle. Their fingers got so numb, they needed a buddy to button their uniform tops.

Not everyone suffers the same level of debilitation. Some people adjust pretty well to being in cold water. I'm one of the more fortunate ones. With my thick build—six foot one, about 205 pounds in the fall of 1998—I held my body warmth better than many of the skinnier guys held theirs. But that was just by comparison. It was unnerving for everyone, feeling that frigid water pushing the body temperature swiftly downward. San Diego Bay is usually a few degrees warmer than the ocean, somewhere in the mid-50s Fahrenheit. But even the bay water could make your teeth chatter and your fingers go numb. And for most people, the open Pacific felt like a countdown to hypothermia, even during a hard, competitive swim.

While BUD/S students were often wet and cold, one thing we weren't was hungry. The recruits were practically force-fed. Bacon, eggs, cereal, waffles, juice, and coffee for breakfast; big platters of meat, potatoes, and vegetables for lunch and dinner. We are not the Army Rangers, where starvation is used as a training tool. SEAL recruits burn so many calories, they constantly need to be replenished. Otherwise we would die. I'm not kidding. With all the physical exertion, a student could literally eat an extra-large, triple-cheese, meat-lover's pizza with a stick of butter on top, call it lunch, and still not have the calories to carry through to dinner.

My classmates and I were constantly measuring ourselves as individuals. But right from the start, we couldn't help noticing something striking about the BUD/S approach: No matter how onerous the demands became, we almost never faced them alone. Our first week of training, everyone was assigned a swim buddy, another student to exercise with, keep an eye on, help along as necessary, and, in a very real sense, share the BUD/S experience with. The class was also divided into boat crews, usually one officer and six enlisted men. These relationships became the foundation for SEAL relationships to come.

My swim buddy was my roommate Matt, a fellow officer candidate from Colorado who remains my closest SEAL friend today. Matt has a razor-sharp mind, amazing leadership qualities, and an infectious we-can-do-this self-confidence. To this day, I would trust

Matt with my life. We pushed each other, motivated each other, joked with each other, and always watched each other's backs. Each week, we and all the other swim-buddy pairs took to the open ocean for a grueling two-mile, a test we'd either pass or fail together.

One duo in our class failed to stay within the required six feet of each other on that swim. When they got back to the beach looking totally exhausted, the instructors handed them a heavy, cumbersome, six-foot rope with a loop on either end.

"This will make sure you stay together," one of the instructors told the pair. "Now go swim it again."

You might not stay with the same swim buddy forever. People leave, get injured, or fall back to later classes or swap to help a struggling classmate. I had four swim buddies by the time I finished BUD/S, including one who was in danger of being dropped from the class because he kept failing his swimming tests. I became his swim buddy and helped to get him through. We understood that once we became fully deployed, combat-ready SEALs, we would all be expected to perform with high efficiency in tightly knit teams. But these relationships, the swim buddies and the boat crews, become over time the very foundation of the SEAL community, direct precursors to future eight-man squads, sixteen-man platoons, thirty-two man task units, and then teams of several hundred men, all of it intricately layered into a rock-solid SEAL brotherhood.

You'll see the results of this personal tightness up and down the SEAL ranks. Two snipers working in perfect coordination, a shooter and a spotter. An errant BUD/S student being told to "hit the surf," supported by four or five of his buddies who just decide to dive in, too. A senior admiral and his force-master chief, not formal swim buddies, but still working in total synch. From the battlefield shoot-out to the barroom brawl, from the family crisis to furniture-moving day, SEALs come to expect it: They can count on other SEALs.

Two retired SEALs can meet for the first time on a street corner. If a crisis breaks out, they'll be working together to solve it, instantly and seamlessly, swim buddies again. That interconnectedness was woven through everything at BUD/S. Working as a unit, seven strong young men could lift a 180- to 200-pound log about the size of a telephone pole and run down the beach—but only if every man was giving his all. If someone wasn't, the whole crew was at a big disadvantage.

The same group dynamic applied, even more so, every time we climbed into our IBSs, or Inflatable Boat Small. Those rugged rubber boats, black with bright yellow trim, looked like they might have come from a white-water rafting company. They were strong enough to handle almost any kind of abuse. They and the students in them were the heart and soul of BUD/S teamwork.

For hours at a time, we'd be out on the ocean or the bay in our IBSs in pounding, maximum-effort races—winning crew gets to sit out the next one. "It pays to be a winner in BUD/S," the instructors kept reminding us. And they made sure it did.

"When you guys get to the battlefield," one instructor told us, "your squad will perform well together or it won't. You'll get the job done, you'll save each other's lives—or you won't. Out there, it'll be a lot more important than a boat race."

When we weren't paddling our boats, we were dragging them, lifting them, filling them with sand, dumping the sand out, and running down the beach with those damn, 110-pound inflatable boats balanced on our heads. Some guys complained they were getting bald spots from the constant rubbing of sandy boat bottoms on their heads.

My boat crew—Matt, Trey, Coop, Mike, and Carlo, plus some rotating others—were absolute animals, studs all. Since Matt and Trey were officers like me, we had three boat crew members who were always ready to lead. That was a solid advantage, and it gave me two real peers to bounce things off of. Depending on each other as we did, our crew got very tight. Even today, some of my closest friends are my fellow Boat Crew III members from BUD/S.

From the start of bud/s, we all knew the numbers, the brutal wash-out rate for the one thousand or so young men who are accepted into five or six BUD/S classes every year. We knew that at some point before graduation, 70 to 80 percent of our class would likely be gone. In most cases, people wouldn't get kicked out. Demoralized and exhausted, they'd choose to leave. Somewhere between the grueling log races, the frigid ocean swims, the small-boat marathons, the endless sit-ups and push-ups, the underwater knot-tying panics, the constant verbal beat-downs from a cadre of barking instructors who never seem satisfied with anything—most of our classmates would soon be asking themselves, What exactly am I doing here? And without an adequate answer they'd conclude that, despite whatever SEAL dreams they'd had, this just wasn't for them. They'd DOR, Drop on Request. They would walk away from whatever crazy abuse they happened to be suffering at the moment and signal their decision by giving the famous SEAL bell the required three rings, hoping never to be so cold, wet, sandy, sleep-deprived, emotionally finished, or physically spent ever, ever, ever again.

In my BUD/S class, we lost a couple on opening day. One of my classmates got up and left during the very first classroom session, even before he'd been asked to do a single exercise. He rang the bell and was gone.

The clang of that bell, along with the barking instructors and the rolling surf, really was the audio track of BUD/S. It rang at all hours of the day and night, letting everybody know: "There goes another one."

The bell was never hard to find. It hung right outside the First Phase instructors' office on the Grinder. Following long-standing SEAL tradition, those who were ready to leave laid their green trainee helmets on the ground in a line beside the bell. Depending on how many classmates have quit already, that line of helmets could be short or very, very long. And then came the rings, each one with its own sad story and its own special sound.

Some exiting students, I noticed, pulled the bell cord as softly as they possibly could, as if they were hoping no one would notice. Others gave it such a fuck-you pull, it was like they were hell-bent on denting the bell or yanking it off the stand. Then there were the ring-once guys. They'd ring the bell once, walk away, come back and ring again, then walk away, then in a final realization that their SEAL training was over, they'd give three resigned rings and glumly leave.

There were some total refusers who said, "I'm outta here, but I'm not ringing any damn bell." This was handled off the grid. Nothing physical—just a bitingly intense conversation. One of the chiefs pulled the person aside and said: "This program and this community are bigger than any one individual—bigger than you or me. When you disrespect the bell and the program, you really have proven you don't belong here. Now go be a man. Ring the bell. Do it right. Don't disrespect the community or yourself." As far I know, that message was always received.

The truth is that many people just aren't ready for this, whatever their level of desire. It is horrible to watch. We've had students everyone was pulling for, just hoping they could get through. But they didn't have the physiology or the athletic ability to perform at this level. We had an expat from Great Britain, a pudgy, little, unassuming guy—five foot seven, maybe 165. He had never been an athlete a day in his life. But he was Richard the Lion-hearted. He gave everything a human could give. He just wasn't physically strong enough.

When he left, one of the instructors sat the whole class down and said: "Some of you have physical attributes that are a gift from God. If you can find inside yourselves half the heart this guy did, you'll be phenomenal SEALs."

Not being strong enough or physically prepared doesn't always mean the dream is over forever. An officer who leaves may never return. But an enlisted man who falls short and leaves can return for another shot. If you haven't gotten through Hell Week, you have to start over from the beginning. If you've made it past Hell Week and then get injured, you can pick up wherever you left off. The rules say you're supposed to sit out for two years before returning. But there are cases, like the young Brit, where instructors write a letter to the commanding officer of whatever ship the person has ended up on, saying, "We want to see that guy back soon."

Most decidedly, that is not a group that includes the bell refusers.

I understood why people quit. Truly, SEAL training isn't for everyone. But I was still sad to see some individuals go. You get close to people in a hurry at BUD/S. My buddy Jason, whom I'd arrived with, left. He had an old shoulder injury that started acting up, and I think a couple of weeks of SEAL training also opened his eyes. "I don't know if this is for me," he told me a couple of weeks in. "I'm not sure I'm one of these guys." He didn't seem all that broken up when he was dropped for medical cause. Still, we'd started together. He was a bright guy and an excellent friend. I definitely missed having Jason around.

At the same time, there was something about hearing that bell ring that was also affirming. It was primal, something deep inside. For those of us who stayed, the sound of that bell actually made us feel good. The bell would ring, and we would think to ourselves, We're still here and those other guys aren't. We're that much closer to the finish line.

After a while, that bell started sounding like a twisted tuning fork—not taunting, not warning, but calling like a mythological Siren to those who remained. Withdrawing was such a public act, it sent a message to everyone: "This place is exactly what you thought it was, a place for the best of the best. That ringing bell proves it."

I knew one thing already: However relentless the instructors, however high the demands, I would find a way to get through BUD/S. I was not going to quit. That's not how I was raised. That's not who I was. I'd waited long enough to be here. I had made my decision carefully. I wasn't just testing the waters. This is what I wanted to do. I certainly wasn't interested in some regular job in the U.S. Navy, which is where I'd be sent if I bombed out of SEAL training. And that positive self-talk, that sense of absolute inevitability, that refusal to even consider anything else—that turned out to be the elusive key to doing well at BUD/S. I was already getting into the SEAL mind-set.

But that early, intense PT was just a beginning. We had much more training to do, and what came next harked back to the earlier frogman days of the SEALs. Soon enough, the instructors were leading us into the Combat Training Tank. It's not that the SEAL teams have been doing so many combat-swimmer operations lately. It's not that future warfare will be fought in masks, fins, and dive tanks. It's that, as the special-operation force of a Navy, the SEALs are intimately linked to the oceans. There's no tougher environment to train in. So every future SEAL must demonstrate a high degree of proficiency in the water. A big part of the proving takes place at BUD/S in the CTT, the SEALs' specially equipped, Olympic-length training pool. The tank is outfitted with various ledges, hooks, and platforms and has windows below the water line like you might see at Sea World or in the shark tank at your local aquarium. Those windows give a great view of the many training ordeals occurring underwater.

To get through training, every recruit has to master the fifty-meter underwater swim, combative lifesaving, and underwater knot-tying.

These are the building blocks to more advanced SEAL skills like af-fixing a bomb or a mine to the side of a ship. For the drown-proofing test, a student has to float in a dead man's position, feet tied together, hands bound behind his back. Tied up like a rodeo calf, each student has to swim two pool lengths with a modified dolphin kick and bob up and down in fifteen feet of water. Sinking to the bottom, rocketing to the top, grabbing a big gulp of oxygen—the trick is to maintain a steady rhythm while getting enough air. It's all about remaining calm and keeping your lungs filled.

These tests aren't easy, but for many students it's the underwater knot-tying or the lifesaving test that strikes the most panic. In knot-tying, you can't shoot back to the surface until your ropes are tied and untied and you've gotten a thumbs-up sign from the underwater instructor. The knots—the bowline, the square knot, the Becket's bend, the clove hitch, and the right angle—are basic enough. But such intricate hand-eye coordination isn't so easy on an underwater breath-hold while the seconds tick painfully by.

I didn't expect the lifesaving test to be so hard. In theory, it wasn't so different from the usual grab-and-go at the local YMCA. But one of the BUD/S instructors just about drowned me. He was under six feet, weighed maybe 150 pounds. I was supposed to grab him in the water and pull him to the side of the pool. How hard could this be? When I played high school water polo, I was the team's hole set or two-meter man, the position reserved for the strongest, most aggres-sive water-treading wrestler.

Never judge a SEAL by his build.

The wiry instructor let me grab him. As soon as I had a good lock, I thought, "I'll have him at the side of the pool in seconds."

To this day, I have no idea how or what happened next. He started kicking and drove me straight to the bottom of the pool. He spun me like a top. I have never experienced such fury underwater when trying to hold on to someone. He was like a bucking bronco. I really thought I might drown. While I managed to hold on and get him to the edge of the pool, I was seriously gasping for air. With my heart still racing, he splashed pool water in my face. All he said was: "You pass. Get out of the water."

There was something different about these SEAL instructors. He should not have been able to do that to me.

But for most students, it is the fifty-meter underwater swim that is the real lung-crusher, the real test of prowess in the water. Each trainee stands at the side, jumps in feetfirst, does a forward somersault, then swims across the width of the pool and back, a total of fifty meters, the same distance at which Olympic medal winners are tested. People pass out all the time on this one. An instructor is assigned to each trainee, shadowing the student in the water from above.

"Here's the deal, gents," one of our instructors said to our group, pumping up the drama just a bit. "When you jump into the water and do your front somersault, start pulling and stroking as fast as you can and get a good rhythm right away. If you are smart, you'll go down to the bottom and stay down there. Your lungs, when they are under pressure, they will shrink, which will give you more oxygen than near the surface. The problem is that, when you start coming back up, your lungs start expanding. You can experience what we call a shallow-water blackout."

He made it seem as if that happened all the time.

"Here's what I'm gonna do because I like you guys," the instructor said. "I don't care if you pass out underwater as long as you hit the pool wall. If you are about to go tits up—if you are about to pass out underwater—and you have enough momentum to hit the wall with a little glide, I'll consider that a pass. We'll pull you up. We'll revive you with the slap of life. And you'll pass."

That didn't sound so great to the student standing next to me. He leaned over and whispered: "Is this for real? Is this guy crazy? I'm not gonna purposely try to pass out underwater." As it turned out, the instructors weren't exaggerating by too much. Quite a few of our classmates had to be slapped back to consciousness.

But that was just BUD/S. If it wasn't one thing, it was another. It was everything at once. Physical, mental, teamwork, students pushed to the breaking point to see who folded and who didn't.

Something unexpected was happening as I got my footing there. I actually started enjoying the experience. It was hard. Many of the physical training evolutions bordered on torture. But as the days rolled on, I felt a growing sense of satisfaction that I was able to meet even the toughest challenges the instructors threw at us. That was building my confidence and my connection to this brotherhood.

The water was cold, but I could stand it. The PT was brutal, but I could do it. Some of the physical challenges actually became fun. You'd never call the SEALs' obstacle course a breeze. But as I began to master it, I could see my own progress, and I enjoyed the way that felt.

The instructors could certainly be relentless. Some of them could be real knuckle-draggers. But still, there was something about them that I couldn't help liking. The unique way they carried themselves. The way they talked. They had a confidence about them, a good form of intensity, a cockiness, almost. They were smart-asses, a lot of them, always making jokes. If you weren't scared of them, I discovered, they liked to banter and have fun. They engaged with the students and each other in a way that said, "I know who I am. I'm comfortable with that. You could probably learn some things by hanging around with me." I never heard any of them say that, not directly. But almost all of them exuded it. Despite their constant demands, I thought these guys were cool. Bring it on.

As I was making my way through BUD/S, I didn't grasp all the nuances of the curriculum. That would take years for me to sort out.

The need for physical strength was obvious. Someday we would all be called to perform even more challenging evolutions in war zones around the world. But until I'd completed BUD/S, joined a SEAL team, been out on fierce combat assault missions, then returned to Coronado as a BUD/S phase officer and begun teaching the things that I had learned, I didn't fully appreciate how brilliantly designed the mental component of BUD/S is.

Only then did every grunt and grind make perfect sense to me. Only then did I come to see that a SEAL's mental toughness is even more important than his physical fitness.

BUD/S embraces that concept in two ways. First, it weeds out people who, while physically strong enough, will never be able to develop the mental strength to be a SEAL. If you can't withstand the pressure of tying a knot in the Combat Training Tank, you'll never keep your cool when someone's pointing a gun at you in Afghanistan.

BUD/S takes people who have the mental toughness and natural aggressiveness to be SEALs, and hones that powerful mind-set. The training builds their confidence. It makes winning second nature to them. It creates a default mental attitude that says, "I can do this. No challenge is too big. Nothing will defeat me. I am part of a seriously elite unit."

That sense of being a part of something so special—a true brotherhood—is what allows a man to get up every day, ready to put his life on the line.

2

BUD/S SECRETS

Weapons are an important factor in war, but not the decisive one. It is man and not the material that counts.
—Mao Tse-tung

I've never seen a SEAL have his gun jam and wonder, What do I do next?

In a wild exchange one morning, one of our .50-gunners was firing from a gun-truck turret when his weapon suddenly jammed. That .50 is a big, heavy, man's gun. It takes two hands to pull the charging system back. As the handles are flying forward and the powerful springs are snapping into place, you could easily chop a finger off. You have to own that gun whether you're shooting it or working on it.

Not wasting an instant, he pulled out a screwdriver and stuck it into the crease between the belt-fed magazine and the gun, when the tip of the screwdriver promptly broke off.

"Get me a screwdriver!" the gunner yelled.

Within a couple of seconds, another team member was reaching up with a fresh one, but the gunner shook his head. He'd already reached his stubby fingers inside the sizzling-hot weapon, moving things around, tossing out a tiny piece of brass, making little adjustments no one else could see, and clearing the jam from the gun.

He was back in the fight just like that.

When you ask your gun to fire and it doesn't, that could be a deadly problem. We train for hours on how to respond to that. Every gun has its own unique malfunctions. The battlefield is an especially unforgiving terrain for a weapon, a perfect swirl of dust, mud, sand, dirt, and grime, all of it just itching to climb inside your gun. Even less forgiving is the enemy, who never waits for us to get our guns ready before he shoots.

At the range, we have special malfunction drills for each make and model of weapon. We load a dummy round inside the magazines that will cause the gun to stop firing. You never know when that bad round is coming through. Now, how quickly can you clean the jam and get back into the fight?

Our basic M4 is not an especially rugged gun. You could carry the enemy's AK-47 through a sandstorm then drag it through the mud. That gun might feel like a rattletrap, but it'll keep on firing. Our guns are built with such precision, they are much more accurate. They are also more temperamental.

So our guys have to be good.

"You have heard the harsh statistics about how tough this place is," I would tell each new BUD/S class after I became the head of First Phase of training. "But here's a number you may not be aware of. If you can make it until Friday of Hell Week, you've got a ninety percent chance of succeeding in this course. Almost all the attrition happens in the first five weeks."

That was true when I went through my basic SEAL training. It's true today.

"So if you can just bang out a little more than a month of really, really phenomenal work," I would say to the students, "you have an extremely good chance of putting that Trident on your chest and being a part of this brotherhood."

That's one of the little-known facts of BUD/S. There are many others, but that's one these SEAL recruits need to hear early in the game. Yes, the course is super-demanding. Yes, Hell Week is as hellish as it sounds, as those who make it that far discover soon enough. But the lethal part of SEAL basic training is concentrated near the start. "If you had to," I would ask students, "couldn't you survive almost anything for five weeks? After that, the brutal numbers will be on your side."

There was so much I didn't understand about SEAL training while I was in BUD/S. I hadn't been to war yet. No student could possibly have perspective in a whirlwind like BUD/S. But I was fortunate. As time went on, I had the opportunity to test what I had learned in some very hairy combat situations. I then became responsible for hundreds of young men who had the same SEAL dreams I'd had. I ran all the major phases of SEAL training, basic and advanced, and guided our training program through some turbulent times. By now, I can say with confidence: I understand the process as well as anyone.

Over the years, countless people have offered their views on what makes SEAL training so effective and how best to survive the experience. Physicians, psychologists, nutritionists, physical trainers, clergymen, military theorists, media commentators, and probably a couple of storefront psychics, too—they've all weighed in with confident pronouncements. Do this many push-ups. Eat that kind of vegetable. Make a vow with your swim buddy that neither one of you will quit. Thanks for the pet theories, guys. But as far as I'm concerned, none of that has ever quite captured the full reality. It's oversimplified, out-of-date, or missing key ingredients. The insights seldom get beyond "Gee, BUD/S sure is tough."

Yes, it is. But it's so much more than that.

Our program is unique in four ways: what we teach, how we teach it, who teaches it, and who we teach it to.

What we teach is pure SEAL. The lessons are simple, clear, and well-defined: They come right out of our basic values. Winning pays. Losing has consequences. Nothing substitutes for preparation. Life isn't fair and neither is the battlefield. Even the smallest detail matters. We are a brotherhood. Our success depends on our team performance. And we will not fail. These precepts are driven home constantly as we make new SEALs.

Whether the students know it or not—and mostly, they don't—these powerful ideas are behind almost everything that happens in BUD/S.

A boat race isn't just a boat race. It's a way of teaching the culture of winning. A room inspection isn't just a room inspection. It's an excuse for the instructors to get all over the students and teach the life-or-death importance of sweating every last detail. It actually does matter if your knife is fully sharpened and sitting just so by the bed. It matters if your dive vest is freshly safety-checked and your fins are resting at a precise 45 degrees.

"All our lessons," the instructors say, "are written in blood."

Translation: Everything our community knows, we have learned because somebody screwed up badly enough that one of us was hurt or killed.

There are so many examples to choose from. Four SEALs were

killed and eight badly wounded at Panama's Punta Paitilla airport in 1989, trying to destroy Manuel Noriega's Learjet. Blame poor planning, too large a force, and lack of communication with a U.S. Navy gunship offshore. I promise you we never made those mistakes again. Under the weight of experiences like that, the message is hard not to grasp: Don't screw up. And when you do, learn from it.

The instructors have some highly vivid expressions for driving their points home. "Congratulations," they'll say pretty much any time a student makes a mistake. "You just got your whole platoon killed."

In my BUD/S class, the instructors especially enjoyed aiming that one at junior officers in training like me: "Good job, sir"—the *sir* still dripping with sarcasm. One day an instructor barked at one of my fellow junior officers: "You forgot to double-check your tank pressure. You and your swim buddy both drowned."

At the beginning of training when they hear those comments, students are surely thinking: "My knife? Come on! I just killed my whole platoon because I forgot my knife today?" But eventually they all figure out the absolute importance of attention to detail. If you forget an essential piece of gear on a mission, it really can get people killed. That's the truth.

In 1983, during the invasion of Grenada, a SEAL forgot a satphone on a helicopter, a radio ran out of batteries, four SEALs drowned in a high-seas parachute drop, and other SEALs had to be rescued by Marines. There were years of painful lessons in that one. A key one: Every tiny detail matters.

BUD/S room inspections are held each Monday. They can be withering. Everyone fails the first time. Matt and I were roommates during BUD/S, and we thought we had cleaned our room impeccably. But when the instructors barged in for that first inspection, they had no trouble finding little specks of dirt here and there. They dropped the mattresses on the gray metal bed frames and noticed small clouds of dust puffing up. They white-gloved the windowsill that we'd wiped ten minutes earlier. The wind had blown some beach sand in.

After the instructors informed the class that everyone had failed, we were hit with three solid hours of punishment exercises. Matt and I made a vow to ourselves. We didn't care if we had to spend the whole next weekend with feather dusters and chamois cloths, we would do whatever it took to ace the next inspection.

First thing Saturday morning, we went to Home Depot and grabbed one of the jumbo carts. We loaded up so heavily in the cleaning supply aisle, the back of Matt's white Ford F-150 pickup looked like a janitor's closet on wheels. Professional-grade degreaser for the door and window frames. Designer floor wax for the linoleum. High-quality buffing pads for the wood furniture. A putty knife to fill the cracks and crevices. We even bought a mini-vac for the hard-to-reach corners of the room. We pushed all the furniture out into the hallway. We super-cleaned every last inch before pushing all the furniture back. It took us nearly fourteen hours working together to clean the tiny room. But when we finally finished, I swear the place was so immaculate, we could have rolled around on the floor in our dress whites and still taken an admiral's twin daughters to a debutante ball. Clean like a BUD/S room had never been clean before.

And when the instructors arrived for the Monday inspection, I think even they were impressed.

"Now, that's clean," one of them said, summoning several other instructors to review what Matt and I had done.

"Clean," the others had to agree.

Obviously, we're not trying to create the world's greatest force of spec-ops housekeepers. We're not going to defeat the terrorists by out-vacuuming them. But there's a tenet that lies at the core of this that really could save a young warrior's life: You have to be willing to do more than the minimum. You have to be willing to sacrifice your rest and your free time to constantly improve.

It matters if all these details are attended to.

Damn right it does.

Just as important as the powerful content of BUD/S is the method we use to teach it. BUD/S is a total life-changing experience, and that requires a relentless, multilayered approach. The program is thoughtfully constructed and, I believe, psychologically sound. The purpose of BUD/S is not torture, though it certainly can seem that way to those going through it. That unbelievable physical regime is not an end in itself. The point isn't simply to get these men into better physical shape, though that's a nice by-product of all the PT they do. In fact, many skills the students learn will not be used directly on the battlefield at all. In our entire history, I don't believe a SEAL was ever tossed into the water by enemy combatants with his hands and feet bound. Rather, there is a purposeful arc to the training.

What begins as a physical training program ends up being a mental assault on what each of these young men can withstand—and how effectively each candidate can work as a selfless member of a team. These training evolutions help the instructors get inside the students' heads and help the students confront the core of who they are. Important decisions have to be made. The instructors are evaluating whether the students have what it takes to join us. The students are deciding if our community is really for them. Both sides need to be armed with the information to make smart decisions. If we don't get this right, nothing else will matter.

Of course, there is rigid discipline. Even a small slipup can have major consequences. The students are supposed to replenish the ten-gallon water jugs inside the instructors' offices. God forbid one of those jugs is ever empty. When I was training, that happened once. The instructor yanked the plastic jug out of the cooler and hurled it across the Grinder. The echo was something ferocious as the jug bounced across the concrete and into the Grinder's far wall.

"How stupid can you be?" a voice came thundering out of the office moments later. "What moron screwed this up? You people can't even remember to replace a simple water bottle. Next, we're supposed to trust you on the battlefield."

The instructor stormed onto the Grinder and grabbed the first two unlucky recruits he saw.

"Get the entire class onto the beach right now," he demanded. The beating for an infraction like that could be brutal, maybe three hours of push-ups in the sand with hundreds of mountain-climber leg kicks thrown in.

Early in BUD/S, students begin to notice that the instructors aren't just demanding. Sometimes they can seem downright irrational. They'll punish a class for poor performance or when someone screws up—yelling, berating, making everyone do an evolution all over again. But just as often, they'll punish the class when everyone performs perfectly. Some days, they'll be fair and judicious, passing out encouragement and even occasional praise. Other days, the slightest little thing will set these demons off. Or it'll be nothing at all. With no obvious provocation, the instructors will just go berserk.

Singling out a trainee for a withering beat-down, whether he deserves it or not, or reacting excessively to small transgressions are examples of what I call "random acts of instructor violence." The violence isn't a literal physical assault. That has no place in SEAL training. But those extra PT evolutions sure can feel like abuse.

"What did we do wrong?" the trainees want to know after some especially grueling evolution.

"Nothing," the instructor shrugs. "Just do it again." And again. And again.

It's brutal. But it does send a message: Fairness is an irrelevant concept in war. Screwing with the trainees' expectations—forcing them to deal with failure, irrationality, and unpredictability—is a vital part of training SEALs. Things won't be fair on the real-life battle-field, where the stakes are infinitely higher.

There the random acts are literally violent.

You can do everything right, and things can still go catastrophically wrong. That's what happened when more than a dozen friends of mine were killed on two helicopter rescue missions in Afghanistan. Lucky shots from insurgent RPGs brought those two birds down, killing everyone inside. No one in either helo did anything wrong.

It's easy to understand how push-ups, pull-ups, and flutter kicks can prepare future SEALs for the physical rigors of the battlefield. But this mental training is just as vital, maybe more so. A SEAL who has faced frustration, disappointment, and changed circumstances a thousand times in training and worked around all those impediments to success is primed to face similar challenges in the real world of battle. Call it muscle memory. Call it mental exercise. It works.

Lesson by careful lesson, a culture of resilience is being baked permanently in. Those random acts of instructor violence in BUD/S, maddening as they can be, are an extremely effective way of teaching focus and composure under the highest-pressure circumstances. It's an inoculation that can save your life.

None of this would work without phenomenally talented instructors. Few of the students now going through BUD/S realize how fortunate they are. Today's instructors have had multiple tours of duty in some very hot war zones. They have Silver Stars, Bronze Stars, and Purple Hearts, often more than one. When these guys tell a trainee, "You just got your whole platoon killed," that's hard to take lightly. All of us have good friends—some of us have many friends—who have been killed in combat.

When I was a student, I wondered, "How many instructors have been in combat?" I didn't have the nerve to ask. There wasn't an easy way of finding out. Only later did I come to realize that hardly any of that generation of rock-hard, tough-talking, world-weary guys had ever actually seen any live combat themselves. They'd trained for it. They knew all about it. They certainly would have been phenomenal warriors if they'd gotten the chance. But Vietnam was over. The War on Terror hadn't begun. Historic events were against them. They were left with a few small skirmishes and lots of opportunities to train.

You'd be mistaken if you thought that diminished their authority or their stature. These instructors were like gods to us.

The instructors are role models, advisors, evangelists, father figures, and disciplinarians. That gives them a huge amount of control over the trainees. And, of course, as a cadre, they do possess the power to block any student from becoming a SEAL. As students, we were in awe of these men. An instinctive instructor uses that fact to push his trainees to the max and beyond.

Students and instructors journey through BUD/S together. But the instructors always have the upper hand. They may seem to be doing the exact same workout the students are doing. But watch closely. The instructor just did one thousand sit-ups with the students. Good for him. Then he sends the class for a run down the beach or into the surf a couple of times. He's exhausting them while he's drinking water and catching his breath. Then he comes back out and just starts pounding on the class again.

A buddy of mine, once he became an instructor, loved to assign an exercise called the arm-hauler. You are flat on your stomach with your hands out. You bring your hands up above your head and then back to your hips—above your head and back to your hips. You're lying on the ground, just swinging your arms like that. But soon the shoulders start to burn, and the agony that takes place after fifty of those things—let alone fifteen hundred—is horrible.

My friend started doing them with three-pound weights, then five-pound weights. He got up to ten-pound weights, and he could do sets of three hundred without a break. He could do arm-haulers forever. No student could possibly keep up.

The students have a term for the most fearsome instructors, instructors who demand the most, yell the loudest, and seem the most impossible to please. They are the "hammers"—loud, hard, and unyielding. They are the opposite of the "huggers," instructors who are warmer, friendlier, and kinder. The truth is that BUD/S needs both. The BUD/S huggers, who'd be considered hammers anywhere else, motivate with support, encouragement, and understanding. The hammers motivate by demanding more and more and more. As the training officer who supervised the instructors, I had to create a balance between the two approaches. A big part of my job was also to insulate the instructors and protect the program from the latest harebrained idea from above.

While I was in charge of First Phase, a new senior officer checked on board. During one challenging and dangerous training evolution, we asked the students to paddle their boats into the rocks in front of the elegant Hotel del Coronado. The boat crews are required to land safely and portage, or carry the boats, over the rocks to dry land. In a January or February class, the water temperature is exceptionally cold. And the evolution is conducted at night. The instructors stand on the rocks, getting pummeled with spray from the water, holding light batons to guide the students to their landing spot.

During the winter months, those instructors stand very close to and sometimes in the water, wearing exposure suits, which keeps them dry from the oncoming waves. The new senior officer at the time said to me as we watched from a distance, "This is bullshit. If we're supposed to be the model for these young men and set the example for them, we should be in the same uniform and be every bit as cold and suffering to show them how it's done."

I responded in a calm and respectful tone: "Let me make sure I understand your recommendation," I said, sounding a little like one of those enlisted instructors I met on day one and their well-barbed "sirs." "You would like me to direct my instructors to put themselves in a position where they'd be out in that cold water so long, their judgment and physical ability to respond will reduce to the point that they won't be able to react to the inevitable emergencies? An emergency in this evolution could mean serious injury if not death, the one thing I am certain would end your career. Do I understand your guidance clearly, sir?"

He just walked away. We didn't change a thing.

As carefully as we pick the students, as well thought out as the curriculum is, as hard as the instructors try, we don't succeed with everyone. That's the other major secret of BUD/S, starting with the right raw material. We have a sense of the trainees we're looking for. We have ideas about where to find them. We have some reliable control measures to keep the wrong ones out. The rest of it is more an art than a science. In the end, it all comes down to the students, even Proto-SEALs like the twins.

Everybody loved the twins. Two handsome brothers from southern Illinois, they looked so much alike, Tim had to bleach his hair blond so we could tell him from Tommy. Upbeat personalities, the same goofy humor, they'd smile through all the toughest training challenges.

No one would ever have bet against Tim and Tommy. "Those are the guys you want at your side in a bad gunfight," I remember one of the instructors saying. "They'll still be smiling then."

One night at low tide, the trainees were too far out from the beach for the instructors to make out faces. All they could see was the glow of the chem-lights the students were carrying.

Suddenly one of the lights came bouncing toward the beach. Only when the light got closer did the face become clear. It was blond-haired Tim, running toward the bell.

Then out of the distance behind him, here came Tommy like a rocket, tackling his brother twenty yards from the beach.

I thought about my brother. I had an idea what they might be going through. The instructors didn't intervene, as Tommy dragged Tim back into line.

What happened next was like a slow-motion train wreck. Barely a minute later, Tim made a break again. And just as before, Tommy came running behind him.

"How can you do this?" Tommy shouted at his brother. "We've been talking about SEALs forever."

"You better get your asses back in line or we're gonna toss both of you," one of the instructors said. But Tim's decision was made. His BUD/S experience was over. He ran straight for the bell.

A chief stepped in front of Tommy, grabbed him by the T-shirt, and said: "Do not let this affect your game. You can get through. He's not ready. You are. This is now your journey, not his."

It all made sense, of course, but it did no good.

Three minutes after returning to the surf, Tommy was also running toward the bell. Both the twins DOR'd.

It's rarely this dramatic. But quitting can be infectious. One quitter will often drag a few others along. As a phase leader and basic training officer, I always encouraged the students not to be dragged down by the decisions of others. They have to make up their own minds.

"Right now," I've said to many new BUD/S classes over the years as they were approaching Hell Week, "you may be sitting next to a guy who just shared with you that he was in the Olympics last year for swimming or a professional mixed-martial-arts fighter who has you convinced he'll be getting through this place without breaking a sweat. You're gonna think that he is what we're looking for. And you know what? He is going to quit two days from now. You're going to see him quit and some of you are going to say, 'If he can't make it, I can't make it.' Don't praise false idols. I promise you—one has nothing to do with the other. I don't care where you're from, what your history or your background is. Every one of you guys can make it through this course. You have the physical capacity to do it. You've proven that by getting here. Now it's on you to believe that's the case and to want it badly enough."

It's very hard to predict that at the beginning. Behavior is the only proof.

"Some guys have no quit inside them, no matter how much is asked of them," I say. "These are the guys we want here. But we never know who's in that category until we throw all of you into the meat grinder and see what comes out. It could be the little guy. It could be the big guy. It's in your hands. It's always the guys who truly want to be SEALs who kick this program in the ass. You have to want to win. You have to want to win so badly, losing is not even a possibility for you. If you feel that way, there is no obstacle the instructors can put in front of you that you won't figure out how to get past."

Not even the horrors of Hell Week.

3

HELL, YES

If you are going to go through hell, keep going.
—Winston Churchill

We'd all seen the YouTube videos. An American or a Westerner is having his head chopped off with a long, rusty bread knife by a savage in the very same neighborhood where we were assigned. Those images were burned in everybody's mind.

"I gotta ask you something," I said one afternoon to five of my closest guys: Big D, Ru, Lope, Cams, and Red. We were on a roof together, catching our breath after an especially rugged gunfight.

"Here's the scenario," I said. "Everybody's dead but you and your swim buddy. You're trapped on the side of a road, and there's no escaping. Two hundred bad guys are bearing down on you. Your magazines are empty. You've expended every round. Are we all in agreement on this? You'll have your knife in your fighting hand and a grenade in the other, pin pulled and ready to go. Better dead than a prisoner."

No one even needed time to think.

"Yes," said Lope.

"Yes," said Ro.

"Yes, yes, yes," said the others.

"Your loved ones back home might call that suicide," I told them. "They may say, 'Let 'em take you prisoner. As long as there is life, there is hope.'"

"There's no hope in that," Big D said. "I'd go out before I'd ever go with them."

"In this era of combat with this enemy," Lope agreed, "I'm not throwing up any white flags."

The bad guys knew who we were. They knew we were the special operators. They knew we were different from the regular troops. The way the Viet Cong knew "the men with green faces," these people knew us. Capturing us, they'd have a bigger prize. Whatever they'd do would be worse. They'd have a better video.

"Dying is definitely a better way to go," Red said. "Being tortured and mutilated and having your body defiled so your family can see it on TV? I don't think so."

Just the thought of what was coming was too much for some guys.

The Sunday night before Hell Week, the instructors put us to bed early in fifty-man canvas tents on the beach. The wind was picking up. Sand was blowing around. I don't think anyone got much sleep at all. Lying in the darkness, imagining how brutal the next five days would be, a couple of my classmates made life-changing decisions right then and there. They didn't say a word to anyone. They just climbed off their cots and hurried out of the tent. Soon enough, the bell was ringing again. No one tried to stop them. If you're quitting in the tent, there's no way this is for you.

Hell Week is BUD/S on steroids with hardly any sleep. From Sunday night until Friday noon, the challenges, mental and physical, never, ever let up. It's evolution after painful evolution of unspeakable intensity with ingenious new abuse layered on. The instructors are extra-maniacal. The exercises are twice as fast. Even the weather often turns to crap for Hell Week. I know that's hard to believe, but I swear it's true. San Diego could have just been enjoying seventy straight days of 75-and-sunny. Eight times out of ten, dark clouds blow in for Hell Week and the temperature drops ten or fifteen degrees. The students shake their heads and mutter: "The instructors must have a switch somewhere."

The instructors think that's funny. One of them always nods knowingly at the coming storm: "God must really love SEALs. He makes Hell Week even harder so only the best men get through."

My Hell Week, like all Hell Weeks, arrived with a bang. Literally.

First, we heard some rustling outside the tent.

Then—*ka-boom!*

Someone tossed a simulation grenade right next to my cot. Suddenly three or four instructors were rushing frantically around, kicking sand, shouting and firing Mk 48 machine guns. The weapons were loaded with blanks. But they were painfully loud, and they were spewing round after round of sizzling hot brass. The shell casings were bouncing everywhere, including down the backs of people's uniform tops. It was a full, five-sense overload in there—whistles blowing, sirens wailing, smoke billowing everywhere—the worst wake-up call ever. Groggy and disoriented, my classmates and I leaped out of our cots and onto our feet. This was Breakout, evolution number one of Hell Week.

"Hit the surf!" one of the instructors shouted, and we all went running for the frigid Pacific. That run was damn near the last time any of us were dry or warm all week.

The instructors called us out of the surf, split us into our boat crews, and ushered us onto the Grinder, which had been transformed into the Southern California version of a live-action urban fire zone. The grenades were going off in all four corners. Smoke bombs choked the square with an acrid haze while huge fire hoses sprayed mist on everyone. A .50-caliber, tripod-mounted machine gun was on the rooftop, blasting away. Instructors were back with their Mk 48s, still spewing brass. The cadre had set up what looked like carnival stations around the Grinder with special challenges at each one. The boat crews moved through the smoke together, locking arms so we didn't lose anyone, performing bursts of flutter kicks, push-ups, squats, jumping jacks, low crawls, and buddy drags.

No student could ever remember how long Hell Week's opening mayhem went on for. But anyone who knew what was coming next would never want Breakout to end.

We had done log PT before. We had lunged with logs, marched with logs at chest level, executed extended-arm log carries, and done log sit-ups. But somehow in the opening night darkness of Hell Week, log PT turned into something truly evil. The pace was stepped up dramatically. Every instructor had a bullhorn and was yelling in our ears. "We're gonna keep at this till someone quits!" the instructors kept saying. And more often than not, someone did. Even when we were doing the exercises correctly, somehow it didn't feel like we were.

Then came the shout, "Surf torture!"—and we headed back to the water again.

A long line of class members stretched down the beach, facing the ocean.

"Lock arms!" the instructor demanded as we linked ourselves in a long human chain of interlocked elbows. We clenched our hands together in front of us.

"Forward march!"

We marched together into the surf. It couldn't have been more than 52 or 53 degrees in there. We walked farther out until the water was chest-high on most of us.

"Halt!" the instructor said.

Then "Take seats!"

That's where the real torture began. We floated along in this arm-locked line, bouncing in the rough surge of the Pacific, catching breaths when we could, as the constant waves smashed over our heads.

Boom, boom, boom. The waves kept breaking over us.

With all the strength we had, we were holding on to each other and trying to keep our heads up in the great wash cycle of the Pacific as our battered bodies were tossed helplessly around. Water was rushing over us, into our eyes, mouths, and noses. Sand and sea life were in the whirling mix. Wave after wave, the surf was pushing this long, floating line of prospective SEALs, who were trying desperately to hold on, closer and closer to the beach.

I'm not sure how this sounds, describing it now. But with the surf pouring over our heads and our bodies bouncing up, down, and sideways and the water as cold as it was, it was a hugely disorienting experience. And that was the point. Seeing if we could keep our cool instead of panicking. Trusting our fellow students to help hold us upright. Going with the flow to ride out the surf. Building the cohesiveness that we would eventually carry with us to the battlefield.

And Hell Week was just getting started. It was amazing how much the instructors could cram into the very first night.

Just to make sure everyone felt sufficiently taunted, the SEAL bell, which had been hanging on the Grinder outside the First Phase classroom, it was hooked to the back of a Ford 4x4 on an L-shaped metal bracket. Wherever we went during Hell Week, the truck was parked nearby. Sometimes, as the bouncing brass bell was pulled from bay to beach to exercise field, you could hear a stray clang or two. It was as if the witches of Hell Week were singing out to the class: "It's here, fellas. The bell is right here for you. It's always here."

Hell Week hasn't changed much over the years. "Surf torture" is now officially renamed "surf immersion," which I guess is more politically acceptable. Most students still use the old name, and believe me, the experience is every bit as torturous as before. You end up with just as much sand and salt water in your eyes, ears, nose, and mouth. But class after class, those first killer days of Hell Week are when the largest concentration of people quit.

Anytime we came out of the surf, the instructors liked to yell, "Sugar cookies!" We knew what that meant. We had to drop immediately onto the dry, abrasive sand. We rolled around down there until our sticky, wet bodies were totally coated in sand. Then we carried on whatever evolution was planned for next. No matter how often "sugar cookies" was called, the instructors seemed to get special glee from the order, knowing how miserable we must feel. All these years later, I still feel itchy just thinking about it. But "sugar cookies" was just an irritation. "Steel pier" felt genuinely life-threatening.

On Monday night, the instructors lined us up single file and marched the whole class onto a mammoth steel-and-concrete pier that extended seventy-five yards or so into San Diego Bay.

Here we go, I thought to myself as I stood with the others on the pier in our green uniform pants and tops. I'd heard about this. We all had. "Steel pier" was legendary.

We began on the concrete part of the pier. Placed every five paces was a fat fire hose and giant industrial fan like you might see spraying mist from the sidelines of a high school football game on a hot Friday night. It definitely wasn't hot on that pier.

They marched us onto the steel grating that led to the water.

"Enter," one of the instructors called. He seemed to mean it. Like a long line of giant lemmings, we jumped one at a time off the edge of the pier and into the bay.

The water was deep there, easily over our heads. The water temperature was a degree or two warmer than the open ocean, but certainly no more than 55 or 56 degrees. As we treaded that icy-cold bay water, our heads bobbing just above the surface, our boots and green fatigues soaked through, an instructor paced on the pier above us with a bullhorn, offering special deals to any students who wanted to come out.

"It's warm up here," he offered, his voice sounding oh-so-understanding. "If you quit now, we got hot coffee and doughnuts in the truck. Don't you like doughnuts? You'll never have to be wet or cold again."

"Quit now, beat the rush," another instructor said. "We'll get you to a warm bed in a hurry."

I knew if we stayed in that water long enough, our body temperatures would fall so low, we'd all get hypothermia. How long were they keeping us there? We didn't know if there was a time limit. We didn't know if they were waiting for the first student to drown. But guys started quitting the program after a minute or two.

From the water, I could see them getting wrapped in towels and led off toward the coffee-and-doughnut truck.

We treaded that water for about ten minutes, I'd say, every second of it horribly numbing and cold. I was sure I was better off than some of my classmates. Look at those little guys, I said to myself, glancing over at a couple of the smaller ones. I'm a big polar bear. They don't carry the body mass I do. I'm in a good position compared to them.

That didn't raise my body temperature one degree or make me feel any warmer. But it did bring some comfort. Plus, I kept reminding myself, that freezing-cold water was working as an anti-inflammatory, healing and helping my body to recover from the previous rounds of abuse.

At that point, a loud whistle blew. The instructor with the bull-horn started to yell: "Okay, everybody out!"

We scrambled out of the water and hustled back up the steel grating onto the concrete pier. The same way concrete gets hot in the summer, it gets cold in the winter. It takes on the temperature of the day. Well, we were all about to get a lesson in thermal conduction right on that pier.

"Take your green tops off," the bullhorn instructor demanded.

We did.

"Lie on the concrete," he said.

"Arms out. On your backs. This is your rest time. Put your arms out so you're nice and cold on the concrete."

Not too restful.

"Don't be warming up by touching a buddy," he warned.

That's when someone turned on the hoses and fans, letting that frigid mist rain down on all of us. So our rest and warm-up break after being in the bay was to lie in a pool of cold water on the pier with fans blowing mist across the concrete and us.

An instructor was walking down the line of shivering bodies, trying to push students' arms flat against the concrete. It wasn't easy. Some people's bodies were jackhammer shivering so hard, they just couldn't keep their limbs down. Their muscles were cramping. Their arms were seizing up. Honestly, it was hard to know which was worse— dog-paddling in that mid-50s bay water or lying on the icy wet slab of concrete.

But there was no time to ponder. "Back in the water," Instructor

Bullhorn demanded, and so we jumped back in, this time minus our uniform tops.

We went back and forth like that, from bay to pier to bay to pier, discarding an article of clothing each round, tossing away our T-shirts, then our boots, then our pants until we were down to our swim trunks and nothing else. The experience brought a whole new level of understanding to the concept of wet-and-cold.

Hell Week isn't designed to kill you. It's designed to make you wish you were dead—or at least to push you to the edge of physical and mental endurance to see how you react. While the demands are mostly physical, the journey through them is all about mental attitude. The harder Hell Week got, the more important that turned out to be. So whatever the instructors were throwing at me, I had the same response: "Fine. I can get through this. I have no doubt I can. Let other guys quit if they want to. I'm not going anywhere, no matter what they put us through."

As a student at BUD/S, I never allowed myself to think, I have a choice here. I never let that concept anywhere into my consciousness, not even the faintest possibility I might not survive Hell Week and BUD/S. It wasn't like I answered the should-I-leave question with "I'm staying." It was that no such question was ever even asked.

Years later, when I began to supervise BUD/S training, including Hell Week, I came to understand more clearly the fine line between tough and torture. We were always careful in walking that line. As instructors, we took precise measurements of the wind speed, the water temperature, and how exhausted the students were likely to be. After years of putting recruits through Hell Week, we know how hard to push them. And we push right up to the edge of that limit.

The random acts of instructor violence really started flowing in Hell Week—more random and more violent every day. Hammers and huggers alike, the whole instructor cadre seemed to believe this was their big chance to break us down, like we were extra ripe now and they didn't want to miss their easiest opportunity. Never gentle before, the instructors seemed genuinely possessed. And the possession always got worse when the sun went down.

During Hell Week, each twenty-four-hour day is divided among three shifts of instructors: Alpha Shift handles 4 p.m. to midnight, Bravo Shift has midnight to 8 a.m., and Charlie Shift takes 8 a.m. to 4 p.m. The later it gets, the crueler the instructors are.

Just before 4 p.m., after eight full hours of Charlie Shift, it's Alpha time. The Alpha Shift instructors load into a convoy of work trucks, announcing their arrival over a bullhorn as they slowly roll up. "The sun is going down soon," one of them will say as the trucks approach the class. "Alpha's here now. No more of this daytime bullshit. The night belongs to us."

They then proceed to prove it.

And whatever level Alpha establishes, Bravo is inevitably worse. "You thought it was bad with Alpha," one of the Bravo instructors is sure to announce before midnight. "Colder, harder, wetter—Bravo time."

"Son of a bitch," the students understand. "The real demons are here." And the minutes keep ticking on.

That round-the-clock relentlessness is eventually what is toughest about Hell Week. Day and night, the evolutions are never over. From one horrible trial to another with hardly any breaks—the demands are trying in deep and profound ways. Between Monday morning and Wednesday afternoon, the only real interruptions are for meals—full breakfasts, lunches, and dinners, and midnight rations. The instructors circle the tables like maniacal high school cafeteria monitors, making sure every student is eating enough.

They yell at anyone who isn't banging sufficient food down, then stand over him until he gobbles several large mouthfuls. Those who won't or can't eat are pulled from training and, if they're up to it, rolled back to a subsequent BUD/S class. I've seen it happen more than once.

Across the full five days and nights of Hell Week, the schedule calls for two short bursts of sleep. We barely got that in my class. Shivering and numb, we were finally taken back to the tents on Wednesday afternoon and invited to collapse on the cots. Thank God no one has found a way to bottle the smell in there. Thirty guys under stinky canvas—raw, miserable, and snoring, some not even bothering to get up to urinate—lay like zombies for an hour or two.

If I had known what I would feel like when the instructors burst into our tent again—blowing whistles, blasting an air horn, yelling as loud as they could—I wouldn't have taken that nap at all. My ankles, knees, and legs were swelling badly. I didn't feel one degree warmer than I had. My nervous system seemed to be going haywire. I could tell my bodily fluids were badly out of whack. We were all young, strong men in peak condition. But humans just aren't built for this.

By the time my class hit the surf again and returned for the next evolutions, pretty much everyone was looking spent. Easily half the class had quit already. At each step, several more of our classmates had decided, "SEAL training isn't for me." In whatever style they chose, they walked to the exit bell and pulled the cord. Now I could see who the real hard-core guys were. They were the ones who were still there with me. It was a steadily shrinking group. There were still a few more who wouldn't make it.

As Thursday night arrived, we put our IBSs in the water for the most grueling multi-leg boat race of Hell Week, the one known as Around the World. By then, all seven remaining members of my boat crew, myself included, looked utterly spent. But Coop, a good-looking kid who'd been a real team player, looked the worst of all. His hands were shaking. His gaze was bleary. His speech was slurred. Our boat team had been burning up Hell Week, winning race after race after small-boat race. That kind of effort is what the instructors are looking for, but it also takes its toll.

Coop was an all-around performer, one of those guys who aren't tops at anything but are strong in everything and work incredibly hard. But every leg of Around the World was hugely demanding. I didn't know how Coop could possibly make it through this one.

"Hey, Matt," I said, nodding in Coop's direction. "What do you think?"

Matt's dad was a doctor. In the first few weeks of BUD/S, he had become the informal medical advisor to those classmates smart enough to listen. He was the one who explained to me how hypothermia works at the cellular level. And now I wanted his seat-of-the-pants diagnosis on Coop.

"He's done," Matt said.

I'm not sure if that was an official medical determination. But I knew what Matt was saying, and I was certain he was right. Now I had to explain this to Coop.

"Coop," I said. "I want you to curl up in the middle of the boat and go to sleep."

Coop tried to protest. "No way. I'm okay," he said faintly. "Just give me a second here." But he didn't have the strength to resist.

He curled up near the bow of the IBS. He fell asleep soon after the race began. As the other six of us paddled frantically, Coop stayed out for more than an hour.

Here was the strange part: Having him balled up like that on the floor of the boat shifted our angle in the water and actually made us faster. We won that leg of Around the World.

When we finally got ashore, Coop had recovered completely. No one else seemed to notice that for this one race, we were a six-man team. But even in victory, Coop seemed devastated.

"I'm so mad at myself," he said. "I can't believe I blew it."

Matt and I both tried to tell him that was ridiculous. "Everyone hits the wall sometime," I said. "You had nothing left in the tank." In fact, Coop's unscheduled nap hadn't been a problem at all. But that didn't console him.

"I feel horrible," he said.

Coop went on to become a legendarily effective SEAL, involved in some of our highest-profile operations. When I've seen him over the years, whatever I say, he still seems slightly chagrined about that Hell Week boat race. That's just the kind of guy he is. Much as I tell him he has nothing to apologize for, he still can't stomach the idea of once having failed to pull his part of the load.

That exact trait is a big part of what makes the SEAL brotherhood so strong. It's guys like Coop who, even thirteen years later in the middle of a distinguished career, will still fixate on what is now an insignificant shortfall—a total aversion to failure of any sort. I've seen it over and over again. Those who get through this training develop an unshakable desire not to let the brotherhood down. They make unreasonable demands on themselves. They are brutal at judging their own performance. Coop felt this would hang with him far longer than it did. We knew who he was, and he had already earned his spot on our team. Once you are part of that team, there is almost nothing we won't suffer for you. We'd pick you up and carry you a hundred miles across the desert. You have earned it. We know you would suffer equally for us.

One thing did change as Hell Week moved closer to the end. The bell wasn't ringing so much anymore.

Lots of people had left already, and the ones who remained didn't seem likely to leave. No matter how grueling or weird the process got, they'd be seeing it through.

And things did keep getting weirder.

On one leg of Around the World, our boat crew was paddling

briskly across the bay when all of a sudden I noticed our teammate Trey was paddling extra-furiously. For no obvious reason, he was pulling twice as hard as he had been a moment earlier. He had what I can only describe as a terrified look in his eyes. Soon our boat was veering wildly. I didn't know what was happening as I tried to steer us back on course.

"Trey, Trey, what's going on?" I shouted.

"We gotta go, man!" he yelled back at me. "We gotta go. Keep paddling. Let's go. Let's go. Let's go!"

I was totally confused. "What? What's going on?" I shouted.

"We gotta haul ass so that clown doesn't catch us," Trey said.

"What?"

"That clown on the bicycle. He's gaining on us. I don't want that sucker to catch us."

Four days into Hell Week, and Trey truly believed that a clown on a bicycle on the Bay of San Diego was going to catch us in our IBS. He couldn't let that happen. He was too competitive. He had too much pride and too much drive. And in a funny way, I understood where he was coming from. A clown on a bicycle gaining on us—that truly was a horrible vision to have living in your head.

And while I couldn't see the clown—believe me, I looked behind us to check—I wasn't exactly sure there wasn't a clown back there. By that point, I'll admit, I was a little wired, too.

Well, shit, I said to myself. Let's keep paddling. I don't want that clown to catch us, either.

Now all of us were paddling as ferociously as we could. We won that leg of the boat race. Again, it paid to be a winner at BUD/S. Clown or no clown, we got to eat our dinner sitting up high on the shoreline in a dry set of greens while the rest of the class ate, in descending order, in wet green tops, in wet green tops and bottoms, and, for the final stragglers, sitting in a foot of water. Believe in him or not, Trey's clown took care of us.

Trey wasn't the only one with an active imagination after so many exhausting hours with so little sleep. In another race that night, another one of my startled boat crew members started yelling at me to steer the boat away from an aircraft carrier that was at least half a mile away. "That carrier's gonna roll right over us!" he yelled excitedly.

I wasn't worried about the carrier. I was steering in the back of the boat, trying to work out in my head how we were ever going to get around a fence I was sure stretched straight across San Diego Bay, a fence I had never seen before and never saw again.

When we get to the fence, I was calculating in my mind, if we all stand on one end of the boat, we'll be able to slide it bow-first over the fence. Matt and I played water polo so we'll get underneath and push the boat over the fence. Then, if we can hold our breath long enough, maybe we can all swim under the fence and get to the other side. Or maybe we can scale the fence with the paddles. Or maybe . . .

It sounds so crazy now. What I thought was a fence must have been the piers across the bay where the big ships are moored. But it's amazing what exhausted eyes and an exhausted mind can see. It sure looked like a fence when we were paddling toward it. And getting past that fence felt so urgent to me.

I asked Matt about it. I'm sure he didn't see a fence any more than I saw a bulbous-nosed circus reject on a two-wheeler. But Matt did what I had done. He instinctively tried to help a buddy deal with an issue, whatever that issue happened to be. I was with a group of guys I could easily see again on a battlefield, guys who were on their way to being SEALs. Our BUD/S class was becoming a brotherhood.

Beyond the powerful bonding and the intense competitive drive, the real salvation of Hell Week was the calendar. No matter how exhausting the superhuman demands, Friday eventually came for my class.

Late that morning, the instructors told us to paddle up to the water line in front of the BUD/S compound. At that spot there were huge sand berms that blocked your view of anything past the beach.

"Line up your boats on the shore," one of the instructors ordered. "Get 'em dressed up and ready and looking sharp." Then the cadre started us on an especially sinister drill—hitting the surf, running back to the sand, hitting the surf again, running back to the sand. They made us all do sugar cookies. Then we had to run into the surf again. We went back and forth like that—it felt like a thousand times.

Finally, one of the instructors met us at the water's edge as we were coming out of the surf again, wet and bleary and cold.

"About face," he commanded. "Look out at the sea. Lock arms. We're gonna get wet again."

Whatever.

At this point, no one was going to quit. If one of the instructors had said, "We just got word from the admiral that Hell Week is two weeks instead of one," no one would have left. These guys would have gone on for a year. Anyone who remained in the class was here for good now. Another round of surf torture wasn't chasing anyone away. We all locked arms as we were told.

Now the orders sounded especially urgent.

"Forward march! Forward march! March forward to the surf!"

But just as the water was licking at our feet, the same instructor said, "Everybody halt."

Then, "About face."

We all turned around. Up on the berm across the beach, I saw something so beautiful, I thought it might be a mirage. Just the day before, Trey had seen a clown on a bicycle. But I swear: Up on the berm was the entire cadre of instructors, dressed in uniform, all the chiefs in khakis. A dozen senior officers were standing with them. One of the instructors was holding a huge American flag, which was fluttering in the sharp ocean breeze.

None of this was a surprise exactly. Everyone knew what was coming. It was almost noon on Friday. But still I needed to pause a second and collect myself.

"This has to be the end," I thought.

Captain Mac was in charge of Hell Week our year. Eight years later, I would serve as his flag lieutenant. He walked us all back to the Grinder and called us into a big huddle. He addressed the class.

Knowing Captain Mac, I'm sure he said something very eloquent. He probably quoted Socrates or Abraham Lincoln or maybe Thucydides. He's a gifted speaker, very well-read.

But I have zero recollection of what he said.

I was sleep-deprived. I was physically exhausted. I was emotionally drained. I was shivering, sandy, and wet. My mind was zooming in five directions simultaneously. I was 100 percent, totally smoked. I was standing there with my arms around my Hell Week buddies on the road to somewhere amazing, exactly where we wanted to be. We were swaying slightly from side to side and leaning on each other for support. As the captain said whatever it was he was saying, I was listening for three simple words.

The captain finally obliged.

"Class two two three," I heard him say. "Hell Week secure."

With that, a tight huddle of hopeful Navy SEALs, fewer than forty of us now, let out a huge, whooping roar. Everyone started hugging each other. Then, like idiots, we turned around, ran to the surf, and dove in.

4

COOL STUFF

Never walk away from your home ahead of
your axe and sword. You can't feel a battle in
your bones or foresee a fight.
—THE HÁVAMÁL

On one nighttime exercise, the members of BRAVO Platoon, SEAL Team Four, were dropping rubber Zodiac boats from two Army MH-60 helicopters hovering eight or ten feet above the water in the Bahamas. Each time, the jumpmaster cut the line, dumped the boat, and shouted "Go!" to the next two swim buddies standing inside the helicopter door. On the jumpmaster's signal, the SEALs leaped into the dark water and swam after the boat.

A K-Duck, this rapid-insertion maneuver is called, or Kangaroo Duck. It is considered a routine training exercise, as well as you can say "routine" about anything that involves a leap of faith from a helicopter into pitch-black water at ten o'clock at night. Routinely dangerous is more like it.

Then came tragedy.

Somehow, one of the boats was dumped prematurely. Instead

of being eight feet off the water, it was 165 feet up. That's the equivalent of jumping off a fifteen-story building. Instinctively, even before hearing the jumpmaster's "Go," the two SEALs jumped into the darkness after the falling boat.

"I had time in the air to think, Oh, my God, we're way higher than I thought we were," one of the SEALs told me later, still shaken by the experience. "And then I thought, Oh, my God, when we finally hit the water, we're both going to die."

He was the lucky one. He broke several bones. He busted some ribs. He got all banged up. But almost miraculously, he managed to survive the fall. And even as he hit the water with such ferocious velocity, he remained every bit a SEAL. Despite his injuries, with the wind knocked out of him, he swam to his buddy's aid, holding him above the surface long enough for the SEAL corpsmen to arrive.

The ultimate swim buddy.

But the other SEAL's injuries were too severe. He didn't even make it to the hospital.

The incident was studied exhaustively. The fundamental causes, concluded Admiral Eric Olson, commander of the Naval Special Warfare Command, were "insufficient situational awareness" and a "predisposition by both men to exit the helicopter prior to receiving a positive 'go' signal from the assigned castmaster."

Yes, all our lessons are written in blood.

Just because it's training doesn't mean it's risk-free. Not even close. Some of our training evolutions can be every bit as dangerous as a war zone, and jumping is where most of the deaths occur. Someone's parachute doesn't open. Two chutes get tangled up. Distances get misjudged in poor visibility. Hardly anything we do is 100 percent safe. With overconfidence comes sloppiness. Constantly, these lessons must be hammered home.

A SEAL chief died on a dive from a SEAL Delivery Vehicle mini-

submersible. On a training exercise in El Salvador, a SEAL commander was killed in a helicopter fast-roping accident one hundred
feet above a concrete airfield. As he stepped out of the Black Hawk
helicopter and reached for the dangling rope, somehow his hands
slipped, and he fell straight down to the concrete. He was an experienced jumper. He just missed the rope.

To say we all felt whipped and beaten doesn't do justice to the
words *whipped* and *beaten*. But Hell Week was over, and I was
still on my feet.

The instructors marched us—more like stumbled us—from the
beach back to the compound for hot showers. That was about as
soothing as boric acid on my scraped-up skin. Everyone got a thorough medical check, which under the circumstances seemed like a
good idea. The doctors and med techs were ready with IVs, bandages,
antibiotics, antiseptic ointments—scrapes, bruises, dehydration, and
profound exhaustion being the most common ailments. No one in my
class needed immediate hospitalization, although that's been known
to happen over the years.

One by one, the Hell Week survivors emerged from the medical
office and walked, limped, or crawled back to the Grinder, where all
the fun had started a few long nights before.

Finally, it was time for a bleary-eyed celebration, which, sadly, no
one had the energy to enjoy.

Following long-standing SEAL tradition, the class below bought
each of us the traditional Hell Week Secure meal—a large cheese-
and-pepperoni pizza and a sixty-four-ounce lemon-lime Gatorade.
The way a McDonald's Happy Meal comes with a prize, each Hell

Week victor got a brown T-shirt with his name stenciled on the back. I unfolded mine.

DENVER.

Now that was something special. The T-shirt didn't look like much, but it was the most important T-shirt I'd ever received in my life. I knew I had earned it.

Up through Hell Week, all BUD/S students wear white T-shirts. After completing Hell Week, the shirts are brown. It's amazing how such a tiny acknowledgment can mean so much.

We ate our pizzas and guzzled our Gatorades, and that was it for the Hell Week festivities. Nobody felt like hanging around. We were helped onto buses and driven straight back to the barracks, where we'd all set up our rooms just so. We hadn't seen the barracks in almost five days. But now there were quite a few empty rooms, all in immaculate condition, all prepared by students who had DOR'd and would never get to use them. Sleep, it's really all we wanted.

The instructors and senior students had given us ominous warnings and specific advice.

"Build up the foot of your bed with pillows so your legs will be elevated and put towels along the side," one of the instructors had strongly suggested. "If you're lying there and your arm falls off the side, it could go septic on you."

"You should leave an empty Gatorade bottle by the bed," several of the previous class's students said. "You won't want to walk even twelve feet to the bathroom."

To my great regret, I somehow forgot that last one. At some point in the night, when I tried to get out of bed to relieve myself, it took me a disoriented fifteen minutes to reach the bathroom and find my way back. Another student discovered Trey dead asleep on the toilet. He had clearly been there a while.

It was a little past one o'clock on Friday afternoon when our heads, arms, and legs finally hit the towels and pillows. I didn't wake up until eight o'clock on Saturday morning—nineteen hours later—and I wasn't the last one up.

AFTER HELL WEEK, we all expected the instructors to ease up a little. And in many ways they did. As the focus of our training shifted from tests of raw strength and stamina to learning the actual skills of war, the overall brutality of BUD/S definitely leveled off—by SEAL standards, that is, and not all the time. A couple of the real hammer instructors still seemed to get some twisted pleasure from riding the class even harder than before. They got in the habit of demanding ridiculous challenges before every meal. When we went out to San Clemente Island for small-arms, demolition, and land-warfare training, it wasn't just "Give me fifty push-ups, fifty sit-ups, run up Frog Hill with your boat crew, run back down—then we eat." They started having us run up the hill with four-by-four metal pallets on our backs like giant wings. The pallets weren't super-heavy, maybe fifty pounds each. But they were extremely awkward to balance. And running down the hill with the pallets, we were supposed to "request permission to land" as if we were approaching the flight deck of the world's dustiest aircraft carrier.

"This is Ensign Denver, flight twenty-one," I'd say. "My wings are level. My flaps are down. Request permission to land." If the instructor was satisfied with my delivery and my run, permission would be granted. If not, the instructor would answer, "Deck is full. Wave off. Wave off." That meant another run up and down Frog Hill.

When the instructors were really dissatisfied or just grumpy for some unknown reason, they'd respond urgently: "Left engine is on fire! Put the fire out!" That meant running the metal pallet eight hundred yards down to the ocean, jumping in, then running back another eight hundred yards to Frog Hill.

It wasn't that we couldn't do it. After the big weed-out of Hell Week, everybody could and would. But nobody liked those before-meal challenges—or the consequences for coming up short. Those who finished first would go right to the mess hall for a dry, indoor meal. The stragglers would have to dive into the surf one more time, then take their meal dripping wet, sitting outside in the wind and elements.

The whole thing wasn't any more painful than what we'd been going through. It was just irritating and uncomfortable. One sinister morning, the instructors were acting especially ornery and mean. "You can all eat outside today," one of them said. As the class grumbled silently, my swim buddy Hoss decided to put himself on the line. He approached the instructors and proposed a deal.

Hoss looked just like his name. Weighed 230, not quite six feet tall, built like a Brahma bull on a pair of tree-trunk legs. Looking at Hoss, you wouldn't think he'd be swift in the water. In fact, earlier in BUD/S, before he and I paired up, he'd had trouble passing some of the swims. He failed enough of them that he was in genuine danger of being rolled back in training. But Hoss was actually a very good swimmer, as strong in the water as he was on land. He just couldn't swim straight. He kept veering off to the right. Once he and I paired up and I could keep him on target, he proved he was one of the better swimmers in the class.

Hoss pointed to a huge link of anchor chain that was on the ground at the base of the hill. The link was so large, a normal-sized man couldn't even get his hands around it. "I think I can carry that link to the top and back down," he told the instructors. "If I do, everyone eats inside. Everyone. If I don't, well, whatever punishment you were thinking of, double it up and make it worse."

Hoss was strong. But the instructors weren't sure he was serious. "That link, that hill—that's a bold call," one of them marveled.

Frog Hill is nearly as steep as a double-black-diamond ski run. Under normal circumstances, if you had to hike it, you'd want to bring a walking stick. And the link must have weighed 120 pounds. But Hoss was serious. And given the way things had been going, most of the rest of us were willing to put our fate on his massive shoulders.

It took two classmates just to lift the heavy link onto Hoss's shoulders. With a few scattered cheers and plenty of moral support, he began his trek up the hill.

He got off to a solid start. One foot in front of the other, steady and slow. But thirty paces or so up the hill, Hoss really seemed to be struggling. He was swaying noticeably. He staggered once or twice. He was managing only the tiniest baby steps. Soon he was shaking his sweaty head in frustration. I guess this bold offer of his was a little bolder than he realized. As I looked at Hoss, he reminded me of one of Hannibal's elephants climbing the Alps or maybe Jesus on Calvary. He was on the side of the angels, but no one was entirely certain that guaranteed success.

The rest of us did what we could to encourage Hoss. We all surrounded him in a tight little circle, giving him just enough room to walk and breathe.

"Hoss! Hoss! Hoss!" we chanted.

He was sweating. He was groaning. He was nowhere near the top.

I was getting concerned. I didn't want Hoss to injure himself. But I knew him well enough to know how much he wanted this—for himself, for the rest of us, for one meal at least completely dry. I knew Hoss would expect me to push him.

"We can take the beating," I leaned in and told him. "But honestly, you can do this, bro. There is no doubt in my mind. You can find a second wind."

Hoss looked at me like I was crazy. Then he scrunched up his face. He gritted his teeth. And he pressed on.

He took another step. Then another. And another. His steps were getting longer now, more like stomps. He just kept plugging until, against all odds, he reached the top of Frog Hill. He steadied his footing up there and somehow found one last burst of strength.

He lifted the gargantuan link off his shoulders and fully up over his head. As his arms went up, he let out a long, slow, guttural growl. *"HOO-YAAAAAAH!"*

The whole class erupted in shouts and cheers. We knew Hoss had finished the hard part. We knew we'd all be eating inside. Literally, it was all downhill from here.

Hoss slid the weight back on his shoulders. He tromped to the bottom of the hill, a whole lot quicker and with a whole lot less strain than he'd made it to the top. When that link finally hit the dirt at the bottom of Frog Hill, the entire class erupted in delirious, congratulatory applause. It wasn't just the promise of a dry, mess-hall meal we were cheering. It was the near-impossible achievement by one of our own. Everyone rushed over to Hoss, who could barely hold up that powerful body of his to accept all the back-pats and hugs. The instructors weren't cheering quite like we were, but even they had to smile.

I'll give the instructors credit. They held up their end of the bargain. We all ate in the mess hall that day—and for most days forward. And another BUD/S legend was born.

The physical and mental challenges of BUD/S are only the foundation of SEAL training. To become the premier warriors on the planet, all SEALs need to master a vast array of war-fighting techniques. In the Second and Third Phases of BUD/S—and in the first year or two after—the new guys need to become experts in the specialized skills of modern warfare.

They need to know the cool stuff. There is a whole lot of that to learn.

Shooting. Blowing things up. Diving. Navigating. Rappelling. Getting in and out of a firefight or an ambush. Surviving in a blistering desert or on a snow-topped peak. Leaping from a helicopter and diving off a moving boat. Sinking a ship or assaulting one. Modern warfare is a complex art and science. The day of the dumb grunt, if it ever existed, is ancient history now. For SEALs, the lessons come fast and furious. How to jump out of an aircraft with combat equipment and night-vision optics. (Like those rearview mirrors say: "Warning: Objects may be closer than they appear"—especially the fast-approaching ground.) How to swim for miles underwater without a single bubble floating up. (Get to know your Dräger rebreather.) How to build a campsite in a snake-infested jungle. (The first question: "Isn't there somewhere else to bed down?") How to blow a house door off its rusty hinges. (If the hinges are already rusty, you probably don't need to blow it off. A crowbar or a sledgehammer will be easier, safer, and quicker. But if explosives are needed, we have quite a selection to choose from.) How to kill a man with a gun, a knife, a garden tool, or a well-placed choke. (It's all about picking the right tool for the job.)

We have some amazingly knowledgeable and experienced teachers in the SEAL instructor cadre who handle all the basics. When we want to go beyond their fields of expertise, we call in some world-class outside talent. Whatever the skill is, we have to be the best, and we find the finest experts who can get us there. One of America's top hunting guides comes in periodically to show us his favorite tracking techniques. For him, a forest is like a digital GPS readout. Every broken twig, each bent grass blade tells him where to go. He is listening, looking, and smelling, every step he takes.

"Once you know what you're looking for," he told us, "the environment almost speaks to you. And everything I'm describing works just as well when you're pursuing human prey."

Better, actually. "Humans aren't nearly as light on their feet as most animals are," he told us.

It was amazing what he could read into a single deer—or Nike—print in the dirt: which way the target was running, how fast, how long ago, and how far he'd likely gotten since then.

A top Baja 1000 racer shared some of his most aggressive off-road driving skills. It was a heart-pounding adventure just riding with him—driver's ed like it was never taught in high school. But he opened my eyes to how counterintuitive so much crisis driving is. Stepping on the gas to maintain stability and safety. Slamming left when you want the vehicle to go right. "It's like the rules of the road were written in reverse," he said with a shrug.

It turns out the back roads of western Iraq aren't so different from those of western Mexico. The driver's profession and ours both place a high premium on maintaining control at excessive speeds when our lives are on the line.

We want to know what all these experts know. We learn from world-class marksmen, knife-fighting pros, computer hackers, explosives gurus, and linguists who know Farsi, Urdu, and the most obscure dialects of Arabic. One group of SEALs flew to the Swiss Alps, where they got to practice highly aggressive free-fall techniques with cutting-edge canyon jumpers.

One of my favorites—and a favorite of many SEALs—is the hand-to-hand-fighting instruction we've gotten from mixed-martial-arts pros. There's a lot of high-tech weaponry out there, but we still can't forget what we call combatives. There are times you won't use a gun even if you have one. Sometimes a fight will break out that shouldn't end with a bullet in someone's head. Or a deadly level of force isn't needed to impede someone's progress. You have to think fast, grasp the situation, and react. Depending on the circumstances, you don't always go for the kill. Several of the top-ranked fighters of the mixed-martial-arts world have hosted our assault teams at their training compounds, and we've hosted them at ours.

"You guys clearly have the physical strength and the motivation," one of the fighters told my group. "But there are some head strikes and choke holds that we've learned in the octagon that could be highly useful to you in a close-combat encounter on the battlefield."

All of us were eager to learn.

He spent the next week schooling us on some of the most lethal takedown moves that have ever been applied to other humans. These guys aren't just amazing athletes. Their brains are packed with deadly knowledge about human anatomy.

"Wrap your arms around the neck just like this," one MMA champ said to a gym full of attentive special operators. "And squeeze—hard. The confrontation will end very quickly."

I have learned quite a few moves from these guys. One of my favorites is the flying neck seal. It's especially effective when an opponent is trying to flee and needs to be subdued. You run up behind him and, as you close the distance, you leap into the air and land on your target's back, simultaneously squeezing an arm around the front of his neck from behind. It's similar to what the MMA people call a rear-naked choke. The challenge is bringing your opponent to the ground in a such a way that you don't kill him—unless you intend to.

If you want to motivate someone not to resist, you'll need submission techniques such as joint locks and chokes to render an opponent noncombative. We use a lot of those during searches. Throw someone into a hold or a choke just to settle them down for a disciplined system of body search. We do this to reduce the threat, to maintain control, and to protect them and us.

Let me make one thing clear: We don't practice this or any of these moves on random civilians or even enemy combatants. We save them for when the need is real. The best way to practice is on a big, aggressive, uncooperative SEAL. SEALs never make it easy on other SEALs—for the training value, of course.

There is some debate in the SEAL community over what kind of combatives program we should have. There are zealots on both sides. Some people say, "You can't pretend you'll be fighting without weapons. That'll never happen. We don't fight our wars in a padded octagon."

Other people say "SEALs should be prepared to fight in the worst-case scenario."

But both those arguments miss the point, I believe. The best thing for the fighting spirit is to fight. Just having those skills builds tremendous confidence in the SEALs.

Becoming a combatives expert fosters toughness. It strengthens character. It builds hardness. It is a historic warrior skill set. The Samurai, the Spartans, and every other fighting culture before us—they've all been proud experts in the hand-to-hand component of the fight.

So are the SEALs.

These various outside instructors really seem to enjoy working with the SEALs. Some call us unsolicited and offer their expertise. Others we have sought out and asked for help. All of them say we are highly receptive students. They know—and we know—that what we're learning could well get an assault team member safely home to his wife and kids.

Often, the world's greatest experts come from our own community, even when we bring outside backup or use someone else's training facility. Over the years, we've developed some unique ways of teaching what our guys need to know. Our guys attend shooting school in Mississippi, North Carolina, and Texas. We have free-fall practice in Arizona and dive training in Virginia Beach, San Diego, and Newport, Rhode Island. We learn mountain warfare in the California Sierras and cold-weather fighting in Alaska. The desert terrain of California's Imperial Valley, we've discovered, is a great stand-in for Iraq and Afghanistan. For MOUT training—Military Operations in Urban Terrain—we go to Fort Polk, Louisiana, and San Clemente Island, California, and sharpen our skills in built-to-scale mock cities, chasing armed bad guys through dark alleys and up blind stairways. This kind of practice made a huge difference when we finally found ourselves in urban war zones.

In Close Quarters Combat, for example, we learn how to barge into a house or a building, clearing and dominating the environment. It is a complex operation. Every spec-ops force has its own way of doing it. The SEALs believe in speed. Breaching the door, going from room to room, fighting in a house or other confined space. How to use a crash grenade as we're storming through a door. How to assault a target so you get the bad guys and they don't get you. It all starts with an effective breach. You have to get through the door. Or the window or the wall or the roof, whatever it takes—you have to get inside.

Learning basic breaching techniques is a twelve-week course. Most doors of virtually any house are a simple breaching problem. We know how to use a prefabricated strip charge or a breaching charge affixed to the door. The breacher detonates the charge so the door will blow off the hinges. In the drama of the moment, we are already inside and moving around.

What's tricky is a building that's fortified. They know you're coming. They've barricaded themselves inside. There are options, mechanical and explosive. Sledgehammers. Chain saws. Hooligan tools, those metal pry bars favored by firefighters and house burglars. Quickie saws and plasma torches that cut through metal. A shotgun blast to blow the hinges off the door. And the entire time that's happening, someone could be shooting at you through the door.

Every training environment has its own unique challenges and its own potential for crazy stories afterward. That's especially true of the air. The array of SEAL jump-training opportunities is simply staggering. As far as I can report, no SEALs have jumped from the Space Shuttle. But otherwise, if it's flying in the sky, chances are SEALs are jumping out of it or hurling something down to earth. The jump training starts with static-line parachutes. Your chute is rigged to a static line connected to a cable inside the aircraft. You go out the door of the C-130, the C-17, or the C-141, floating down at whatever speed your body weight and that big round parachute will let you go. No cord to pull. No brake, no steering. You'll go wherever the whims of the wind, temperature, weather, and terrain want to take you, into a field, a forest, or a big, gnarly Tijuana cactus with needles sticking out. That'll ruin your day. I never caught a cactus, but plenty of guys did. They spent the next two hours with a pair of pliers, pulling needles out of their hands, arms, neck, and any other exposed body parts. Since much of jump training is in the desert, we also have to watch out for bugs, scorpions, rattlesnakes, and other unfriendly species. This is their home territory. We are literally just dropping in.

The ground is hard. If you spread your legs and try to anticipate the fall but you time it wrong, that's when you will break an ankle or blow out a knee. But if you keep your feet and knees together and your eyes on the horizon, that will keep you upright. You'll survive every jump you ever make.

It's amazing what we can parachute to earth: Jeeps. Humvees. Assault boats. Giant supply bundles. Everything SEALs need to survive through a mission. We have gotten very good at safely and accurately dropping heavy objects out of aircraft.

But the real control and precision comes with free fall. Every SEAL must learn to run his own jump. You pack your own chute. You check your own rig. One, two, three, the light goes green. You're one foot away from a twelve-thousand-foot drop. It's one of the great leaps of faith humans have ever invented. On the jumpmaster's call, you hurl yourself out of a plane and believe you will live. Turning in the air. Checking your altitude. Doing a couple of hand drills. Pulling the rip cord to open the chute, hoping you packed it right, and then—wham, the shock of the chute slowing you down. Seeing a bunch of silk over your head. You're at terminal velocity until you're not anymore. It's an amazing feeling, being in the sky with such control.

There are so many ways to jump out of a plane. You can fly as a group—six, eight, ten SEALs, in a diamond or a wedge so everyone can see each other. You open your chutes as a group, and you don't get fouled with another jumper. For combat purposes, it's always at night. You're flying in a stack, heavier men at the bottom. You already know each other's drop rate. Like a big accordion in the sky, you're following each other, all ending up in the same preplanned place. It takes a lot of practice, but it's a beautiful thing.

And it goes on from there. To HALOs, High Altitude–Low Opening jump. You're jumping out at 25,000 feet or higher but pulling the rip cord at plus or minus 2,000 feet. Not much room for error there. And you're less detectible by sound or radar. You can very quickly hit the ground and be up and running. On HAHO jumps, High Altitude–High Opening, you're pulling the cord as soon as you're out of the bird—and the wind carries you from there. Fifteen guys under parachutes, floating in at night. They could travel forty miles across Afghanistan, propelled only by the wind, undetectable to anyone on the ground.

Underwater diving is at the core of SEAL training. It's where we began. It's still the toughest environment on earth. These days, SEAL combat diving is almost never done with regular scuba gear. We rely on the LAR V Dräger Rebreather, a closed-loop system that doesn't use hissing compressed-air tanks and, most important of all, sends no bubbles to the surface. That's crucial for anyone on a clandestine dive. Nothing gets you caught like bubbles.

The Dräger is ingenious. It scrubs the carbon dioxide out of your breath. Instead of regular air, it returns pure oxygen. But it takes some getting used to. Once you get the rhythm going, the rebreather becomes almost like a second set of lungs. Even the air that's in your dive mask is pure oxygen. With a Dräger, you can stay discreetly underwater for hours. The members of SEAL Team Four who blew up General Manuel Noriega's personal gunship swam undetected into Balboa Harbor on Drägers. They could never have done that with regular scuba gear.

After a couple of weeks in the training tank, it's time to take the training to open water. Using a compass. Plotting a route. Learning to control depth and buoyancy.

It's surprisingly easy to fall off course. At the start of Dräger training, everyone keeps screwing up. Getting turned around. Becoming lost. Crashing into pilings and other swim pairs. It takes a lot of practice before anyone begins to look like a Navy SEAL.

Communicating underwater is never easy. Radios and cell phones don't work down there. Two swim buddies must speak the language of nods, waves, and gentle shoves, everything this side of Vulcan mind melds. But even on the best-planned trips, you can always count on surprises. One time, a buddy and I were diving in San Diego Bay when, all of a sudden, the water started shaking. Twenty feet down, it felt like an earthquake. The rumbles got louder and more violent. The water was swirling all around. I had no idea what it could possibly be. My ears were filled with what sounded like a giant growl. It was as if some huge horror-movie sea monster was coming straight at us.

That's what it feels like to be diving when a tugboat passes overhead.

Tugs don't look so threatening. They don't move fast for their size. But their massive diesel engines and huge propellers are strong enough to push an aircraft carrier or a barge piled high with steel. As this one came roaring our way, we didn't know what to do. We dove right to the bottom of the bay, into the mud and muck, and stayed down there until the sea-monster tug had chugged along. But sometimes, there is no place underwater to hide.

There are other unexpected dangers underwater.

The bay is home to the Navy's Marine Mammal Program, where dolphins are trained to help with port security. With their intelligence and size, they have a special knack for running interference against a hostile swimmer. But every once in a while, a SEAL swim pair is physically assaulted by one of these dolphins. The closest thing I can compare it to is being sniffed by a frisky neighborhood dog—if the dog weighed six hundred pounds and was dead set on getting cozy.

No SEAL has ever been nuzzled to death by a runaway bottlenose, and we've never had to use deadly force to defend a teammate from one. But there is nothing fun about one of the most athletic and headstrong animals in the water making an aggressive pass at you. It's funny, but only if it's happening to someone else.

Off the Virginia coast in Little Creek, someone sank one of those giant shipping containers like you'd see on the back of a semitrailer or a train. That one box has produced countless hours of panic and amusement. The sunken box is open at one end, and it's easy to swim in there by mistake. More than a few trainees have. The box is all metal, which makes your compass start doing crazy things. If you swim into that box not knowing it's there, it feels like you have flown into a coffin. That's not hard to do when you're training at night and the only thing you can see is the tiny glow of the chem-light that is illuminating your attack board. Down there, it's darker than the dark side of the moon. And all of a sudden, you're surrounded by metal, and your compass is jumping all over the place. You're wondering, What the hell is going on here? It's like you're in some vortex somewhere.

People laugh about it later. "Yeah, I hit the box one time," one team member told me. "I was in there for half an hour trying to figure out what the hell was going on."

All this training is exhilarating and fun. But it is also vital to our survival. Lesson by lesson, day by day, SEALs work hard to be the best at every imaginable battlefield skill. We train. We practice. We make mistakes and correct them. We push ourselves some more. Eventually, the raw SEAL recruit becomes something other men can only dream of—a warrior in every sense of the word.

5

YOUNG WARRIOR

As long as you brothers support one another
and render assistance to one another, your enemies
can never gain victory over you. But if you fall away
from one another, you can be broken like
a frail arrow, one at a time.
—Genghis Khan

If I had a fresh platoon of poorly trained recruits, I'd have given them a gung-ho speech. Standing around a bonfire the night before we deployed, I would have quoted Roman or Spartan mythology. Plutarch said, "The Spartans don't ask how many are the enemy but where they are." I would have done everything I could to pump them up, mentally and physically, for the fierce battle ahead.

But there is zero need to do that with a bunch of SEALs.

Standing on the beach in a tight, quiet circle with Ro, Big D, Cams, Lope, and the others, I talked about balance instead. "Before we step on that bird tomorrow and begin this campaign," I said, "we need to be sure everything at home is taken care of. Your finances are in order. Your families have what they need. Nothing back here is left unsaid or undone. Where we're going, we all need to take care of each other. So if anyone has something that requires attention at home—bills, house repairs, kid stuff, whatever—I can help take care of it now. Or Chief can. Let us know. From here on out, we can't be looking backwards. We have to be present every single second we are over there."

There is never an issue of getting SEALs motivated. They can't wait to see for themselves where the enemy is and then confront him. Some people are born for this. It is such a part of their being, they are incomplete without it. They are warriors.

I was born a warrior. It just took a couple of decades to make the designation official. I grew up in the 1970s and '80s in northern California, thirty-five miles south of San Francisco, in a place called Los Altos. That's Spanish for "the heights" or "the foothills." When I came along, Los Altos still had a few apricot and peach orchards where the old Spanish land-grant ranches used to be. But the gently rolling terrain was being transformed into sprawling suburbs. The Silicon Valley, people were calling the area, for all the computer companies that were popping up. Apple, Adobe, Intuit, Hewlett-Packard—they all had facilities nearby. There were lots of smart kids in Los Altos and, as time went on, some very rich adults.

My dad, Tom Denver, was a partner at a busy law firm, a very disciplined and focused man. He rowed crew in college and still runs every day. He loves marathons and off-road races and is old-school in a lot of ways, hard and just—and brilliant. I don't confer that on many people, but *brilliant* definitely applies to him. Yet he's always been down-to-earth and accessible to anyone. At night when we were kids, he would read books to my younger brother and me: *Jason and the Argonauts, Hannibal and the Elephants, Alexander and the Macedonians, The Hobbit, Lord of the Rings.* They were stories of struggle and war and cavalry, tales of individual hardship and adventure. In those stories, the protagonist was often a leader whose fortitude and character were being tested in some deep and profound way. Looking back, I know those stories planted ideas in my head, ideas that would have a huge impact on my future. I learned a lot from my father, including the importance of working hard, being strong, and trusting yourself.

I definitely owe the stork who delivered me to Deanna Denver. My mom has always been a dreamer. She's had every job on earth. She's been a dental hygienist, a PE teacher, a wedding photographer, an inventor, a family counselor—you name it. She is a talented artist—painting, woodworking, producing beautiful stained glass, creating amazing craft gifts every Christmas. She's an excellent tennis player, an aggressive downhill skier, and a constant free spirit, very much her own person, always up for an adventure. Her brothers Dick and Dave convinced Grandma to name their sister after the spunky girl-next-door star Deanna Durbin. She instilled in my brother and me the idea that anything is possible in life.

My brother, Nate, is three years younger. He and I were close when we were little, and we've never drifted apart. He's a musician, a songwriter, a carpenter, a champion stair-climber, a world traveler, a sponsored snowboarder, a bike racer, a poet, an author, an artist—as much a Renaissance man as anyone I've ever met. He has shockingly perfect posture and always carries himself like a gentleman. Nate was a much more natural student than I was. But we shared an intense love for sports and for hanging around with each other. We had endless fun together. My brother has always been my closest friend.

Our closeness growing up is a big part of the reason that years later I felt immediately comfortable in the tight-knit SEAL brotherhood.

Teammates, swim buddies, boat crews, never leaving a fallen SEAL behind—because of Nate, I understood all of that instinctively. If I ever needed Nate but the labors of Hercules were placed in front of him, he would knock them out in a day and then be standing at my side, fresh and ready to rumble on my behalf. He's my forever swim buddy. Whatever might happen, I always knew my brother had my back.

When we were five and eight years old, we had adjoining rooms on the lower level of our house. One day, I decided I'd give my little brother a haircut. Trusting as he was, Nate sat quietly while I snipped away—until I almost cut off his left ear. He yelped so loudly, my mom came running. Her footsteps on the stairs sounded like serious trouble to me. Without even thinking, I hopped out a window and bolted down the street. She saw Nate's ear. But Mom being Mom, she kept her cool and grabbed some bandages from the bathroom. She managed to stop the bleeding in a minute or two. When she asked what had happened, all Nate would say was that he accidentally cut himself. He wouldn't rat me out. I confessed later, but I got it. The little dude was looking out for me, and I had to be sure I looked out for him.

I struggled academically, especially in the younger grades. I was plenty bright, my teachers said. But my mind was bouncing everywhere. Kids like me they used to call hyperactive. It's what people now label ADHD. I had trouble focusing well when it came to academics, and that left me vulnerable to ridicule from other kids. I always liked to read. But I was clueless with math. Still am, actually. The only time I thought I might be in trouble in SEAL training was on the physics and math part of my diving qualification. I had to take a makeup test and got through only with my roommate coaching me all night.

But there was one area where I always excelled. Sports. Even as a little kid, the field was my natural habitat. Sports focused my undirected energy. It's where I was finally one of the cool kids, where I knew what I was doing, where I wasn't on the outs anymore. Put a ball in my hand, and I was in control. I had basic, raw talent. I was strong and fast for my age. And I was constantly competing, absolutely driven to win. I'm not sure if I loved winning so much or I just really hated to lose. Whatever the combination, my mom still tells stories about the horrible temper I had as a child. I was inconsolable if I lost at anything. Shooting baskets, kicking a soccer ball, playing a board game, whatever it was—I could ruin the day for everyone if somebody else came in first. My free-spirit mom didn't feel like she instilled that in me. My dad didn't, either. He focused on discipline and working hard—but never pushed the idea that winning was everything. That supercompetitiveness, I'm convinced, was just me, buried somewhere deep in my genetic code.

We lived on a cul-de-sac. Our street, Mariposa Avenue, was rough asphalt laid out in the shape of a lima bean. At my fifth birthday party, we had a running race. Five or six kids, once around the cul-de-sac. I was in the lead most of the way, and then this other boy pulled in front of me. No! I had to win so badly, I dove across the finish line Superman-style, scraping my hands, knees, elbows, and chin against that ragged asphalt. Pain, blood—I didn't care. The thought of losing was so much worse.

My dad says he knew something was different about me as far back as my youth soccer team, the Silver Streaks. We were playing in a big game, which ended in a tie. The game had to be decided with an overtime shoot-out, three kicks for each side. The coach's son was also on our team, and he took the first kick. It was way off to the left. The coach's son took the second kick. That one bounced against the goalie's chest. His son now 0 for 2, the coach called me in.

Before I approached the ball, I glanced over at my father, who was standing on the sideline like he always was. My dad gave me a signal he'd given me before. He lifted both his hands and shook them as if to say: "Just stay loose. Nice and relaxed."

As my dad tells the story, I approached the ball cold as ice. The ref blew the whistle, and I sent the ball flying right into the goal. The Silver Streaks briefly had the lead, but it wasn't enough to win the game. The other team scored, and the match ended in a tie. When I came off the field, I ran right over to my father. "If they'd let me take all three, we woulda won," I said. My dad still marvels at that. "There was a confidence there," he told me years later, "a level of self-assuredness you don't see in many eight-year-olds."

That was around the time my parents divorced.

I never doubted for a minute that my mom and dad loved Nate and me. My mother especially made sure we knew that. "This is an adult problem that has nothing to do with two perfect boys," she told us. We lived with Mom, but Dad stayed close to us. Twice a week, he would pick us up at school and take us out to dinner. I don't remember a single sporting event of my brother's or mine that our dad didn't attend. But with our parents' divorce, we were very much on the lower end of the economic spectrum at Bullis-Purissima Elementary School in the booming Silicon Valley. We weren't living in our car or eating out of Dumpsters or anything like that. Mom was a genius at stretching a dollar and maxing a credit card. She managed to take us on regular ski trips and summer-cottage visits with the relatives back east. But we definitely didn't have all the luxuries a lot of other kids had—the video games and designer sneakers and spring-break trips to Hawaii.

You know how cruel some children can be, drilling mercilessly into other kids' insecurities. They'll always find something to exploit. Well, there was a group of boys in my school who really started giving me a hard time. To this day, I still appreciate two adults who stepped forward for me. Both of them happened to be Marines.

In sixth grade, I was a Cub Scout. Once a week, I had to wear my Scout uniform to school. At my school, that was not considered too cool. None of the bullies were in the Cub Scouts, and they loved making fun of my uniform. I wasn't going to take that passively. I started lashing out, getting into scrapes that kept getting me sent to the principal's office. One day, Mr. Barry, the principal, called my dad at work.

"Rorke's been suspended for fighting," he told my father. "But Rorke did the right thing. Those little rich kids were asking for it." That was it. I was so sick of the teasing, I threw my Cub Scout shirt in the garbage and told Mr. Barry and my dad that I wasn't wearing my uniform to school anymore.

But Mr. Barry had one last move. "Wait a week before you give up on this," he told me. "Would you be willing to wear your uniform one more time?"

Okay, I told him, not too enthusiastically.

That next week, we were standing at assembly for the flag-raising. I had on my Cub Scout uniform. I could tell the bullies were already eyeing me. Mr. Barry came in late, and he sure caused a stir. He was wearing the dress blues of the U.S. Marine Corps with full medals and a sword. It was insane. No one at school had ever seen him dressed like that before.

"Raising the flag," he announced to the assembly, "is a very special duty. I need an assistant to join me today."

He looked out at the students.

"Me, me, me!" the kids shouted, their hands shooting up. It seemed like everyone wanted this job.

"Let me review the troops," Mr. Barry said, sounding even more serious than he usually did. "I have to see who makes muster."

He walked up and down the ranks of students, stopping several times before moving along. Then he stopped next to me. "To raise Old Glory," he said, "it should be another man in uniform."

He and I marched to the front of the assembly. We raised the flag and saluted together. He took a medal off his uniform and pinned it on my chest before I returned to stand with my class.

That alone didn't quiet the bullies completely. But it gave me a much-needed shot of confidence, and I was never afraid to wear my Scout uniform again.

Over the years, my mom dated some great guys and some real colorful characters. My dad was my biggest adult-male influence, but I've always felt I was the product of many fathers. My mom's boyfriends and my various coaches definitely influenced me as well. From them, my brother and I learned some of our very best lessons about how to be—and how not to be—a man. Thinking back, I can barely imagine how hard it must have been for the mom of two overactive boys to be working, attending grad school, and keeping a love life going, too.

Russ was a 250-pound, retired-Marine tough guy who worked as a deputy sheriff. It was Russ who taught me how to look a man in the eye and give a firm, confident handshake. He was big on that sort of thing. He gave Nate and me military-style crew cuts. We hated that. He was always trying to pit us against one another. He must have gone home scratching his head because, try as he might, he could not split us apart. He certainly wasn't the most paternal guy. But he did like competing, and he definitely liked to win. So when my mom told him about the trouble I was still having with the school bullies, he decided to teach my brother and me some basic boxing moves. "Just in case," he said. We thought that was fun. When Russ heard a special Career Day was being held at my school, he really sprang into action. Other kids' parents would be telling the students what it was like being a doctor or a lawyer or a computer executive. My mother's burly boyfriend said he'd come and show the kids what boxers do.

I don't imagine Mr. Barry was too charmed by Russ's kind offer. Really, how many Bullis-Purissima students would be pursuing boxing careers? But there was big Russ arriving at school with a duffle bag of Everlast boxing gloves and a large, shiny bell. He set up a temporary ring on the playground, where he gave a quick talk on the boxing basics—hooks, jabs, crosses, and uppercuts—before the practical demonstration began.

"We will fight one-minute rounds," Russ announced. "Winner stays in the ring."

He just so happened to pick me for the first bout. He paired me up with Ernie, one of my least favorite bullies. Several other parents who were there for Career Day wandered out to watch. I will never forget the excitement I felt as Russ clanged the opening bell.

I went at Ernie fearlessly. *Pow! Pow! Pow!* At his chest. At the side of his head. Straight into his face. Yes, training in advance can be a huge advantage, a lesson I am happy I learned so young. I wasn't quite ready for the Golden Gloves finals. But I was Mike Tyson compared to my bewildered classmate. Within fifteen seconds, the bully-boy's nose was bleeding, and soon he quit the fight. I then proceeded to beat, bloody, or bruise—sometimes all three—the next four boys I was paired against. One by one, they left the ring demoralized. The only bummer was that the last kid I fought, Ishmael, was someone I actually liked. I had to make it look like I was pounding him while making sure I didn't hurt him at all. It was a special day for me, and I did not take any grief from any of my classmates from that point on.

Sports kept serving me like that, helping to build my confidence and my sense of identity. On the court, on the field, or in the pool, I always felt comfortable and naturally in charge. In the years to come, I don't think I played on any athletic team without being chosen captain. That's where I got my first tastes of being a leader. I liked that role, I learned, and many people did not. I might have sat in the back of the room in math class and hoped the teacher didn't call on me, but I never hung back on the field. I wanted to be the lead guy. I wanted to have the ball when the game was on the line. I liked taking the final shot when everything was riding on my shoulders. That's a lot of responsibility. Most people worry that everyone will be mad at them if they fail. I just felt comfortable in that position, and I grabbed it every chance I got.

"Just shoot," I remember my dad telling me on the basketball court one day. "You won't win the game by not shooting. Someone needs to put the ball into the net. Someone needs to take the shot."

Without even knowing it, I was setting myself up to be an officer in the Navy and a commander in the SEALs.

It wasn't until I got to Los Altos High School that I began to find my place in the crowd. Our school had lots of cliques, as many high schools do. The brainiacs. The cool kids. The stoners. I got along with most groups. But I found my footing in sports, even though I wasn't exactly a stereotypical jock. I got physically stronger in my freshman year. I started playing water polo and really enjoyed it. I grew my hair long, my own personal rebellion against Big Russ's junior-Marine fantasies. I wore corduroy pants with sandals. I liked vintage pullover and colorful T-shirts. We didn't do our shopping at high-end Nordstrom like the wealthier kids. But I had my California casual attitude, and I never liked seeing other kids get picked on.

Water polo is a tough, physical sport, kind of like wrestling for a couple of hours in the deep end of a pool with hardly any breaks. It takes a lot of stamina to be good at water polo. Freshman year, the coach asked if I wanted to play for the varsity squad. I talked to my dad and a couple of other people and decided, "No, I'll play JV instead." To this day I've regretted that decision. The varsity team was much stronger, and I think I could have held my own with the big guys. Always I pushed myself harder than anyone else on the team. That was a huge advantage over my peers. The voice of my dad was inside my head: "You can do this. Just give it your all."

During practice, I would never lose a sprint late in a workout. Everyone else would be exhausted, and I'd just push some more. It was basically a test of who had the most guts. When I was a senior, it was known that you were not going to keep up with Denver at the end of a workout. Then one day, we were running pool-long sprints. It was the varsity and the junior varsity together. On each sprint I could see one other boy on the far side of the pool get to the wall just a split second after me. He'll drop off soon, I figured. I won't see him much longer.

But on the final sprint, he was still there, and we were body lengths ahead of everyone else. When we hit the wall that last time, barely a second apart, I finally looked over at who'd been able to keep up with me. It was my freshman little brother, Nate. Always pushing hard—that's who the Denver boys were.

I was getting looked at to play water polo at most of the big-name college programs in California. But by the time I had to make a decision, I wasn't sure I wanted to go that way. Back in eighth grade, at a summer cabin with my cousins in upstate New York, my mom had bought my brother and me a couple of lacrosse sticks. We didn't know the game, but Mom taught us the basics—how to use the sticks to scoop up the rubber ball and toss it back and forth. When my high school started a club lacrosse team my sophomore year, I signed up. Most kids who go on to play Division I lacrosse in college have been playing since they were big enough to hold a stick. I'd only played three years. But I went to a one-week lacrosse summer camp at Syracuse University, where both my parents and my grandfather had attended college. At the end of the week, I was recruited by the coaches there. Lacrosse bumped water polo aside.

Syracuse has one of the most dominant lacrosse teams in the nation. Johns Hopkins, the University of Virginia, and Princeton are always in the mix, as are a few other East Coast schools. Syracuse has more NCAA National Championships than any other school. I knew if I decided to go to any other major power in the lacrosse world, I most likely would have cracked the starting lineup my freshman year. I also knew that if I went to Syracuse, I would have to scrap it out with the best of the best, and that appealed to me.

I was one of the very first kids from California recruited to play for a major East Coast lacrosse power. As the sport has grown, all the big programs have recruited players from all over the country. But I was an anomaly back then. And when I showed up for my recruiting visit, I didn't look too much like a typical northeastern high school jock. I was much more California in my surfer T-shirt, hiking boots, and thick, dark hair down my back. Don't go looking for any ancient photographs. I've already burned them all.

I was honored to wear the Orange jersey, number 16, and play as a long-stick midfielder and close defender for legendary Coach Roy Simmons Jr. in the Carrier Dome. Coach Simmons taught us many things. None was more important than an utter disdain for mediocrity. I became incredibly close to my Syracuse teammates Colsey, Photo, Sammy Dukes, Toby, K-9, and my closest friend, Oak. Like my brother had, those guys taught me lessons about being a team member and looking out for each other. In my four years at Syracuse, I was a member of two national championship teams. I was a team captain and all-American my senior season.

It was at Syracuse that I got the nickname that stuck with me all the way through my SEAL days. I arrived on campus at 180 pounds. When I realized that wasn't big enough for the type of Division I player I wanted to be, I started spending extra time in the gym. That spring, when we divided the team for an upstate-downstate practice game, I was up to 200 and feeling strong.

About halfway through the game, an upperclassman who used to rag on me for being from California was breaking out on an outlet pass. The goalie lobbed the ball to him. As he looked over his shoulder, I had an open, ten-step shot at him, as clean a hit as there is in lacrosse. It was a dream moment for me, a chance to legally crush someone who'd been busting on me. I dropped my shoulder and hit him so hard he fell to the ground, looking dazed.

Coach Simmons ran over.

"Man, I'm not sure what hit me," the upperclassman said.

"It looks like you got run over by a diesel pickup truck with California plates," Coach Simmons said.

At dinner that night, the team was still talking about that hit of mine. "Damn, Denver," said Ricky, one of the team's real stars, "you're twenty pounds bigger than you were. Coach was right. You are a diesel pickup. From now on, I'm gonna start calling you Diesel." And it stuck. At Syracuse and later, Diesel sometimes got shortened to "D." My family still calls me Rorke. But hardly any of my friends do.

Being from California and looking a little shaggy when I arrived weren't the only things that made me stand out from my hard-charging Orange teammates. I wasn't a drinker, and that was definitely unusual in the world of college lacrosse. I've never minded if other people drank. Most of the people I know, including most of my relatives, like to take a drink. But I never have. I never believed drinking would make me a stronger athlete, and I'd gotten to know a couple of problem drinkers, including one of my mother's boyfriends. I just never wanted to start.

Not drinking could have been a real problem for me at Syracuse. Lacrosse is a famously hard-partying sport. If you made the travel team as a freshman, you got invited to a party run by the seniors. It was called Rookie-Bring-a-Bottle Night. Each new freshman was expected to come to the party with a bottle of hard liquor, and you'd better choose it carefully. Chances are, you'd be drinking most of it by the time the night was done. I wasn't planning to start drinking that night. But based on the excitement of the seniors, I was pretty sure I needed a plan.

The toughest man on the team was one of our captains. Reggie was his name. My locker was right next to Reggie's. He was a beast and one of my idols. He came from a local family of legendary tough guys. He was a lot bigger than I was, a former wrestling champion. But I'd given him a solid hit one day in practice, and I think it earned me some grudging respect. "You know, Denver," he'd said to me that day, "you're a lot tougher than we thought you'd be, coming from California."

I found out Reggie liked Jack Daniel's. I brought a bottle with me to the party house, arriving a little late. I could see the seniors eyeing me as I came in. I had a pretty good idea what they were thinking.

I walked past everyone and found Reggie in the back. I placed the bottle of Jack on the table in front of him.

"This is for you," I said. "I don't drink, and I am not starting tonight. If you all want to test that, it is going to take all of you. And whoever gets their hands on me first is going to regret it."

Reggie just smiled. He didn't say a word.

I walked back out to the porch, where most of my freshman buddies were already well on their way to drunken oblivion. I waited for whatever was coming next. From the porch, I could see four or five seniors, all consulting Reggie. I couldn't hear what they were saying. But I liked their body language. Reggie seemed to be telling them that if they wanted to get me, have at it. But he was not interested. Nobody touched me that night. Which is lucky, I know. I could have held my own against most of the lacrosse players. But brawling Reggie would have been tough. It made for one of the greatest nights of my life, proving that almost anything was possible with a well-thought-out plan.

I ended up choosing fine arts as my college major. My athletic-academic advisor had suggested speech/communications, saying some Syracuse jocks had discovered it wasn't too time-consuming. But I wasn't looking for the easy way out. I took a couple of art and art history classes. I liked them, and I kept taking more. I loved being exposed to great thinkers and great ideas. Fine arts isn't too common a major for serious lacrosse players or future SEALs. But it ended up serving me well. The rest of my life I'd be surrounded by quantitative types, who had studied math or science in college and tended to see the world in black-and-white. Every organization needs some of those. But studying fine arts made me far more comfortable dealing with the nuances and complexities of real life, as any leader must.

Until senior year, I never thought seriously about joining the military. Not too many people from my high school or my college had shown much interest in enlisting. Neither of my parents served that way. During the Vietnam War, my dad had gone down to the Army recruiting office to enlist. But his thick glasses and poor eyesight medically disqualified him. After a short stint as a college crew coach, he went off to law school.

We did have a war hero in the family, and I'd heard some stories about him. My father's father, Thomas Rorke, was an Army Air Corps navigator in World War II, flying a big battle plane called a B-24 Liberator. After a very successful run, he was killed in operations in the Pacific Theater. I never knew him, of course. My dad didn't either. He was two months old when his father was killed. When my dad was ten, his mom married a New York City police officer named Dan Denver, whose name she and the children took. Yet my father grew up always knowing his father was a war hero. As an adult, my dad didn't talk about his father all that much. But he and my mom did name me for that side of the family. And when my father got together with his uncles and his cousins, they loved telling wild family stories. The Rorkes were a tough, fun, brawling breed of Irish immigrants who came to America from County Offaly. My great-grandfather was a New York police inspector. Even beyond my name, I think I have a lot of Rorke in me.

But ancestry alone didn't open my eyes to the idea of military service. That took a book in the mail from my father. All through college, he sent books to me. I thought of them as sequels to the *Elephants*, the *Argonauts*, and those other books he'd read to us as children. Senior year, he sent me a copy of *My Early Life*, by Winston Churchill. I knew Churchill had been the prime minister of England and an important figure in World War II, but I'd never read that much about him or anything he'd written. I certainly wasn't patterning my life on his, and I'm quite sure that wasn't my father's intent. But in the book, Churchill wrote about his time in the field as a young, frontline officer in the British Army and as a war correspondent overseas. The way he described that world, it sounded unimaginably exciting and profoundly consequential to me.

> *There is nothing like the dawn. The quarter of an hour before the curtain is lifted upon an unknowable situation is an intense experience of war. Was the ridge held by the enemy or not? Were we riding through the gloom into thousands of ferocious savages? Every step might be deadly. Yet there was no time for overmuch precaution. The regiment was coming on behind us, and dawn was breaking. It was already half light as we climbed the slope. What should we find at the summit? For cool, tense excitement I commend such moments.*

He talked about his days at the Royal Military Academy at Sandhurst and the excitement of being a real-life combat leader in Cuba, South Africa, and the Sudan. With the benefit of hindsight, he laid out the strategies behind his battlefield decisions and the impact they had. He explained in moving detail what was going through his mind as he went off to war and then came home. He shared his hopes and disappointments about the state of Britain's large but fading empire. He described his techniques for psyching out the enemy and motivating his men. He detailed the high standards he set for himself and felt responsible to meet. There was a level of focus and a higher purpose and, yes, a sense of romantic adventure in Churchill's words that struck me like a lacrosse stick across the head. He thought so deeply. His command of the English language was so strong.

It sounds presumptuous, I know, to say I felt like I'd found a kindred spirit in Winston Churchill. But he was saying things that resonated profoundly with me. He shared his reactions across a spectrum of insight, emotion, and spirituality that I had never experienced before. I swear he was talking straight to me.

Come on now all you young men, all over the world. You are needed more than ever now to fill the gap of a generation shorn by the war. You have not an hour to lose. You must take your place in Life's fighting line. Twenty to twenty-five! These are the years! Don't be content with things as they are. "The earth is yours and the fullness thereof." Enter upon your inheritance, accept your responsibilities. Raise the glorious flags again, advance them upon the new enemies, who constantly gather upon the front of the human army, and have only to be assaulted to be overthrown. Don't take no for an answer. Never submit to failure. Do not be fobbed off with mere personal success or acceptance. You will make all kinds of mistakes. But as long as you are generous and true, and also fierce, you cannot hurt the world or even seriously distress her. She was made to be wooed and won by youth. She has lived and thrived only by repeated subjugations.

Confronted with such eloquence, all I could think was, Where do I sign up?

Churchill believed that being a soldier in the British Empire was absolutely a requirement for being a statesman later in life. He described that process of preparation in a way that made total sense to me. To seek adventure, honor, and glory—all those things appealed to me. He, like me, felt a responsibility to share what he had been so privileged to learn.

Reading Churchill, I knew immediately that one day I would serve.

6

RAW MATERIAL

*Of one hundred men, ten shouldn't
even be there. Eighty are just targets. Nine are the real
fighters, and we are lucky to have them for they
make the battle. Ah, but the one: He is a warrior and
will bring the others back.*

—Heraclitus

The platoon I took to Iraq, it was scary how well we knew each other. I knew how every one of them moved, how they breathed, how they smelled at night. It could be pitch black in the woods. We could be on night-vision. A guy got up and started walking around. It was just a silhouette against the darkness. I knew exactly who it was. Everyone in the whole platoon knew. We were running so hard, working so long, risking so much together, there was no way to have secrets in that group. We all knew whose crazy uncle was putting pressure on him. We all knew who was having trouble with his wife or girlfriend— and the one dumb bastard who was having trouble with both.

I wasn't one of the boys. I was the officer. I had their lives in my hands and the weight of command. For a military unit, we had a fairly casual rapport. They didn't call me sir. They didn't call me Rorke. The might say "LT," for lieutenant, or "Mister D."

The senior Army or Marine officers in Iraq, that kind of thing made their skin crawl. They called each other by individual rank, even in private. We were not too particular about that detail. We had a nontraditional approach to our battle gear. Guys made individual choices. I wore a pair of Solomon assault shoes to run onto a target as opposed to Army desert boots. Another guy wore Oakley boots because he liked them. Someone else was wearing Nikes. Another guy had a hat on backward underneath his helmet. It was good luck for him. That would never fly in a regular unit.

We were obsessive about a thousand things—the condition of our weapons, the details of the mission plan, how we were going to keep everyone alive on a treacherous battlefield. We were deadly serious about war. But making ourselves comfortable in the small, individual ways we could—that could only make us better fighters and more confident men.

Desert boots or Nikes, LT or Mister D, I'm pretty sure the enemy wasn't deciding whether or not to kill us based on those kind of details.

Every year, thousands of young men across America look into the mirror and see a future U.S. Navy SEAL. However the notion is planted—a TV report on SEAL adventures, a friend just back from war, a kick-ass score on a shoot-'em-up video game, or even a book in the mail—the question is always the same.

"Why not me?"

They come seeking excitement. They show up hoping to test

themselves. They are drawn to the SEAL mythology. They want to be part of a consistently winning team. They may or may not already be serving in the Navy or some other branch of the military. But somehow or another, they've convinced themselves they just might have what it takes to be a SEAL.

And some of them are right.

In fourteen years of evaluating, training, and leading SEALs after becoming one myself, I've learned that it's almost impossible to predict in advance who will and who won't succeed. Often, they're not the ones you'd expect.

We've had guys from Kansas who'd never seen the ocean become phenomenally talented SEALs. We've had Olympic-level swimmers who quit on day one. On one of my very first days as a SEAL training officer, we accepted a brainy kid from Michigan who was a master-level chess champion. He proved himself a brilliant tactician even when the battlefield wasn't laid out in sixty-four light or dark squares. Then we rejected a future NFL star. He didn't strike us as a real team player. Turns out we were correct.

Spend any time around SEALs and you can't help but notice: We're not all six-foot-three musclemen. We do have our share of jacked-up gym rats, but SEALs come in many shapes and sizes, and we like it that way. You can't spot the SEAL just by glancing down the bar or across the mess hall. In any group of SEALs, there will be big dudes next to wiry guys, people from a variety of places and backgrounds. There could be a boxer from Oregon next to a coal miner from Pennsylvania next to a cowboy from Texas next to an astrophysics major from New Hampshire next to a Churchill-reading, California-born lacrosse player like me.

Most SEALs don't talk a lot about why they became SEALs. Only recently did I ever ask Matt why he joined up. He ticked off four reasons. "The people, see the world, do unique things, and serve"—in that order. But I have noticed over the years some quintessential SEAL profiles, and they do keep coming up again. We have what I call the Smurf SEAL. Five foot five, he was a starting linebacker on his high school football team. But he knew he was every bit as tough as the bigger guys, and he proved it all season long. We have the Rough-Upbringing SEAL, who came out of South Boston or the ganglands of Los Angeles or the barrios of Houston, where being tough was just a way of surviving. Joining the SEALs was a healthier way to move his life forward. There's the Brawler SEAL. A guy like that, you just know: If he weren't here, he'd be in prison. Brawler SEALs aren't pure antisocial thugs. A real thug would never have the focus or the discipline to meet our training requirements. There's no one bad enough to stare down thirty, forty, or seventy SEAL recruits enforcing our code of conduct.

Someone we've seen a lot more lately is the Gamer SEAL. They've spent an inordinate amount of time playing first-person shooter, blast-'em-up games like Call of Duty or Tom Clancy's Splinter Cell or SOCOM: U.S. Navy SEALs or whatever's in beta test now. These gamers have gotten a taste of virtual warfare. They want more action-packed adventure than even the best games provide. I just have to remind them: "You realize, in our line of work, we don't get twenty lives."

Then there's the Ivy League SEAL. They're the Rhodes scholars, the straight-A honors graduates, the military academy standouts. At some point they say to themselves, "I could make a killing right now on Wall Street, but I want something more meaningful." Military service, especially joining an elite military organization like the SEALs, appeals to them. These Ivy SEALs are a key part of our officer corps. But they have to convince the other SEALs they aren't here just to give their high-gloss résumés some military spit-polish.

And don't forget the Legacy SEAL. In our nation, military service is often a family tradition, and these candidates had a father or an uncle or a brother who was a SEAL. They know the culture. They understand the expectations. They aren't caught off guard by the sacrifices. Second- and soon third-generation SEALs are some of our best performers. But there's also a flip side to these family traditions, a question we always have to ask recruits with SEAL pedigrees. "Is this your dream—or your father's?" Whatever they say, we'll learn the truth in training.

And of course we also have people I like to call Proto-SEALs—those rock-hard, Greek-god characters you'd expect to see on a SEAL recruiting poster or maybe a Wheaties box. In many ways, they exemplify the SEAL qualities of strength, pride, honor, and a little battlefield intimidation. Believe me, Achilles, Hector, Ajax, or Alexander the Great didn't show up on the battlefield with droopy shoulders and beer guts. Their fellow warriors knew immediately a champion was fighting beside them. The enemy knew it, too.

As for me, I always considered myself a SEAL mutt, a mix of several breeds.

This kind of diversity makes us different from many other elite organizations. The vast majority of people could never play in the NBA, even if they worked hard their whole lives to achieve that goal. Almost everyone in that league has a certain height and jumping ability. To be an Olympic swimmer, it really helps to be built like Michael Phelps. There are unyielding genetic requirements in many of these exclusive clubs. That's not exactly true for us. You can be five foot two, hideously ugly, and still become a Navy SEAL, although I've heard from young women over the years how ruggedly handsome they thought my SEAL friends were. My mom certainly noticed when I brought her to the SEAL Christmas party in Coronado, California, one year. All the guys had showered and combed their hair. "That's a very good-looking, self-assured group of young men," she said, adding with a laugh: "Have the SEALs ever considered doing one of those beefcake calendars for charity?"

Mom was joking—I think.

But however we get here, it's an extraordinary individual who even considers entering the SEALs. These young men have all risen above their backgrounds and circumstances and decided they want to take on a challenge they know will be exceedingly hard. For such people, that extreme difficulty is a big part of what makes the challenge such a draw.

FIFTEEN YEARS AGO, I was one of those wannabes.

As senior year rolled along at Syracuse, Churchill's words were still banging in my head. The future prime minister had gone from serving as an officer in the British Army in India, the Sudan, and South Africa to being the most important statesmen of his generation, rising all the way to 10 Downing Street and leading the United Kingdom through its darkest hours in World War II. He was convinced that his early experiences in the military had uniquely prepared him for all that. I wanted to deposit those kinds of experiences in the bank. That's how I would build up credit I could withdraw later in life. I knew I had to do my part, as Churchill had, and I was eager to start as soon as possible, before my own life and the rush of events passed me by. For me, as for Churchill, military service was the obvious path. The stakes are the highest. So are the risks. The rewards of my labor might mean not coming home. But protecting my own nation from its outside enemies seemed like the purest form of service. What an honor that would be.

But which branch of service? In what kind of role? I knew I wanted to be an officer, not an enlisted man. From all my years playing sports, I fell naturally into the role of leader—and I thought I was good at it. But it wasn't as if the young Winston had slapped a sticker on the back cover of *My Early Life:* "Hey, if you want a life like the British Bulldog's, here's who you should call." He was writing about the British Empire at the turn of the twentieth century. I was living in America at the turn of the twenty-first. He couldn't see the challenges ahead for his beloved nation any more than I could see what lay ahead for mine. As we each began to chart our courses, unimagined wars were brewing for both of us—the great world wars for Churchill, the post-9/11 conflicts for me. Neither of us could possibly have predicted the fierceness of those wars, their duration, or their scope. All we could do was be in the right spot and prepare ourselves fully for whatever the future might hold. Churchill had a desire for action, just like I had. We both assumed it would come somehow.

I knew the SEALs were special-operations commandos in the Navy, and they got a lot of respect. I'd heard that the name SEAL was a smash-up of the words *SE*a, *A*ir, and *L*and, all the places the SEALs could operate. But I'd never actually met a SEAL. And I certainly didn't know that in the same speech where President Kennedy vowed that Americans would walk on the moon, he announced an unconventional-warfare initiative that led the Navy to establish a beefed-up counterinsurgency force, staffed initially by combat swimmers from the old Underwater Demolition Teams. That was eleven years before I was born.

When I was seventeen, I'd read a book that was a compilation of four or five stories about special-ops forces—Green Berets, Air Force paratroopers, and Marine snipers, I believe. There was a SEAL story in there, too. It focused on how crafty and mysterious the SEALs were. That intrigued me. My sophomore year in college, I read *Rogue Warrior*, Richard Marcinko's riveting account of "the men with green faces," as the Viet Cong called these crafty American warriors who didn't follow the usual rules of combat. Marcinko described how tough the Vietnam-era SEALs were, fierce fighters uniquely set off from typical American soldiers. Most of what these commandos did seemed to be shrouded in mystery. That made them even more compelling. I remember thinking, This is cool: a clandestine force of naval frogmen who can sneak out of the water and attack targets onshore, then go back into the water. And not only that, they free-fall from aircraft into dangerous territory and use wild technology and combat arts to get to targets and kill people.

SEALs weren't just in books, either. It seemed like half the tough guys on 1970s and '80s TV—Lieutenant Commander Steve McGarrett in *Hawaii Five-O*, the Tom Selleck character in *Magnum, P.I.*, and on and on—were SEALs or ex-SEALs. Network scriptwriters sure seemed convinced: SEALs were the toughest, shrewdest, most devious, most physical, most expertly trained warriors around, a breed apart from any other commandos you'd want to stack them up against. It was one powerful mythology, and it seemed to have the extra advantage of actually being based in truth.

There were other elite military units I could have joined. But I kept coming back to the idea of the SEALs. They just seemed like the best to me. They were constantly getting into the middle of the action, just as Churchill had. I also liked the idea that the SEALs came from the ocean. The ocean was something I'd grown up around and was totally comfortable with. I'd heard that it might be difficult getting accepted to the SEALs officer training program. But I was determined to try.

As graduation neared at Syracuse, career recruiters kept coming to campus, offering attractive positions in finance, accounting, and various other fields. They told us about how much money we could earn and the great contacts we would make if we went to work somewhere like Wall Street. The Syracuse lacrosse team has a strong alumni network, and those folks seemed eager to help. I tried to be polite. But I had zero desire whatsoever for that career path. I just wanted to be an officer in the SEALs.

When I told my lacrosse teammates what I'd decided, I don't think any of them even looked up from their video games. They said, "Yeah, that kind of makes sense." By that point, they knew me pretty well.

OVER THE YEARS, young guys have asked me many times: How hard is it to be accepted for basic training in the SEALs? Often they are surprised by my response. "Getting *through* SEAL training is really difficult," I tell them. "It's the toughest military-entry program anywhere. But getting *in*—I don't want to call it easy, and it's been getting harder over the years. And it's nothing compared to what you're facing once you get there. Want to give it a try?"

There are some basic entry requirements. In general, you have to be a healthy male between eighteen and twenty-eight years old, have vision that can be corrected to 20/25, and be mentally sharp and able to learn. You don't need to be a trained warrior or a world-class athlete. But you do need to pass our pre-entry Physical Screening Test.

Forty-two push-ups in two minutes, fifty sit-ups in two minutes, six pull-ups with no time limit, a five-hundred-yard pool swim in twelve and a half minutes, and a 1.5-mile, eleven-minute run.

Be aware of this, though: If you're just shooting for the bare minimums, you're approaching this all wrong. It sends the wrong message to an organization that treasures its hard-earned elite status. And if you're struggling just to reach the minimums, you'll have an awfully rough time making it through basic SEAL training even if you are invited to try. To be competitive, you really should aim significantly higher than the minimums, even if it means pushing yourself beyond what you thought were your limits.

There are many exercise regimes that can help you get fit. I'm a believer in an open-source program called CrossFit, which is beloved by firefighters, police officers, and quite a few special-forces guys. But in recent years, a whole industry has grown up—books, tapes, websites, and personal-trainer programs, a few of them designed by ex-SEALs. They promise to guide their students toward SEAL-level fitness, whether the user is hoping to join up or to just look like they could. Some of these resources are good, some not. The truth is you don't need to spend a dime or hire anyone. If you're looking to become a SEAL, what you should do is get yourself in the best shape possible before you knock on our door.

Instead of just barely passing the Physical Screening test, go for 75–100 push-ups in two minutes, 75–100 sit-ups in two minutes, and a quick burst of 12–25 pull-ups. The lower numbers are considered "average." The higher numbers are "optimal." Aim for the higher end of that range—like a SEAL would. And try to get the five-hundred-yard swim in eight to nine minutes and the 1.5-mile run in nine to ten. That way, once you arrive for basic SEAL training, you won't be spending every last ounce of effort just getting through the physical basics. You'll have something left in the tank for all the mental and psychological challenges that are absolutely coming. Just arrive healthy, fit, and rested—and ready to go.

When people ask, I tell them that playing sports in school does seem to provide an edge. Athletes understand how to push themselves and what it means to be part of a team, although I'm not saying you couldn't learn something similar from the debate squad or the Boy Scouts.

Going by past experience, five sports provide especially good foundations for being a SEAL—rugby, wrestling, lacrosse, water polo, and triathlon. Those big five offer an ideal mix of training, toughness, and teamwork. I hadn't given a thought to the SEALs when I started playing lacrosse or water polo. But you can't do much better than those. They develop the skills and mind-set that could be useful on a future military assault raid.

But far more important than trying to analyze background patterns and sports rosters is understanding what you're getting into. Anyone who's interested—or any parent with an interested son—has to recognize from the start: This occupation is an all-consuming lifestyle. It's all about sacrifice. It's much more than a job. It's different from almost anything else you'll decide to do. You can't do it half-assed. If you don't give it everything, you won't do it well and you almost certainly won't get through.

During basic training, you'll be away from your family for about a year. You might get home at Thanksgiving or for Christmas. Other than that, don't expect to see your family until the day you graduate. Then, when you get to a SEAL team, you'll be in advanced training. That'll keep you away from home for most of the next year. And once you are assigned to a SEAL platoon and you deploy, you'll be out of the country for six or seven months at a time. Even if all that doesn't dissuade you, please, don't think of doing this for the money. Our pay scale is based on regular Navy compensation, which is appallingly low for the work we do. You could be chasing a top al Qaeda chief across the most dangerous terrain on earth—and taking home less than a night manager at McDonald's. Our guys do get something extra for being dive-, free-fall-, and demolition-qualified. Those extras are significant, but not enough to make anyone rich. Our headquarters may be on ritzy Coronado Island, where many CEOs and retired admirals have lavish homes. But believe me, none of us will be buying those houses anytime soon.

Truly, there's only one good argument for joining this challenging brotherhood: Because the idea is so compelling, there's no way to convince you not to.

I was rejected the first time I applied to be a SEAL officer. I can't say the Navy recruiter didn't warn me.

"Don't even bother applying," he said when I went to his office in downtown Syracuse and asked about becoming an officer in the SEALs. "I've never had an applicant accepted for a SEAL officer billet."

"Just humor me," I told him. "Let's do the paperwork anyway."

I didn't have any friends who were SEAL officers, so I tried to find someone who could offer me some guidance or advice. I called the brother-in-law of my father's law partner, who had been a Vietnam-era SEAL and had retired as a commander. Al was his name.

"I'm Rorke Denver, Tom Denver's son," I told him. "Your brother-in-law Peter coached me in water polo. That's how I got your number. I'm going to apply for a SEAL officer billet. I wonder if you have advice on how I could do it effectively."

Al replied in a deep, booming voice without a hint of encouragement.

"My brother-in-law said you might be calling," he said. "I don't want to waste your time or mine. Even as I talk to you, I frankly don't imagine you have what it takes to be a SEAL officer. I wouldn't bother applying."

Then he hung up.

I couldn't believe he had done that. The short conversation rattled around in my head for a week or so. Then I called him back.

"I just wanted to get back to you," I said when he picked up the phone. "I didn't want to leave it hanging. I don't think I really need your help. I'm gonna put the application in anyway. So thanks for nothing." Then I hung up on him.

Two days later, he called me back. This time he was laughing. "Well," he said. "You know, you might actually have what it takes to be an officer on a SEAL team. Let's talk."

About halfway through our conversation, he said: "You really, really gotta have thick skin to do this job. It's a very competitive and wild group of guys. If you're gonna be in charge of SEALs, you need to be a man among boys and have something special. I'm not quick to help people through this thing. It's your own path to walk. But if I can be of service and answer questions, I will. It's gonna be an uphill hike."

"Great," I said. "That's why I'm interested."

He gave me the number for the SEAL recruiting office in Washington, D.C., to make sure I was filing the right application.

The recruiter in Syracuse administered the physical test. He gave me the intelligence assessment, which was like a modified SAT, and a basic psych exam. He didn't have much guidance to offer. But I wasn't too worried. I was a Division I college athlete in excellent physical shape. I had solid grades and glowing letters of recommendation from my coaches. Plus, I had a burning desire to serve. How many candidates like that could they get every year?

The recruiter sent my application package off to Washington. And then I heard nothing for months. I graduated from college. I moved out to Colorado, where my mom was living. I figured I'd get the call any day, telling me an officer's spot was waiting for me in the next SEAL class. I was working out day and night. Running every morning in the thin air of the Rockies. Lifting weights at the gym every afternoon. And before I collapsed in bed at night, I was reading military strategy books, moving on from Churchill to *On War* by Carl von Clausewitz, who warned so vividly about "the fog of war," and *The Art of War* by Sun Tzu, the brilliant Chinese strategist, doing my best to climb inside their sharp and challenging minds. Napoleon Bonaparte wrote: "Read over and over again the campaigns of Alexander, Hannibal, Caesar, Gustavus, Turenne, Eugene and Frederic." It's the only way to "master the secrets of the art of war."

Churchill had done the same: "I ordered Hamley's *Operations of War*, Prince Kraft's *Letter on Infantry, Cavalry and Artillery*, Maine's *Infantry Fire Tactics*, together with a number of histories dealing with the American Civil, Franco-German and Russo-Turkish wars, which were then our latest and best specimens of wars," he reported. "I soon had a small military library."

Then I heard.

The letter went to my dad's house in California. "There's no easy way to break information like this," he said when he reached me in Colorado. "You didn't get chosen, I'm afraid."

Damn.

It was like I'd just been kicked in the gut. I thanked my father for letting me know. Then I told him I had to go. "I can't stay on the phone," I said. "I need to train some more. I have to be in better condition when I put my next application in."

It would be another year before I finally joined the brotherhood I'd been dreaming of. I just kept on plugging, making sure I did better the second time. One of the first calls I made was to grumpy Commander Al.

"Hey, I didn't get picked up," I told him. "But without question, I'm applying again. Anything you can tell me about how to do it better this time, I'd sure appreciate."

Al sounded immediately energized. He seemed happy to hear I wasn't dropping the idea, and this time he had a couple of valuable, practical suggestions.

"My recommendation," he said, "would be you go do your PT test out in Coronado, out at headquarters. The guy in New York might have done it poorly. You'll have the opportunity to meet some SEALs. It might help your package a little."

I asked Al if he'd be willing to write a letter of recommendation for me. He sounded a little hesitant about that. "I'm not gonna make you look like a super-candidate," he warned. "I only know you so well. But yeah, okay."

I followed Al's advice and took the physical at SEAL headquarters. Actually, I took it twice in one week. The first time, on a Tuesday, there was a scheduling screw-up, and I had to race over there in half an hour in my beat-up Jeep—and no excuses, but I really blew the test.

"I know my scores were nowhere near where they need to be," I said to the lieutenant who was interviewing the candidates. "That doesn't reflect what I can do. I guarantee you, if you'll let me take the test again, I can double my scores. I know I can."

The lieutenant took a deep breath and leaned back in his chair. "I'll make an accommodation," he said, "and let an instructor test you tomorrow. But I'm using the scores from tomorrow whether they're better or worse."

"Fair enough," I agreed.

I came back Wednesday morning, and I crushed the test. The push-ups, the pull-ups, the five-hundred-meter swim—I did better than even I thought I would. "Holy shit," said the instructor who administered the test. "That's impressive to come back the next day and smoke it like that."

My scores got sent off with Al's recommendation. A month after that, some good news finally came in the mail. I had been selected for the Navy's Officer Candidate School in Pensacola, Florida, with follow-on orders to SEAL training.

Now the real work was about to begin.

PART TWO

Doing It

7

TEAM PLAYER

Remember upon the conduct of each
depends the fate of all.
—ALEXANDER THE GREAT

"SEAL TEAM," the cap said.

Not "SEAL TEAM ONE" or "SEAL TEAM THREE" or "SEAL TEAM ANYTHING ELSE."

Just "SEAL TEAM."

And that wasn't the only thing that seemed a little off about the man who pulled up the stool at the far end of the bar. The combat boots, the commando jacket, the aviator shades—none of it seemed quite necessary for a stop at a suburban burger-and-wings joint. It wasn't even Halloween.

Our whole platoon was out to dinner when he walked in.

"You know the guy in the SEAL cap?" I asked the waitress.

She rolled her eyes.

"Oh, yeah, Billy," she said. "He scares people."

"Well, this is your lucky night," Chief Hall told her.

Phony SEALs are everywhere, people who crave the attention or the tough-guy cred of being associated with the SEAL teams. Some of them have turned these claims into elaborate, decades-long ruses. It's probably not the worst crime in the world, but to many real-life SEALs, this kind of imitation isn't the sincerest flattery.

The chief dispatched baby-faced Irish.

"Excuse me, sir," Irish said to Mr. SEAL Team at the bar. "Are you a SEAL? They're some of the greatest warriors in history."

The man looked up slowly from his beer. "Look, son," he said, "don't be pestering me all night. But yeah, I'm a SEAL."

Irish's eyes widened. "I won't take much time," he promised. "What SEAL team were you on? What was your job there?"

"I'm what they call a demo god," the man said. "A demolition expert. Killing people with explosives. I was at SEAL Team C4. Out of Groton, Connecticut."

Now, Groton, Connecticut, does have a naval base. They launch submarines. I'm sure a SEAL has been to Groton. But there aren't any SEAL teams there. And C4 is a plastic explosive, not the name of a SEAL Team.

"Booby traps," the blowhard went on. "Planting bombs on cars, on motorcycles, in houses, under buildings."

"Well," Irish said, "my buddies and I would like to buy you a beer." The man nodded our way as Irish walked back to the table and recounted the conversation for us.

When the waitress returned, the chief asked her: "Would you bring a beer to Billy over there. Tell him it's from a real SEAL combat unit—not some make-believe bullshit."

"Happily," the waitress said.

We all watched as she delivered the beer.

The man's confident nod melted into confusion and then to something that looked like abject fear. He glanced over at us again. We all grinned and waved.

He probably should have just gotten up and left the restaurant. Instead, he sought refuge in the men's room.

Ron, our leading petty officer, who is six foot five and 270 pounds and I'd say a little intimidating, followed him in.

Nothing violent happened. I can promise you that. But in less than a minute, the man came bolting out of the restroom and headed straight for the parking lot. He wasn't wearing his cap anymore.

Somehow or another, that cap ended up on the wall in our team room. The blade of a combat knife was jammed through the bill.

"SEAL TEAM," the cap said.

The day I checked into SEAL Team Four, I half-figured I would walk onto Naval Amphibious Base Little Creek in Virginia Beach, Virginia, and a couple of senior guys would pull me aside. "Okay," they'd say, "here are all the top-secret missions." And by the next afternoon, we'd get an urgent page and be on our way to Bosnia or Afghanistan or Somalia on some clandestine operation the world knew nothing about. Maybe the instructors at BUD/S had been keeping the wild stuff under wraps because we didn't have our security clearances yet. If they told us, they'd have to kill us or something.

I know that sounds kind of crazy now. But the SEAL mythology is that strong.

Back at BUD/S, the instructors had repeatedly asked us: "You going East Coast or West Coast?" As a SEAL recruit, you don't automatically get to choose your first team assignment. But the leadership tries to accommodate people's general preferences. Chances are, you'll stay with that first team for four or five years, and the first team you go to is usually the one you'll always identify with. I've spent more time on the West Coast than the East, but since I started on the East I'll always think of myself as an East Coast SEAL.

Both coasts have their own personalities and their stereotypes, wildly exaggerated but not totally unfounded. East Coast frogs would say, "If you want to have dyed hair and play volleyball and surf, you should definitely stay on the West Coast. If you want to go to war, go East Coast." Believe me, the West Coast SEALs didn't see it like that at all. They thought they were every bit as hard. The East Coasters just never learned to let loose and have fun. And to be fair, the West Coast guys were doing a whole lot more than playing volleyball.

I put in for East Coast and got assigned to SEAL Team Four.

Despite my eagerness for action, we wouldn't be rushing quickly off to war. Given my timing, there weren't any wars to rush to. These were the days before 9/11. None of us had any idea what was coming next. The War on Terror was simmering on a back burner somewhere. America wasn't engaged yet in Afghanistan or Iraq. So for the time being, I was in Virginia Beach. For now my job was to stay in better shape than anybody else and do whatever it took to become a world-class warrior. To shoot harder and straighter than anybody. To blow things up more effectively. To dive and jump with pinpoint accuracy. To be prepared for the call whenever it came, which I was constantly hoping would be immediately—if not sooner.

But mostly what we did was have hard, rollicking fun. I woke up every morning, climbed into PT gear, dragged a razor across my face, and worked out at the team compound for two hours with a great bunch of guys. On any given day, we might walk out the back door of the command and take a fast boat out in Chesapeake Bay or chase a ship on an attack exercise. We had a helicopter to take us fast-roping onto a boat deck. We went rappelling and running on the beach. We were always training, always traveling. We practiced shooting in Mississippi and North Carolina. We had diving adventures in Newport, Rhode Island. We went on demolition trips. It was like going to summer camp in your twenties with only the cool guys. We'd hit the bars at night, and every weekend have massive barbecues on the beach.

Really, it was like being a member of an excellent fraternity, the greatest man club in the world. Maybe the last one. Virginia Beach wasn't quite the year-round vacation paradise that San Diego was, and it was nowhere near as large. You couldn't go into a single coffee shop, bar, or restaurant in the Virginia Tidewater region without bumping into five other SEALs, from your team or another. But even that made the experience more intense. What we were doing was totally enjoyable. You couldn't escape the teams if you wanted—and really, why would you? We were young guys, mostly single, having the time of our life.

Whenever I could steal a little quiet time, I would get back to reading the classics of war. Every warrior should. I dove into *The Personal Memoirs of Ulysses S. Grant* and Thucydides's *History of the Peloponnesian War.* I challenged myself with the just-war theories of two brilliant Catholic saints, Thomas Aquinas and Augustine. They wrestled thoughtfully with serious questions about when war is morally appropriate.

"War is justified only by the injustice of an aggressor," Augustine wrote, "and that injustice ought to be a source of grief to any good man, because it is human injustice."

"In order for a war to be just, three things are necessary," countered Aquinas. "First, the authority of the sovereign. Secondly, a just cause. Thirdly, a rightful intention."

I devoured the ancient Greeks, Socrates, Plato, and the Stoic philosopher Epictetus. I read Steven Pressfield's *Gates of Fire*, which was already on its way to being a modern warrior classic. Every time I reread Churchill, he sounded more prescient to me.

I had one unexpected side trip that turned out to serve me extremely well in my career. While I waited for another cycle of advanced SEAL training to begin, I was dispatched to Fort Benning, Georgia, for Army Ranger School. I was totally blown away by the Rangers. Their two-month infantry leadership course was vastly different from BUD/S. Instead of jumping in and out of the ocean and racing boats, prospective Rangers march for endless miles with heavy rucksacks and subsist on starvation rations for days at a time. But these guys are amazing experts when it comes to infantry warfare skills: That training gave me a huge leg up when I got back to my SEAL team at Little Creek, and I have proudly worn the Ranger tab on the left shoulder of my cammie top ever since.

Each Friday afternoon back in Virginia, the SEAL team would end the week with a hard-core ten-mile run through First Landing State Park and back out to the beach. If you were new to the team, you had to earn your reputation on those runs. When we first started, the command master chief, a legendarily hard SEAL named Tommy, said to us: "You young bucks better win every one of these races." I figured he meant it. On the very next group run, three of us young guys broke away from the pack. I don't think I have ever held a pace like that for ten straight miles. It was like we'd packed the BUD/S conditioning runs into a one-hour sprint. When we got to the finish line, I could barely talk I was breathing so hard.

"What the hell just happened?" I asked my friend Ice. "Why did we run this fast? We were way ahead of everybody else."

"I don't know," Ice said.

"Me neither," said our teammate Fish. "I thought you were picking up the pace so I picked up the pace."

SEALs never miss a chance to compete. If we don't have something real to compete over—don't worry, we'll dream something up. If three SEALs are going on a run, it's not a run anymore. It's a race. SEALs get bloody noses during pickup games of Horse. For me, this hypercompetitiveness didn't seem strange at all. It went back to those birthday party footraces in my childhood cul-de-sac. Some boys never grow up. Any SEAL who doesn't want a physically crushing challenge had better play alone—and stay out of the SEAL team van. You never know when a van brawl might break out.

Everyone knew the rules for a van brawl. There was only one: No striking, hurting, or otherwise coming into contact with the driver, who at that moment was trying to deliver his high-spirited male cargo on a dive trip, a jump exercise, or some other training opportunity.

What was the point of brawling inside a moving van? Put it like this: When bored, aggressive, overgrown male children are forced to sit so close to one another for hours at a time, their already excessive testosterone will pump into overdrive, and sometimes they just can't resist beating each other up.

I do not believe regular people do this with their colleagues. Clearly, we were exceptional in many ways.

SEAL van brawls were no joke. The carnage routinely included busted teeth, cracked ribs, and grotesque bruises. Senior officers sometimes tried to calm everyone. But good luck with that when eight or ten frenzied young beasts were punching, choking, kicking, and fishhooking each other in the mouth. Hair-pulling and eye-gouging were considered less than manly, but I've seen both employed.

Van brawls broke out for pretty much any reason or no reason at all. Someone spilled a drink. Or the trip was long and boring. Or some stupid debate—what was the best comedy movie ever or the worst defensive line in football?—grew just a little heated. Every once in a while, some twisted chief would turn in his seat and shout, "Van brawl!" just to see what his guys were made of.

By the time you made lieutenant or platoon commander, you were expected to abstain from van brawling. But when I was a young ensign at SEAL Team Four, I was every bit a party to those fights and a functional fighting member.

It was all just part of SEAL culture. As the new guys got acclimated to life at Team Four, the seasoned SEALs were constantly offering advice. It was like learning life lessons from your big brother or your crazy uncle. How to handle yourself in a bar fight: "Hit first. Hit hard. And be ready to move." How to behave around women: "Date strippers. Don't marry strippers." Some of the advice was sage. Some of it could just as easily get you killed.

The underlying message in all of it was the potency and importance of the SEAL brotherhood. There seemed to be a special SEAL answer for everything, and you'd better know what that answer was. One day I was in the training room with three of my SEAL mentors who had been in the teams a long time. I'd grabbed a copy of the Yellow Pages.

"What are you doing?" asked Jos.

"I just bought a Dodge 2500 diesel pickup," I told him. "I want to put a cap on it so I can keep all my gear back there. I don't want it to be an open-bed pickup."

"I hear you," he said. "But what the hell are you doing with that book?"

This was pre-Google. Where else was I supposed to find a truck cap? "I'm looking for a place that sells caps," I said.

"Let me tell you," Jos said. "The best Yellow Pages on the face of this earth are the SEAL teams. Close that book."

I closed the book.

"Stand by, Young Viking," he said. "Let me prove this to you."

He got on the phone with me sitting there. He dialed the quarter-deck for SEAL Team Eight. I heard him say, "This is Warrant Officer Jos. I need you to put something out over the 1MC," the command microphone system. "Anybody who has a connection for getting caps for the back of pickups, here's my number. Tell him to call me back."

He hung up the phone. He didn't stop. He called the quarterdecks of the other Little Creek teams, Two and Four, and delivered the same message. "Get back to me," he said.

He had just hung up from the last call when the telephone rang.

"Yeah, this is Jos," he said. "Okay, give me his number. Where's he at? Corner of Virginia Beach Boulevard and Independence? Great. I appreciate it."

He hung up the phone and looked at me like he was looking at a child. "Okay, prepare to copy," he said as I broke out a piece of paper and he repeated a phone number to me. "Jim is my friend Billy's uncle," Jos said. "He sells caps on the corner and for team guys will do a fifty percent discount and installation for free. He's waiting for you right now. Go."

Ever since that happened, I don't think I've ever actually had something I needed that I didn't get through the teams.

But I wasn't at Little Creek solely to learn SEAL culture and hone SEAL competitiveness. You're not a SEAL if you don't have your Trident, the shiny gold insignia that tells the world, "U.S. Navy SEAL." And we didn't have ours yet.

The Special Warfare Insignia, as the SEAL Trident is officially known, is one of the most widely recognizable warfare specialty pins in the U.S. military. A golden eagle clutching an old Navy anchor, a trident, and a flintlock pistol—you'll sometimes hear SEALs refer to the Trident as "the Budweiser," and it does vaguely resemble the famous logo of another powerful American institution.

By any name, that tiny Trident is packed with symbolism. The old anchor reminds SEALs that their roots go back to the valiant Underwater Demolition Teams of World War II. The trident, the scepter of Neptune or Poseidon, king of the oceans, emphasizes the SEALs' connection to the sea. The eagle, the classic emblem of America's freedom, refers to the SEALs' ability to swiftly insert from the air. The eagle's head is lowered, suggesting the SEALs' humility. The pistol, which is cocked and ready to fire, points to the SEALs' capacity and readiness for fighting on land. Heritage, sea, air, and land—the SEALs.

When the Trident was first issued in 1970, there was a silver version for enlisted men and a gold one for officers. But that distinction was quickly abandoned. Now everyone gets gold, one of the very few Navy badges issued in a single grade. And even that has meaning. It highlights how SEAL officers and enlisted men are trained and deployed side by side.

Before receiving my Trident, I had to get through one last hurdle, my Trident Boards, a written exam followed by an intensive oral and practical test. I'm not saying the grilling I got was the sit-down equivalent of Hell Week. But it was tough and precise and insistent, and it went on for a really long time. Then came one of the best days of my life.

My dad and my brother flew out to Little Creek. Lots of the other soon-to-be SEALs had family there as well. It was the day I'd been dreaming about for more than three years. That Friday morning, the whole team was together for an extra-strenuous PT. We did a loop through the Little Creek O-course. And then while our families waited near the water and had refreshments, we did another ten-mile run through the state park that eventually brought us back to the beach. You knew we'd all be diving in. The guys who already had their Tridents hit the water in shorts and fins. We newbies kept our full cammies on. We had a final swim down the beach. For three of us, the swim was extra-vigorous. We had to carry a breaching sledge-hammer on our backs. That was a fun treat.

Even knowing the day would be special didn't quite prepare us for the greeting we got when we pulled ourselves out of the water. The commanding officer of SEAL Team Four, whom everyone on the team knew as Father War, was waiting for us on the beach. Lined up with him were officers and enlisted men, the entire team. The families were standing behind them.

Father War is one of the super-legends of our community. A former Marine officer, he went through SEAL training at age thirty-six. He lost a leg in a free-fall jump and didn't let it slow him down one bit. He attached a fin to his prosthetic leg for swimming and used a different leg with a shoe for running. He went on to command virtually every tactical unit in the SEAL teams and retired a captain. His lessons on how to lead men inspired me and set an extremely high bar.

We waited in knee-deep water as the commander stood in the water with us. He delivered a truly moving speech about becoming part of the brotherhood.

"It's a struggle, a tough struggle, to earn your place in this warrior community," he said. "You have worked incredibly hard. You have shown incredible commitment. Now you are part of this brotherhood, and now the real work begins. You have earned your Tridents. You are real team guys now.

"There is only one reason this Trident is polished to such a high gold shine," he continued. "That is so each person does nothing to tarnish it. Everybody carries his weight. Everyone lives up to that expectation. Everyone takes care of one another. The nation is counting on you to do that job. That is not a slogan. It is not something you just read on a poster. That is real."

Standing there, having completed some of the most difficult training there is to join this exclusive group of American warriors, I know all of us felt that. I'm sure Father War believed it. It was a simple but perfectly stated and sincere welcome to the brotherhood.

He passed down the full line of us in the water and pinned the Trident on each man's cammie top. Then, as the families looked on proudly, every single member of the team came up and shook hands with us. It was as genuine a handshake as I've ever received from anyone. It felt very, very special, celebratory and serious all at once. At that point, you're a made man in this elite brotherhood. I felt the pride of that—and the weight of it.

To this day, I feel incredibly fortunate to have started my SEAL career with Father War. He took a special interest in all of us, dealing with issues large and small. It even fell to him at one point to rein us in after one memorably rowdy van brawl. Seat cushions had been ripped open. Windows had been smashed. Doors were knocked off their hinges. After this particular trip to Land Warfare Training in Fort Knox, Kentucky, Father War demanded to see BRAVO's three officers.

"You guys are in the running to be the best platoon at SEAL Team Four," he said. "But you have destroyed more vehicles in a shorter period of time than any idiots I have ever seen. The next vehicle you mangle in any way—I don't care if someone slams into it while you're parked—you three will pay for the fixes out of your own paychecks.

"Now get out of my office."

In large part, Father War made me the officer I am. His guidance, his experience, his insight, his constant openness to creative thinking, and his hands-on style of command—the time I spent with him changed the trajectory of my life and career.

Other things fell into place as well. I was tremendously fortunate to be picked up by BRAVO Platoon. B, the platoon commander, really was one of the last clean-cut superheroes. He and Chief Petty

Officer Hall, who day to day ran the platoon, were creative, driven, and committed to doing things right.

It's a special relationship between a chief and a young ensign. In theory, on the day he's sworn in, a brand-new ensign outranks the most senior master chief, who is a noncommissioned officer. But no master chief in the U.S. Navy would ever take any crap from the likes of me.

Least of all Chief Hall. He had been around so long and knew so much about the day-to-day practical operation of the SEAL teams, he could get almost anything done. Everyone the chief served with, officers and enlisted alike, were loyal to him, and he earned it the old-fashioned way. He was phenomenally good at taking care of the boys, making sure we all got the newest gear and the good-deal trips, knowing every angle in the system to get everything we needed, always making sure he got the best new guys for his platoon.

BRAVO Platoon had just come off a very active rotation, and they were down a few members, including that teammate who'd stepped out of a helicopter in a training exercise 180 feet above the water and was killed. They had to pull some new blood in. The chief assembled an amazing group. Frog was one of the most effective snipers and field-craft experts you'll ever meet. You did not want him tracking you in the woods or the jungle. When we would go on a two-mile swim in the ocean, he'd be the only one on the team swimming without fins—and he'd finish in the top two or three.

Eddie was a good-looking Cuban-American, BRAVO's all-time class clown. Always telling jokes, making crank calls to commanding officers of other military units—harmless stuff but hilarious. Half the platoon met their wives through Eddie. He was the best wingman you could ever have.

Irish and Toro were the two youngbloods in the platoon, barely a year or two out of high school. They weren't short enough to be

Smurf SEALs, but they certainly weren't large. Yet size didn't hold them back. It was these young bucks who carried the heavy M60 machine guns, running through woods, across rivers, and over hills. They had great personalities. Everybody loved them. They were what the twins from BUD/S would have been if the twins had made it through.

Sonny and Josh were muscle-bound Proto-SEALs, the recruiting poster picture of a strongly built physical specimen. Sonny, an explosives expert, had so little body fat, he would actually sink in cold water. I never heard him complain once about anything. To this day, the very definition of cool—that was Sonny. Josh was gregarious, fun, intense, competitive, just an uncontrolled ball of testosterone. He was like a hound dog, totally loyal to his buddies, always chasing tail. You did not want to be on the opposing team when you saw those two guys running at you with big machine guns.

There was nothing Face Man didn't seem to be good at. He was a talented shooter. He was extremely fit. He was bright tactically. He could land his parachute closer to the X than you could every time. And he never looked like he was trying that hard. Face Man probably should have been an officer. As an officer, I loved him and wanted to kill him, too. I was constantly saying, "Face Man, you're right. But can you please shut up so we can move forward here." He was one of my favorites.

Jersey is still one of my closest friends. He was a total free spirit. He wore sandals in the middle of the winter. He played guitar. He loved to surf. He would sometimes go to an Indian sweat lodge on a vision quest. He was one of the few who could find a way around the Navy regs to grow a beard and long hair. He had a wild, infectious laugh. He was brilliant. If you were a friend of Jersey's, there was nothing he would ever fail to do for you.

Jersey faked some paperwork to get into the advanced civilian driver course, which was supposed to be limited to candidates with professional driving experience. One student had six courses in tactical driving. Another had driven on the NASCAR circuit. When the teacher asked about Jersey's driving credentials, he was prepared.

"I'm from Jersey," he answered.

When the teacher did a double take, Jersey added, "Exit 7A."

We did almost everything together. All sixteen members of BRAVO Platoon drove to Kentucky for a six-week land-warfare course at Fort Knox. One night, a group of us went out together to a bar in Louisville called Have a Nice Day, me drinking my usual bottled water, Eddie dancing with every young woman in the place. His dance partners included a tall, stunning, wholesome college student and one of her roommates.

Eddie could see me looking over—and not at him. He gave a big wave.

"I'll have my boy D come over here," he told the young woman, whose name was Tracy. "I'd like you to meet him."

She knew that drill. Okay, she thought to herself—she told me later—this is when the not-so-good-looking-out-of-shape-wallflower friend comes up. I'm sure this D will be a real prize.

Truly, I had no agenda, and I learned that neither did she. I was coming off the worst relationship in my life. She was still in a terrible relationship, and out for a Friday night of dancing with her friends.

I came over and joined her on the dance floor. From that moment forward, I didn't see anyone else in the place. "You've been dancing all night," I told her. "Sometimes it's nice to have a bottle of water."

As we stood at the bar, one of her friends walked up. I'm not sure if the friend was drunk or jealous or what. But she said, "You know, she has a boyfriend."

I didn't care. He wasn't there.

At the end of the night, seven other BRAVO Platoon members

and I drove the young women back to their dorm. Tracy and I got out of the van with all my buddies looking on. I have zero idea what possessed me, but standing right outside the van, I lifted her hand and kissed it like a gentleman from a hundred years ago. I'd never done that before and never have since. Something in the way she looked at me, I could tell it made an impact. I think the impromptu gesture in front of my friends got me a first date.

We took it slowly. We phoned back and forth. I visited Tracy in Kentucky. For spring break, she agreed to come out and see me in Virginia Beach. I thought that was a good sign.

But the day she was set to arrive, BRAVO Platoon was put on a last-minute alert for a training exercise. An exercise like that could take a day, an evening, or a week. Even before her first visit, Tracy was learning about life with a SEAL.

I had to give quick instructions to a buddy of mine. He went and picked her up at the airport. "Hi, I'm Rorke's roommate. I'm sorry to tell you this but his team's working in the field. He won't be back any earlier than Wednesday. Let me set you up at our apartment, unless you'd rather go back home."

Tracy stayed, and I've considered myself lucky every day since.

8

PEACETIME WARRIOR

The two most powerful warriors are patience and time.
—LEO TOLSTOY

I don't think the police officer liked my attitude.

"Pasaporte," he said in Spanish.

I handed him a Xerox copy through the two inches I'd opened the window. I made sure the door was locked.

"Get out of the van," the officer demanded, glaring at me.

"No."

Whap! He smacked the door with his nightstick.

"Absolutely not," I said.

We were in Ecuador teaching combat techniques to the local military, part of our duties as the on-call platoon for the U.S. Southern Command, or SOUTHCOM, helping to build the South American nation's counterterror force. It was Irish and I and nine other SEAL teammates. No one was even supposed to know we were in Guayaquil. We'd been warned by our partner force, the Ecuadoran marines, that the local *policía* had been extorting hefty bribes from visiting gringos. Any problems, the Marine *capitán* said, call right away.

Irish and I had just left his headquarters and were driving back to our hotel.

"If you do not get out of the van, we will shoot," the grim-faced officer threatened, pulling his gun out. I moved my hand slowly toward the SIG Sauer P226 in my concealed belt holster, as the officer's partner radioed for backup and pointed a shotgun at us. Very slowly, Irish reached for his cell phone and dialed the Ecuadoran cavalry. Sitting on his lap was a backpack holding a compact Heckler & Koch MP5-SD submachine gun. In two seconds flat, that thing could be in Irish's hands and cleaning the whole neighborhood.

"No," I told the cop again, as two more police cars pulled up and I fingered the cold butt of the SIG.

I had always wondered what it must feel like being on the other end of a SEAL rescue. To be a U.S. citizen sprung dramatically from a squalid foreign lockup or a desperate hostage when one of our assault teams came rushing through the door. That night in Ecuador wasn't quite the equivalent. But I sure did like what I saw in the rearview barreling our way.

It was a large, open troop truck, squealing around a corner with thirty-five Ecuadoran marines. They were jammed in the back, shoulder to shoulder in helmets and flak jackets. Half a dozen others, some holding machine guns, some gripping machetes, were hanging off each side.

The truck slammed to a stop right up against the first police cruiser.

The marines leaped off their truck and came charging at the five local cops, kicking them, punching them, slamming them with gun butts, shoving the outnumbered officers brutally to the ground. It was like something out of an old biker movie, a combat-boot ass-kicking that left the surprised *policía* a bloody heap on the ground. It was hard to imagine any of them just walking away.

"You picked the wrong gringos to bother," I heard the *capitán* say.

As he walked to the van, I finally lowered the window and eased my hand off the SIG.

"I don't believe this will happen again," he said in near-perfect English. "Please have a safe ride home."

Our first overseas deployment, to Roosevelt Roads Naval Station in Ceiba, Puerto Rico, made us the on-call SEAL platoon for all of SOUTHCOM. We covered the nineteen countries of Central and South America and the Caribbean, fully one-sixth of the landmass of the world. The SEAL piece of anything that happened south of Mexico and north of Tierra del Fuego—that was ours.

We pitched in on America's drug war, teaching the locals how to conduct ship searches and other antismuggling operations. We trained their military units, including those big-hearted Ecuadoran marines, in modern counterinsurgency techniques. We kept a constant eye on FARC guerrillas in Colombia, Shining Path revolutionaries in Peru, and international drug smugglers everywhere. And we kept up our own training like maniacs.

The United States wasn't at war with anyone in the region. We didn't know it yet, but this was our last big chance to be special-ops warriors in peacetime. That didn't mean the neighborhood was quiet. Quite a few bad actors were out wandering around. They just weren't organized enough for a legitimate war. From Roosey Roads, as everyone called our base, we worked with the militaries of Colombia, Ecuador, Chile, Bolivia, Trinidad, and other nations, sharing our combat expertise and always trying to stay below the local radar.

We taught the local special-operations forces to rig explosives, plan raids, and shoot more accurately. Their skills varied widely. The Colombians were knowledgeable and experienced. The Ecuadorans were appreciative but raw. The Chileans were good on land but not so good on water.

Wherever we went, we wore civilian clothes. We tried not to flash our weapons in public. We invented elaborate cover stories to explain why a dozen athletic-looking American males in their twenties and thirties might be staying for weeks at a business hotel in Santiago, Quito, or Bogotá. In the coastal Colombian city of Cartagena—a fun-loving place—we put out word that we were a group of soccer coaches from North America polishing our skills. My guess is that no one believed us.

"I'll hold your pistol for you until you finish dancing with that beautiful Colombian woman," I had to say to more than one of my teammates in the bars at night. "I don't want her patting your waist and feeling metal. And who's the guy who keeps eyeing you from the far corner of the room?"

That's how it was all across the region. Fun and friendly on the surface but with an overlay of danger in the air.

Cartagena was a deceptively beautiful seaside resort, home to drug lords, guerrilla leaders, and international business operators, legitimate and not. They all mixed easily on the beaches and in the restaurants. There was a lot of money floating around. And once in a while, with no specific warning, real trouble broke out.

The ATM across from our hotel blew up in a huge explosion. Several of the SEALs had just withdrawn cash from there. From then on, we did all our banking inside the bank.

One afternoon, Sonny, Irish, and I were in a taxi when we thought that maybe we were being followed.

"Turn left at the next corner," I told the driver in my basic Spanish. But a black Mercedes stayed right with us.

"Turn right and another right—now speed up," I said.

The taxi driver did everything I asked. But the Mercedes was still right there, even though by now our route was totally senseless. By that point, our driver looked truly alarmed.

We stopped at a light, and in a flash, Sonny leaped out of the taxi and raced for our driver's door. He yanked it open and shoved the startled man across the seat. With the driver shouting frantically, "No, no, no!" Sonny took the wheel—and went charging through the crowded streets of Cartagena, safety be damned.

A few fast blocks and a few sharp turns later, the Mercedes was nowhere in sight. We got out of the taxi, paid the driver triple his fare, and disappeared swiftly into the pedestrian crowd.

All across the region, we needed little tricks for everything.

How to keep prying desk clerks guessing. Move hotels. How to find our way through unfamiliar neighborhoods. Bring a trusted local along. We also needed a way to speak discreetly among ourselves.

All of us struggled with basic Spanish. We reached a point where we could communicate fairly well with the locals as long as the people spoke slowly. But when they took off with rapid-fire words, suddenly we were lost again.

"What if we try the reverse?" Sonny suggested.

It was a brilliant idea. When we didn't want to be understood, we didn't bother with secret phrases or complex codes. We just spoke English really, really fast.

"Look-at-the-guy-standing-on-the-corner-in-the-yellow-shirt-I-think-he-has-his-hand-on-a-gun." I'm not sure if the code-cracking linguists at the Pentagon would be impressed by our ingenuity. But we reached the point where we could get those words out in half-a-fast-breath, and only a super-fluent English speaker could possibly follow along.

Two days before we left Chile, the special-operations unit of the Chilean navy threw a good-bye barbecue for us, their way of saying *gracias* for the tactical and explosives training we'd given them.

But during the barbecue, Frog and Duke got into a heated discussion with one of their senior commanders. The *commandante* was complaining bitterly about the United States. To hear him tell it, Washington had caused every single ill in the region over the past two hundred years—and a few big ones still to come.

Frog and Duke were not too charmed by the man's critique. In fact, it took almost the whole team to hold them back and keep the encounter from turning physical.

But the boys ultimately made their point. The next night, the SEALs and the Chilean special-ops team were putting on a final, joint demonstration for the higher-ups. Still irritated at the America-bashing the night before, our guys packed up a mammoth load of C4, detonation cord, smokes, and extra rounds, a rat's nest of explosives. Then Duke invited one of the top Chilean admirals to set off the underwater charge.

"Would you like the honor of pushing the button, sir?" Duke asked.

The instant the charge detonated, a plume of water shot up from the ocean 150 feet into the air. The vibrations were strong enough to break half a dozen store windows. The boom was momentarily deafening. I swear, five hundred stunned fish came floating up to the surface.

"We were going to leave all our extra explosives behind for you," Duke said with great satisfaction. "But after last night, we decided we'd blow them up instead."

Yes, we had some work to do. But the Caribbean beaches were perfect. The water was crystal clear and a whole lot warmer than in

San Diego or even Virginia Beach. We'd "go bugging," we called it, fishing for lobsters with our hands. From Roosey Roads, the San Juan nightlife was a short drive away. With memories of BUD/S not so far in the past, we built our own SEAL-worthy obstacle course on an abandoned dry dock that remained a military legend years after we left.

Our superiors in Virginia seemed a million miles away.

As a junior officer, I was starting to assume some command authority. "Hey, Diesel, run this mission," B, the platoon commander, told me frequently. "It's yours."

"Thanks, brother," I'd say. "I'm on it."

It might have been something minor—a training evolution in the jungle or a ship-boarding to search for drugs. But I was in charge of it, and I liked how that felt. As the months ticked by, I was being folded seamlessly into the team leadership. Chief Hall was constantly watching my back, in the usual veteran-chief, young-officer way. Instead of taking orders from the latest whiz kid, it was more like he was raising me, another junior officer gradually learning to lead and train men. The trust between us was something money, rank, and college could never buy.

Up until then, if I screwed up, I could always give the "ensign shrug."

"I'm a new ensign—what do I know?"

But as a deployed officer and a member of SEAL Team Four—and with Chief Hall watching and judging me—I was slowly expected to know what I was doing out there. I was representing my country, my platoon, and my team. I was becoming a leader. I'd better not screw up.

"Look," Chief Hall said as he pulled the van off a dirt road and into a bushy spot on the far side of the bay. "I know you guys are green, and I don't want to put any extra pressure on you. But that backpack isn't the only thing you're swimming with tonight. You're also carrying the reputation of BRAVO Platoon."

No pressure? Thanks, Chief.

The van was a piece-of-junk '85 Toyota with tinted windows, a cracked left taillight, and local plates. A plastic Blessed Virgin dangled from the rearview, and some kind of Latin music—merengue, I think—was playing on the AM radio. The whole point of the van was to blend into the neighborhood, getting us to the water's edge without calling attention to the fact that two scary-looking men in wetsuits would soon be crawling into the tranquil bay in the dead of night.

"Combat-swimmer missions are our heritage," the chief said solemnly, his voice still as scratchy as North Jersey asphalt even after two decades away. "They go all the way back to the naked warriors who cleared Omaha Beach. That was in World War II."

"Yes, Chief," Toro said.

"Those guys didn't even wear wetsuits," the chief went on. "They slathered grease on their bodies, slapped masks on their faces and knives in their belts. They had no idea what a Dräger was. They took whatever demolition equipment they needed to clear the beaches and get the landing force ashore."

"We know the story," I said.

Chief Hall was a powerful man, right at the twenty-year mark in his career. We were his sixth platoon. Physically, he was all banged up. He busted out a knee in a free-fall mishap. He broke one ankle in five places. He had a way of holding his back. It was hard for him to run-and-gun with the boys like he loved to. He'd paid the price of so many years going so hard. But even now, nothing got his juices flowing like a mission as bold as the one he was hoping—praying—young Toro and I could somehow pull off.

We were FNGs, Fuckin' New Guys, which I eventually figured out was half an insult and half a term of grudging endearment. We had only recently earned our Tridents. This was the very first deployment for either of us—anywhere, ever. I was SEAL Team Four's most junior officer. And Toro, not so long out of high school, looked like he might need a note from his mom just to be here. If you ran a bar, you would definitely card him.

But kitted out like we were—black wetsuits, blackened faces, black dive masks, and black fins—we did look pretty fierce as we stepped out of the van that night. I checked the limpet mine I had in my backpack. All snug. It was secured with ingenious little magnets designed to hold it there until we were ready to slide it out of the pack and ease it delicately onto the steel skin of a giant ship that was docked on the other side of the bay.

"You're both strong in the water," the chief said just before we stepped in. "You're aggressive guys. So get out there and be aggressive. You have to execute."

With that, Toro and I pulled our masks up to our faces and began the long, quiet swim across the bay. We used a classic combat-swimmer recovery stroke, a low-in-water sidestroke we had learned our first week in training and had practiced almost every day since. It allowed us to cover great distances efficiently and without stirring up the water too much.

We knew there was a concrete pier jutting out from the harbor, just shy of one mile away. That's where the target vessel was waiting, though we couldn't even see its outline yet.

"No margin for error on this one," I whispered to Toro a few yards out from the shore.

"Could be our first—and last—op ever," he agreed. "Shortest two careers in SEAL history."

There's a reason sitting ducks are called sitting ducks. Swimming in hostile water is one of the most vulnerable places a warrior can ever find himself. The moment you are discovered, the balance of power shifts horribly against you. The bad guys are above you. You're below. They have cover. You don't. You can be shot with no fair chance of returning fire. If you manage to dive underwater, antipersonnel grenades can easily find you there. By far the best defense for a combat swimmer is not being detected at all. Being noticed is often just another term for getting killed.

Our underwater breathing equipment would have made this mission so much easier, letting us swim beneath the surface without any bubbles floating up. No one would have a chance of seeing us, even staring right in our direction with binoculars or high-mag scopes. But no Drägers on this swim.

As Toro and I hit the halfway point, we could finally see the outline of the target vessel on the far side of the pier. The moon wasn't full but it was bright enough for some visibility. And a string of high-watt floodlights ran the full length of the pier.

Even from this distance, the ship looked huge, far more massive than either of us expected. Silhouetted against the pier, it was high and dark and ominous. The bridge shot up from the stern like a prefab apartment complex. Flags were fluttering from the bow. The deck was mostly empty except for a crane and some other large machinery. A ship like that could haul an immense load of gear.

Toro and I decided to turtleback the rest of the way in. That would be quieter, swimming on our backs with our blackened faces just above the water, kicking in powerful, smooth strokes.

It was right then that we got our first lucky break. On the pier between the target vessel and the shore we noticed that two of the floodlights were out. That created a clear, dark stripe all the way across the water. To us, it looked like a perfect entrance ramp.

Shielded in the darkness, no one spotted us as we got closer and closer to the ship. Soon we were close enough to hear the voices of the sentries up on the pier.

"Any sign?" one of them asked.

"Nothing," another said.

They had to be talking about us.

We followed that darkened path until we were underneath the pier, maybe three hundred yards from the bow of the ship.

It's always eerie under a pier at night, the perfect environment for a couple of adventure-seeking SEALs: the shadows from the pilings, shafts of light slicing through the grates above, the echoes that the tidal surges cause. Our first few weeks of combat-swimmer training, it seemed like all we did was swim in and out of the underbellies of creepy wood and concrete piers. This one was typical. I spotted a couple of old fishing nets torn on barnacles and a busted, half-open crab trap someone had left behind, ideal for snagging a swimmer's wetsuit. We could hear footsteps and voices over our heads.

Those sentries, we knew, were on high alert and actively looking for us.

A ship at night has its own rhythm, its own special heartbeat. Especially in port, a ship this size can sound like a living thing. And this one almost seemed to be talking to us. Creaking against the rubber bumpers on the pier. A huge bilge pump disgorging water. Fuel lines taking on diesel. Machinery groaning like human digestion. There were bells and whistles and voices shouting. Gulls and other seabirds were squawking away.

We wanted to reach the aft of the ship, where the propeller, the propulsion system, the power plant, and the engine would be. If an explosion went off there, the damage would be catastrophic. That part of the pier also happened to be lit up like a high school football field on Friday night.

Our best shot, Toro and I decided, was old-school. We would have to swim underwater, piling to piling, slowly making our way under the pier. The pilings were thirty yards apart. I knew we had enough lung capacity to easily swim twice that distance underwater if we could see where we were going. But this water was shoe-polish black. If our aim was off even a little, we'd be totally exposed.

"Heroes or zeros," Toro said with a shrug.

We both took several deep breaths. On my count, "One, two, three," Toro and I slid below the surface and swam with locked arms. We didn't want to risk losing each other. We aimed for the next piling and hoped for the best. Signaling with arm tugs, we came to the surface one at a time. We made the first piling perfectly. On the second one, we were just a few inches off but not too bad. Then I crashed into the next piling, slamming my right shoulder and head.

Man, that hurt.

And just to make our piling-to-piling journey even more difficult, every five minutes or so a small fishing boat came circling through, sweeping a high-beam searchlight beneath the pier.

Every time that happened, Toro and I had to hold our breath again and duck below the surface. Only when the boat had passed could we slide back up for air.

One time, just as I came up, I saw the search boat moving toward us and I shot back down, holding Toro under with me. It was just like we were back in SEAL training again, doing our underwater knot-tying drills in the combat-training tank. Those forced breath holds hadn't gotten any easier since then.

I couldn't see the look on Toro's face. But I knew exactly what he was thinking: "I want to kill you, sir. I'm running out of O_2 down here."

A few more pilings and we were there—not just at the target vessel but directly beside the ship's stern.

"Get this limpet off my back and ease it in place," I whispered.

Treading water inches from the ship's hull, Toro slid the limpet mine out of my pack. He swam down on another breath hold and gently placed the mine against the hull, a good four feet below the waterline.

I swam down to check the magnets.

"Secure," I said to Toro, surfacing briefly.

Then I swam back down and attached the time fuse.

"Capped in," I said.

We both let out a huge sigh of relief.

Now all we had to do was get the hell out of there.

IT WAS THE final challenge in an elaborate port-security exercise at Roosey Roads. They had plenty of warning. The Navy's ship's commanders knew we were on our way. They were on full alert and waiting for us. Several times in the pre-planning briefing, the ship's executive officer had used the phrase "when we catch the SEALs." Not if. When.

Getting to the ship had gone far more smoothly than we had any right to. But we needed our good fortune to continue. We still had to get out of there and safely back across the bay. Really, the only choice we had was getting out exactly as we had gotten in. Piling to piling, on breath holds, then quietly turtlebacking out into the bay. That's when I really feared we were about to get caught.

Just as we broke the cover of the pier, we saw four sentries standing immediately above us. They were out there smoking cigarettes, staring almost directly our way. This is a lesson our enemies often fail to heed. When you smoke cigarettes, you kill your night vision. You've got the glow of the cigarette distorting your eyesight. The smoke is floating into your face. And people who are smoking usually aren't paying such careful attention to what's going on around them.

"Don't look at 'em," I said under my breath to Toro. Humans have an innate sense of when people are staring at them, the way you can almost feel it when someone's eyeballing you in a restaurant or across a crowded room. I didn't want to risk that.

"Just don't give them any reason to tap into that sixth sense," I told Toro.

It worked. None of the smoking sentries noticed a thing, and we made our way swiftly back across the bay.

Toro and I didn't say a word to each other until we were three-quarters home. Kicking on our backs in the water, staring back at the scene of the crime, we were both superstitious enough not to want to jinx it. Finally, I broke the silence.

"Holy shit, we did it," I said.

"Amazing," Toro agreed.

As soon as we hit the far shore, we called our chief on a radio we'd hidden there.

"Please tell me, 'Mission complete,'" the chief said.

"It's done," I told him.

"Five minutes, I'll meet you at extract."

In five exactly, he pulled up in the junker van.

"My boys!" he said with a huge grin on his face. Our wetsuits still dripping, Toro and I climbed inside.

The chief drove straight to the guard post at the front gate of the port's main pier. "Hey," he told the sailor at the gate, "we need to talk to the officer of the deck right now. Let him know the SEALs are here."

The sailor must have misinterpreted what the chief said. He seemed to think the chief meant that the SEALs had been captured during the training mission—not that they had succeeded in planting their dummy bomb. The guard called his executive officer and announced into the phone: "We got the SEALs," he said.

"All right, you got 'em," we could hear the XO saying. "Where did you catch them?"

At that point, the sailor looked past our chief and saw Toro and me standing there. With our faces still covered in camouflage, we were a scary-looking pair. When the sentry got a clear look at us, he must have realized we hadn't been caught at all. Staring at Toro and me, he quickly revised his explanation on the phone.

"Um, actually, sir, I was mistaken," he told his XO. "The SEALs are *here*."

"Tell him the SEALs planted a bomb," the chief whispered.

"As I understand it, sir," the guard said, "there is a bomb on the ship."

There was dead silence coming through the line. After a moment, I heard a cold, commanding voice: "Show them up to the bridge."

No other victory came close to what I felt as I walked along that pier and onto the bridge of that huge Navy ship. We marched past every single sailor with a gun, including the four who had been smoking cigarettes. I had to stop myself from saying, "You four are the ones who should have caught us."

We were still dripping water with every step we took. As we walked along, everyone seemed to be curious. I could hear people ask, "Did we catch them? Where did we catch them?"

The sailor who was escorting us shook his head glumly. "No," he had to say, fifteen times at least.

When we reached the bridge, there was the XO who the night before had briefed everyone on the port security exercise and what would happen "when" they caught the SEALs.

"I thought for sure we'd get you guys," he said.

"We know, sir," I told him.

"So what's the deal?" he asked, the gravity of the situation finally sinking in.

"You have a bomb on your ship," I told him. "Look, sir, you've got to run your security drill tighter."

He had to wake the captain, who had left orders to be alerted specifically if something like this occurred.

A couple of minutes later, the captain stepped calmly onto the bridge. Under the circumstances, I thought he was extremely gracious and cool.

He looked at Toro and me and said, "Did you get us?"

"Yes, sir," I said.

"Well done," he said, as he began firing off orders to his crew. "All right, XO, launch the emergency action drill and get boats in the water. I want the EOD techs out there. I want everybody." For the next thirty minutes, we just sat there with the XO and the captain, listening to their whole drill. Eventually, word came back over the radio.

"We have an explosive device on the skin of the ship."

That's what they were hoping not to find, undeniable proof that the SEALs had won.

If that had been an active limpet mine and it really went off, the ship would have suffered devastating damage, and the captain knew it. He was making sure everyone else on the ship knew it, too.

These dangers are frighteningly real.

Something not so different had just happened in the Yemeni port city of Aden to the USS *Cole*. The U.S. Navy destroyer, feeling safe and secure in port, was hit by suicide attackers in a small boat packed with explosives, killing seventeen American sailors and injuring thirty-nine others. It was the deadliest attack against a United States naval vessel in more than a decade, and it exposed major weaknesses in port security.

"I really appreciate it, boys," the captain told Toro and me. "Let's wait until tomorrow and you guys can debrief us on how you got it done."

"Sounds good, sir," I said.

It was after 2 a.m. when Toro and I and the chief got back to the team. But all of BRAVO Platoon was up celebrating. People were cracking open beers. The chief pulled a couple of cigars out of his pocket and handed one to each of us.

Our relative inexperience didn't go unnoticed. I loved it when I heard one of the senior guys say, "I guess these FNGs are good to go."

I would hate to have been aboard the Navy ship that night as the captain and the XO were grilling their crew, the ones who were so certain they would get the SEALs.

"Really, how did they do that?" I'm sure they were saying, scratching their heads.

9

TERROR AGE

*The only reason a warrior is alive is to fight,
and the only reason a warrior fights is to win.*
—Miyamoto Musashi

When you're at war, you live a lot on instinct—hunch, feeling, and instinct. Pair that with obsessive training. It's the only insurance you can get in a battle zone. A fishy bump in a field, a pile of trash on the road, a house that just looks different from the other houses. Will it get your whole platoon killed or is it nothing at all? Your brain at war always cycles at a higher rate of interpretation.

Something like this happened almost every day. We were in our Humvees on the way to a target, driving a planned route through an area that we knew. All of a sudden, "Shift right!" the lead driver shouted over the radio as his truck and then the other three screeched into a hard-right turn at fifty miles an hour, veering onto a small dirt road no one even knew was there.

Everyone stayed with the lead guy, even when we didn't know where he was going or why.

"Vehicle One, what the hell was that?" I radioed up from Vehicle Two.

"I don't know," he said. "It just didn't feel right."

"Roger."

Everyone understood exactly what he was talking about. Everyone was 100 percent good with that.

It was just another day in paradise, September 11, 2001. That's how it started, anyway. One of the chiefs was in his little cubby in the back of our platoon hut with the TV on. "Hey, Diesel," Chief Hall called out as I walked in after my morning run along the water. It was a few minutes before nine, Puerto Rico time.

"Come in here. You see the tower?"

At first, I wasn't sure what tower he was talking about. Then I heard the news anchor say that a plane had hit the North Tower of the World Trade Center in New York City. No one seemed to know at first whether it was an accident or something more ominous. But when a second plane hit the South Tower, all doubt was gone. And the attacks kept coming. A plane at the Pentagon. Another plane on the ground in Pennsylvania.

"This is the real deal," I said to the chief.

He just nodded.

The whole world had changed for everyone. Or so I thought.

Word flew across the base at Roosey Roads. In five minutes, ten team members were standing in front of Chief Hall's TV, all staring intently.

Soon enough, "Did you hear?" was giving way to "Where are we going?" and "How soon do we leave?"

We were combat-certified warriors, U.S. Navy SEALs, trained, equipped, and ready to roll. Responding quickly to crises—that's who we were. Within a few more minutes, the team members were trading theories about the likely first stops. There were so many possibilities.

Pakistan, so torn. Yemen, so tragic. Syria, so brutal. Somalia, so out of control. Iran, that great enabler of terrorism.

"Cheney's been talking Iraq lately," someone suggested.

"Maybe Venezuela or something down here. That would be wild."

This was all the rankest speculation. But if we were about to be trading theaters, it was impossible not to wonder what was next. There were so many troublesome countries that could have launched the terror attacks or given aid and support to the zealots who did. We wouldn't be the first responders. That job belonged to the heroic firefighters, police officers, and medics in New York. But we would be the first international responders. We could just taste it.

We double-checked our flyaway bags, one for every conceivable environment: A jungle-warfare bag with light cammies, drain-hole boots, and insect repellent. A cold-weather bag for mountainous terrain. It had everything in layers plus climbing gear and snowshoes. A bag for ship attacks with wetsuits, hooks, and other maritime-assault gear. We needed to be ready for anywhere.

We all gasped together, watching those towers fall. But I'd be lying if I said that moment didn't stir something else in me. As a wave of sadness and patriotism swept across America, I knew as SEALs we'd be called on to render justice. Within hours, we figured, President Bush would issue an order. That order would slide down the chain of command. A C-130 would be gunning its engines on the Roosey Roads runway. Forty-eight hours, seventy-two hours max, we'd be flying like bats out of Puerto Rico, going wherever the most urgent action was.

There wasn't a SEAL anywhere on the planet not thinking exactly the same thing: Let's take the fight to the people who did this—right now.

And then, nothing.

No call. No plane. No gunning engines. No counterterror mission to Pakistan, Afghanistan, or anywhere else. Not for us.

Hours became days. Days became weeks. And once we got to weeks, we had a pretty good idea the members of SEAL Team Four, BRAVO Platoon, weren't going anywhere anytime soon. We'd likely be cooling our jets at Roosey Roads, covering our usual turf in Latin America, while all the real action was occurring first in Afghanistan, eight thousand miles away, where the president had just sent troops to attack the al Qaeda terror network and topple the fundamentalist Taliban government. The higher SEAL command had decided to send units that weren't already deployed somewhere else like we were.

I lay in my rack at night in the Roosey Roads bachelor-officer quarters, torturing myself.

What a waste, I kept thinking. This is wrong. We have to change this somehow.

But the Navy had other ideas.

Puerto Rico was perfect until America was at war. Then all of a sudden it felt like a prison with swaying palm trees and SPF 30. We'd done our log PT. I'd read my warrior books. You can't be a peacetime warrior when your nation is drawn into war, not a happy one.

Every twelve minutes, it seemed, another team member was walking into the command.

"Anything new?" they would ask. "When do you think we're gonna fly?" I had no answers for any of them. I had the same questions they did.

"This sucks," said Frog, one of our snipers.

"Don't get me started, I want to kill bad guys," said Ron.

"I can't believe this," said Chud, another sniper.

I couldn't say they were wrong.

We got an extra slap in the face when one of our Air Force combat controllers, a radioman we'd been working with and loved, and an Air Force parajumper who was one of our medics both got called to Afghanistan.

Unbelievable.

They were going to Afghanistan with Army Special Forces while we were working on our suntans at Roosey Roads. I was certain the war would be over before BRAVO Platoon could ever cycle in.

We did what we could.

We practiced ship-boarding maneuvers in the open sea, imagining we were searching for terror suspects. We ran maritime-blocking exercises with fast-attack boats, gaming the counterterror challenges of commercial-port security. This was an excruciating time to be leading a SEAL platoon so far from the battlefield. As the weeks turned into months, all we could do was deliver empty pep-talks to the team—then repeat them to ourselves.

"Let's not expend all our energy in anticipation," B, BRAVO's platoon commander, said. "We'll keep PT'ing. We'll go to the range. We'll make ourselves the warriors we know we can be. When the bubble goes up, when the pager goes off, we'll be ready."

That was one speech. I had others. "We can't control history," I said. "We can't control what leadership is going to do. All we can be is prepared."

And maybe if I said that stuff often enough, I would eventually start to feel it.

It never happened. The war on terror revved up with BRAVO Platoon shoved over on the sidelines. SEALs, Green Berets, and other special operators were making an impact in Afghanistan. The Bush administration was hinting strongly about a war in Iraq. We stayed in

Roosey Roads until our deployment was over in 2002. Then we returned to the SEALs' East Coast headquarters at Little Creek. My
journey of frustration still had a couple of stops left.

About that time, the top SEAL leadership was creating two new
teams, Team Seven on the West Coast, Team Ten on the East. Like
an NBA expansion draft, other teams contributed platoons to fill out
the new rosters. My boys in BRAVO Platoon were shifted to the new
Team Ten, while as a junior officer with low seniority, I remained at
Team Four.

I hated to split up with those guys—Jersey, Toro, Irish, Face Man,
Sonny, and the others. They'd have been a sterling crew to go into
battle with. To this day, I truly regret that we never had the chance. I
suppose all leaders have a soft spot for their first platoon, but these
were world-class warriors, and I've stayed close with many of them.

"What a missed opportunity," we still tell each other when we
connect.

I went out to sea in March 2003, just as the Iraq War was getting
started, as a SEAL liaison officer on one of the Navy's big Amphibious Ready Groups. Led by a new 844-foot, 41,000-ton Wasp-class
assault ship, the group included two other warships and a landing
force of 1,900 Marines, plus everything they would need to prosecute a
sizable invasion: thirty helicopters, half a dozen Harrier ground-attack
aircraft, Humvees, troop carriers, light-armored maritime-capable assault craft, 25 mm Mk 38 cannons, and a Sea Sparrow missile system.

I'm an officer in the Navy. I appreciate the power and the majesty
of a well-run ship, and this one was epecially awesome, barreling at
22 knots across the Mediterranean with its geared steam turbines
running at full blast. I pray we never give up our dominance of the
sea. But a long ship deployment really wasn't what I was cut out for. I
found shipboard life confining. I wanted to be out hunting bad guys
in a more face-to-face way.

Here we go again, I said to myself as I settled into my SEAL-liaison duties with my chief and communications expert. "One war is raging in the mountains of Afghanistan. Another is starting in mostly landlocked Iraq. And I'm stuck on a ship at sea." I didn't even have a SEAL platoon along. There'd be nothing for them to do all day. Their gear was on board, but the men would come from Rota, Spain, only when they were called. This was starting to make Roosey Roads look like Action Central. None of it felt to me like a quick route to war.

A classic gung-ho, *Semper Fi* Marine commanded the expeditionary unit on the ships. Colonel Franklin was a short but amazingly fit 300-PFTer. Every year he got a perfect score on the Marine Physical Fitness Test. That's a challenge for a young man let alone a colonel. He was a focused, driven commander. I liked the fact that he seemed to be itching for a way into Iraq. But I don't believe he much enjoyed having a young SEAL officer in and around his staff. He seemed to think of SEALs as unruly cowboys and not quite deferential enough. He and I butted heads immediately. Him being a colonel and me a lieutenant, he was always right.

I could have been a valuable asset to the colonel. Through my SEAL team network of brothers, teammates, and friends, I had strong connections to the special-operations forces on the ground in Iraq. I knew things that could have been useful to him and his staff: Where the action was heating up, where nothing much was going on, where the insurgents were gathering strength. I could also have provided a SEAL element to join his Marine contingent. Hitting the ground together would only have boosted everyone's combat effectiveness. But the colonel wanted nothing to do with SEALs or with me or any of my ideas. He had his own theories about how to go to war in Iraq.

Colonel Franklin was a helicopter man. Which was fine. But he didn't want to approach Iraq from the south, the route the Army's 4th Infantry Division was taking along with other mechanized units.

Instead, he decided to fly his Marine contingent in from the far east-ern Mediterranean, over Turkey, into northern Iraq, landing near Mosul.

The plan bothered me. The northern region wasn't Saddam's real stronghold or al Qaeda's. I tried to offer my advice. "I'm talking di-rectly to special-operations forces on the ground," I told the colonel. "Can I share with you what I'm hearing?"

"Nope," he said.

I offered to connect him with special-operations forces in the north, if he was dead set on going in that way. I told him I would go in with his Marines if he'd like to help coordinate. "Maybe you can gin up something with our spec-op guys," I said. "They know the region."

"Nope," he said. "We'll be fine, and you're staying here."

"Roger, sir."

The colonel grabbed all the aircraft he could and roared his Ma-rines into northern Iraq. It did not go well.

I wasn't there. I heard some colorful descriptions from my friends in the sandbox and from some of the colonel's boys about their adven-tures in the north. All I can say for certain is that, eighteen days later, the colonel and his Marines left Iraq unceremoniously and returned abruptly to their ships. I had missed another chance to go to war. Literally and figuratively, I was still at sea.

Then a phone call came that no one was expecting. We might be needed in Liberia. The West African nation was spinning out of control.

Liberia has a unique history. An active participant in the African slave trade, the region was colonized beginning in 1820 by free blacks from the United States, most of them former slaves. They believed they'd find greater freedom and equality in Africa. Even the name they chose for their new country echoed that hope. Liberia's govern-ment was modeled on the ideas of James Madison and Thomas

Jefferson, and the capital city, Monrovia, was named for James Monroe, the fifth American president and a prominent supporter of their cause. Many of today's Liberians are the descendants of those former American slaves.

By 2003, Liberia had spiraled into anarchy. Murderous rebel factions, feuding diamond thieves, armed drug thugs—the country was the shame of West Africa. Two hundred thousand Liberians had been killed in a civil war. Millions of others had fled to refugee camps. Monrovia was a homicidal playpen for crazed and thuggish gangsters. The soccer stadium was a Red Cross medical center. Bodies were piled in the streets. The country's despotic president, Charles Taylor, an international pariah, had fled not long before.

It wasn't the war zone I'd been expecting. The catastrophe unfolding in Liberia wasn't even officially a war. Most Americans were glued to Iraq and Afghanistan. But I found myself steaming across the Med to help save a proud nation from self-destruction, and I couldn't have asked for a more eye-opening experience. This was too big a mission to leave to a Marine colonel or a Navy captain. This was a major military operation. The Liberia mission was handed to a much larger Joint Task Force, run by Army Major General Thomas Turner. The general and his staff came on board.

As our three ships neared the Liberian coast, the U.S. embassy in Monrovia was a last-ditch holdout of sanity and stability. The Americans had already been evacuated in a helicopter rescue by members of SEAL Team Four, who'd flown in a week earlier. But the streets were still in chaos. It would clearly take a much larger U.S. force to calm the unrest.

I knew we'd be landing a full contingent of Marines in Liberia, the perfect force for this kind of mission. And I knew from SEAL history and personal experience that getting them ashore was something the SEALs were uniquely qualified for.

I was excited. I called up the SEAL chain of command.

"At a minimum," I said, "I'll be generating a request for a legitimate, real-world hydrographic reconnaissance of pointed locations on the Liberian coast. I might be able to also get an actual request in for a boat drop," parachuting rigid-hulled inflatable boats and operators into the sea from an aircraft. The SEALs had been training for that, as had the Special Warfare Combatant Craft crewmen who operate high-speed assault boats better than anyone in the world. But we'd never actually done a live drop in theater.

There was silence on the line.

"We're actually doing an exercise drop here in the Med," the senior SEAL said. "There's a bunch of bigwigs here. I can't cancel that."

"We're saying no to a real-world mission for the sake of an exercise?" I couldn't believe it.

"That's correct," he said. "Do your hydro. We'll fly the platoon to the boat. You're not getting the airdrop."

Now, that was bureaucracy.

The drop wasn't mission critical. It was mission enhancing. And chances like this one rarely come along. But still, there were many firsts in Liberia.

The Liberian coast was piled with thousands of smooth, flat rocks, the discarded ballast from long-ago slave ships. The water in Monrovia Harbor was teeming with reef sharks and hammerheads. But twenty SEALs working together would have to find a way to get those U.S. Marines ashore without getting wrecked, shot, bombed, or eaten alive.

The plan came straight out of SEAL history. We'd be doing something not too different from what the Underwater Demolition Teams had done before the Normandy invasion in World War II: a full, jump-in-water hydrographic survey of Monrovia Harbor and two beaches nearby, hammerheads be damned.

I was finally beginning to feel like a SEAL.

. . . .

"You crazy bastards are going in that water?" a Navy master chief asked, shaking his head as we prepared to slide two rigid-hull inflatable boats off the side of one of the group's warships. From the launch platform, he could see the sharks circling in the water. To be honest, so could we, and we were the ones about to climb in.

"That's how it's done, Master Chief," I said. "We take the RHIBs in to the surf line. Then the beach party—the platoon commander and three other SEALs—swim up to shore for an initial recon. When they're satisfied, they signal the RHIBs and the rest of us swim in. It takes about sixteen of us to get the hydro done."

He wasn't offering to come for the ride.

Once the RHIBs were in the water, we linked up with a couple of Marine Zodiacs and their reconnaissance operators. All four boats began motoring in. But as the boats were reaching the surf line, things started going badly.

One RHIB lost engine power. It came close to getting swamped. The other RHIB did an amazing job towing the first one out of the impact zone. But as the four SEAL swimmers and two Marines dropped into the water for their swim to shore, one of the Marines lost a fin and almost drowned.

He made it to shore, but the SEAL lieutenant didn't like the way any of this was going. "This reconnaissance does not have to happen tonight," he said from the beach. "We'll do it tomorrow. We're swimming back out."

Two SEALs tried to swim the suffering Marine back through the surf to the boats. But he was having real trouble. They turned around and swam back in. Finally, the lieutenant called for a helicopter to carry the landing party back to the ship, while the RHIBs and Zodiacs retreated as well.

The rocky start left General Turner reconsidering all this pre-launch secrecy. "We should be showing the flag," the general said.

He ordered the three enormous U.S. Navy ships to move closer to shore, within easy sight of Monrovia. "I'd like the people to see we're here," the general said. The next morning, he said, the SEALs would take their fast Zodiacs straight up to the beach.

"I want the Liberians to understand the American operators are on the ground and able to handle anything that goes wrong," the general said.

In the light of day, thirteen other SEALs in three Zodiacs launched toward the coast near the U.S. embassy. As we came over the horizon into the surf, there were, I swear, six thousand Liberians on the berm above the beach. They were jumping up and down.

We didn't know if they were going to charge or hug us.

THEN MEN, WOMEN, AND CHILDREN came running excitedly into the water to greet us, smiling, splashing, and pulling us onto the shore. They were singing and waving.

"Americans!" they shouted. "Please, help us. Get rid of these criminals who are destroying our country."

Seeing and hearing that, it was impossible not to be moved. "We're here," we told them. "The Americans are here to help. More of us are on the way."

We took a look around. We found a couple of promising locations for the Marine landing, pending the results of the hydrographic survey. We told the people we'd be returning. Then we got back on our Zodiacs and motored out to the ship.

We got the survey done quickly the next day. It was something to behold, fourteen SEALs in the treacherous water off Liberia with grease pencils, whiteboards, and fishing lines. The fishing lines had weights on the end and depth markings every foot.

The SEALs formed a straight line, perpendicular to the shore, six feet apart from each other, standing, bobbing, or treading water. With his grease pen, each SEAL recorded careful measurements of water depth, bottom condition, and any obstacles he found. Then everyone stepped or swam six feet forward and took another round of measurements. They did it again and again. In a little more than two hours, they had produced three intricate survey charts.

The sharks kept their distance.

Based on those surveys and measurements, we chose the most promising landing spots for the Marines. They made their landing safely. They swept triumphantly into Monrovia. The drug runners, diamond thieves, and Charles Taylor loyalists stayed away, just like the sharks. Order was at least temporarily restored.

The SEALs accompanied the Marines on shore, providing ground security. But they didn't need too much of that. The vast majority of Liberians seemed thrilled to see us there, welcoming the Marines like arriving heroes.

We didn't fire a shot in Liberia. Our gun battles were still to come. But we stuck our toes into chaos in one of the most intense places on earth, and we did some good. We all returned safely to the ships.

10

MISSION IRAQ

War is an ugly thing, but not the ugliest of things. The decayed and degraded state of moral and patriotic feeling which thinks that nothing is worth war is much worse.
—John Stuart Mill

The inside of the C-17 looked like a cross between a flying moving van and a flying flophouse. Boxes of ammo, piles of communication gear, all our weapons, half a dozen large shipping containers—anything we might need for a long deployment in an unpredictable war zone was packed inside this giant transport aircraft. There were seats and tiny windows along the sidewalls. But some of the guys had strung hammocks between the shipping containers or laid out bedrolls on the floor. Why not catch some rest on the way to Iraq?

I was too keyed up to sleep.

When we landed at the Habbaniyah airfield and the huge ramp swung down, there was no mistaking how far we'd come. It wasn't just the 102-degree furnace we were stepping into. It wasn't just the dust and the fumes. There was a dull, mechanical roar on the tarmac that I would soon recognize as the grinding sounds of war. Gears catching. Jets overhead. Random pops in the distance. Half a dozen SEAL gun trucks pulling to a stop.

I felt like I'd just stepped into the opening scene of *Platoon*, where Charlie Sheen and the other fresh soldiers arrive in chaotic Vietnam to the shocking sight of body bags and soldiers clearly ravaged by the horrors of war.

It's always the dumbest clichés people reach for at moments like these. "We're not in Kansas anymore," one of my teammates said. And we'd barely learned to pronounce Habbaniyah. *Habba-KNEE-yah*.

We were dressed in light fatigues. Most of our guns and body armor were still packed away. The SEALs who came to meet us were outfitted for the apocalypse. Full body armor, helmets, gloves, assault rifles, and machine guns. They had their heavy gunners in the turret of every truck except for the open one where our gear would ride. Their radio-signal jammers were running full blast. They had come to collect the new class, but they were cocked and ready for anything.

On the way out, we stopped briefly at the airfield's heavily guarded exit gate. We spoke to one of the MPs who was standing there. He knew we were the new SEALs, come to join the fight.

"Go get 'em," he said. "Hope to see you on your return."

As we pulled out and I got my earliest glimpses of this country that would be my new home, the MP's words lingered in my head. I'm sure I read too much into what he said.

"Hope to see you on your return." As if he weren't entirely sure he would. As if the people he saw arriving didn't always fly home alive.

never felt so peaceful as when I finally got to war. The acrid smell of gunpowder was almost sweet to me. The random boom of mortar fire was oddly soothing. The sunsets in western Iraq, filtered through the smoke from burning buildings and scattered piles of trash, were some of the most stunning I had seen, and I came from California. The bite of the sandstorms, the three-figure temperatures, the knowledge that an IED or a sniper could easily be waiting around the next blind curve—everything harsh and unnerving about being in a war zone was energizing and exciting to me. Whatever the challenges, this was where I wanted to be.

I had no illusions about the deadly business we had come to Iraq for or the godforsaken patch of that country where we'd been sent. I don't believe in sugarcoating these things. We were there to kill or be killed, and that kind of agenda has a way of focusing the mind. From the moment we arrived, all the little complexities of life back home melted away. Twenty-six hours earlier, I was drinking a latte in Starbucks and worrying about the cable bill. Suddenly everything was stripped-down, simple, and clear. I felt like I'd just been handed a free ticket to a wild and exciting adventure, a chance to roam armed to the teeth through one of the most dangerous and exotic places on earth. Here in Iraq, a different part of me was coming out.

Camp Habbaniyah was an old Royal Air Force station on the banks of the Euphrates River, fifty-five miles west of Baghdad, a rugged place with built-up berms and crash walls around it and heavily armed guards at the gates. The Brits were forced to abandon the facility after the Iraqi revolution of 1958, and nothing much had been updated since. I knew Alexander and his Macedonians had come through this valley in the summer of 331 BC. They crossed the Euphrates and walked right into town. Just being there, in the same business as Alexander, elevated everything in my mind. It gave me energy. It made me hyperaware. It put extra pressure on me. You asked for this, I reminded myself. Only once can a warrior go to war for the first time.

It was already brutally hot when we arrived—and I don't just mean the temperature. Twenty-eight hundred coalition troops had been killed in the war already, more in the Sunni strongholds of Ramadi, Fallujah, and Habbaniyah than anyplace else. There were Saddam Hussein sympathizers everywhere. They pretty much had the run of the whole area. I didn't know it yet, but Bronze Stars, Silver Stars, and a Medal of Honor—they would all come out of our time there, as the men of SEAL Team Three imposed our will on the region. Our deployment would become quite legendary and help shift the momentum of the war effort, as fierce and as violent as any SEAL deployment since the jungle days of Vietnam. And we truly brought it on ourselves.

Indian Country, we called the territory outside the wire, like back in the Old West. Dusty. Lawless. Rugged. Wide open. We used that term respectfully. I always felt I had a special connection to Native American culture. Lacrosse, the sport that got me through college, came from Native Americans, who believed it was a gift from the Creator and engaged in contests for the purpose of preparing for war. Our patch of western Iraq was a haphazard mix of rural and urban, and the bad guys we faced were far better armed than the forces of Cochise, Crazy Horse, or Geronimo.

Nothing about the terrain was hospitable. There was sixty feet of green on either side of the Euphrates, but everything else was parched and dry and gray. The newer houses were built from tan cinder block. Almost all of them sat behind high walls, even the side-by-side row houses. Whatever life was happening inside, you couldn't see or hear much from the street. Clearly, the people felt vulnerable and they had for a long time.

In the daytime, the heat never eased much. At night, the electricity was often out and, with it, all the streetlights. We were either squinting into the glare of the desert or seeing the world through the pale green glow of our night-vision optics. Either way, the place felt surreal and otherworldly, with dangers large and small.

You always had to be careful where you stepped. That brownish puddle might be a brownish puddle or it just as easily might be the outflow of an open sewer. One afternoon with waste-caked boots and soaking socks was all it took to teach me always to walk carefully. Mangy dogs were everywhere. At first I couldn't put my finger on what made Iraq's stray dogs different from the ones I'd seen back home. Then I figured it out. The Iraqi dogs had been barking so long and with so little relief, their barks had all grown hoarse. They sounded as forlorn as the landscape looked.

If our goal was changing the battle space, we knew our commitment had to be intense and relentless. So every day, we'd go out on operations, the Iraqi Scouts and us. Walking from palm grove to palm grove. Taking fire from bad guys who could be almost anywhere—across the Euphrates, in a cluster of houses, from places we couldn't even see. We'd find the bad guys. We'd make sure they knew we were there with our invisible targets on our backs. We'd just start getting into fights. It really was the only way to smoke the enemy out. We weren't fighting the Iraqi people. We were fighting for them. In a war zone like this one, you can't simply open fire on the first scary-looking person who strolls along. Just by looking, there was no way to tell who was on what side. But there was one line that was easy to recognize: When someone began to shoot at us or was clearly about to, we quickly started shooting back—with overwhelming firepower.

Our idea of patrolling in the daytime was highly unorthodox for SEALs. Back home, our approach was a source of some controversy among armchair military critics, including some retired SEALs. Special operators, they said, go out under the cover of darkness. The light of day, they said, is for conventional troops. Daytime patrols, they said, are a waste of the SEALs' special talents. But in western Iraq before the Tribal Awakening, daytime was where the action was. So daytime was where we made our stand. If SEALs were going to be problem-solvers, the most creative warriors on the modern battlefield, we had to go where the problems were. Hell, we'd have patrolled in our pajamas if that's what got the job done. We briefed our senior leadership. To their credit, they said yes. And the results were impossible to argue with.

The first month we were there, 160 mortar rounds landed inside the perimeter of Combat Outpost COWBOY. The second and third months, it was down to forty. By the fourth month, the number was down to two. We had taken away the gunners' free-fire license. Already the momentum was beginning to shift.

THERE WAS NOTHING as quiet as the courtyard of a house at the end of a dark road before BRAVO Platoon rammed its way inside. As we made our stand in the daytime, we didn't ignore the challenges of the night. The night in western Iraq was a whole different world.

The stars above. The moon reflecting off the Euphrates. The light rhythmic breathing of the U.S. Navy SEALs and Iraqi Scouts.

If you didn't know what was coming, you'd never expect anything until, without a hint of warning—and that was precisely the point—the night exploded in stomps, screams, and the sound of busting hinges and shattering glass.

On this night, we weren't just raiding a house. We were looking for a sixteen-year-old budding insurgent named Kamal, who we had strong reason to believe had shot and killed an Army medic named Blakley. Kamal's older brother, Abu Roma, was a well-known terror lieutenant suspected of running a sniper cell in Khalidiya. The way the story went, Blakley was with a group of Iraqi and American troops who had arrested yet another of Kamal's brothers, and Kamal had gone out seeking revenge.

We thought we knew where the young suspect was hiding. As we pulled up in our blacked-out gun trucks, we had a full escape team ringing the block and an extra set of eyes in the sky, an F/A-18 aircraft flying overhead with night-vision capabilities. Also invited along that night: Blakley's major, whose name was Roberson. I knew the major took Blakley's death extremely personally.

Big D was such a skilled breacher, I swear he could have blasted opened a bank vault with half a roll of kiddie caps. With a well-placed charge and a click of the initiator, he blew the front door open. In a flurry of shouts and sharply barked orders, the four-man initial-entry team burst inside.

What unfolded next was more a ballet than an onslaught. Okay, it was probably a bit of both. All of us could feel the whole team's movement.

"Clear left!" one of the assaulters shouted.

"Clear right!" shouted another.

"All clear!" came back the answer, as the entry team completed the initial search of the first room and moved on to the next one.

Then, the other eight of us and the twelve Iraqi Scouts went rushing inside, clearing the house with businesslike swiftness and few spoken words. On nods, hand squeezes, and shoulder pats, we moved through every room. It was the same kind of nonverbal communication we'd learned back in diving training. Who needs words to talk?

One team member opened a door. A teammate joined him to search that room. "All clear," one of them announced. The assault team went like that from room to room, down each hallway, up the stairs, dominating every corner and section one by one. In a matter of a minute or two, we owned the house.

"Target secure," one of the assistant officers said over the radio.

In one room we found three women, one older man, and six children. We separated the man from the women and children, carefully identifying everyone, being alert for weapons and for any intelligence that might be extracted. Even for experienced operators like BRAVO Platoon, so much is easy to miss. A false wall or a trapdoor hiding people or weapons. Explosives rigged into the house. We found none of that this time.

And no Kamal.

It was then that the F-18 pilot radioed my communicator, Lope, who was standing where he always stood, immediately at my side.

"Squirter on the roof," the pilot said, using the term for someone trying to escape. "Squirter on the roof."

Roberson and I raced immediately to the top of the building. My chief, Frank, beat us up there.

Still no Kamal.

The squirter team, which had the building surrounded, hadn't reported anything, and there wasn't much on the roof except for a large water tank. It was the only place up there a person might conceivably hide.

Cautiously, Frank approached the water tank. He stood beside it and listened.

At first he heard nothing.

Then he heard something strange.

It was the unmistakable sound of bubbles rising through the water.

The chief had time on his side. He could breathe all night if he had to. But whoever was in the tank underwater could hold his breath for only so long.

A few seconds later, the squirter came bursting to the surface, gasping madly for air.

It was a dripping-wet Kamal.

Roberson was elated. "I can't tell you how much this means to me and my unit," he said as the chief put the cuffs on. We gave Roberson the honor of walking the prisoner to the truck.

WE ALL HAD our ways of going into battle.

"I want a couple of grenades right here beside me in the truck," one team member said. "I don't want 'em in the back. I want 'em right next to my water bottle and the patch from my buddy's fire department."

We all had things that were special to us. There were so many variables on the battlefield that none of us could control. We had trained as a cohesive group. We were issued the same uniforms. But our dress, our weapons, the placement of our gear, our pre-battle rituals—those were individual choices.

Not being a heavy-weapons gunner, I wasn't on the Mk 48 or a .50-cal very often. My primary battle weapon, the one I've spent the most time with, was my M4. It became an extension of my body. The M4 is the standard, special-ops battle rifle—a gas-operated, air-cooled, magazine-fed assault rifle that traces its heritage to earlier carbine versions of the M16, all of them based on the original AR-15, designed in the 1950s by the visionary firearms engineer Eugene Stoner. The M4 is fast. It's light. It's accurate. It's highly modifiable. It has a rail system that can handle lights, lasers, scope—you can dress it up like a Christmas tree if you want. It fires a .556-caliber round from thirty-round magazines, and it has a flat, predictable shooting trajectory. Mine was tricked out the way I liked it. I used several different sights. My favorite was an Aimpoint red-dot with very low magnification. Our snipers tended to use much higher mag. They needed that for their long-range targets. If I felt like I needed a little more magnification in the field, I would use a Trijicon ACOG scope. But most of the time I preferred a wider view.

I wouldn't say the M4 was my favorite gun. The gun I really liked was my teammate Rob's M14, a World War II throwback that I used a lot of the time. On an overwatch from a rooftop or on any daylight patrol, I always carried Rob's M14. He had it camouflaged. He had a red-dot scope with a little mag. I love that gun. It just has a lot more bang for the buck than the M4 does. The M14 fires a .762-round, a much heavier bullet. If I laid the two rounds right next to each other and asked, "Which would you rather be shot with?" you wouldn't need to know anything about ballistics to say immediately, "I'll take the one on the left," the smaller M4.

For most SEALs, the big Rambo knife is mostly a myth, and I never carried one. But like most warriors, I always had a fixed-blade knife with me, an SOG Desert Dagger with a six-inch blade or the slightly smaller SOG Pentagon with a five-inch blade.

I have buddies who are knife pros. They've convinced me that a folding-blade knife is a broken knife, great in your pocket at home, not so great in battle. Fixed is just stronger. I used it to cut a line, open a package, slice open a mattress in a hunt for hidden weapons. That knife was in action many times a day. The handles and the grips are easy to hold whether hands are wet or dry.

I hung my knife vertically on my body armor, handle up, blade down. That way, if someone came at me in close quarters in such a way that my hands were pinned against my chest, I'd still be able to grab the handle of the knife. It would have to be a highly motivated bad guy to still hang on as I was slicing at his hands or his eyes.

We had the newest generation of Kevlar body armor. When we got over there, some of the team members were talking about the advantages of a body-armor system they called chicken plates.

"They're thinner, they're lighter, and they aren't nearly as hot," one guy said. "These plates will stand up to AK-47 fire even better than Kevlar does."

We'd been wearing the chicken plates in the field on and off for a couple of months when one day Ro said: "We should probably test these things. We've just been taking them on faith."

We took a couple out to the range and fired an AK47 straight on at the chicken plates. The rounds went through metal like a hot knife through butter.

"Uh-oh," Ro said.

"All of a sudden, Kevlar's looking very light and cool," I said.

My most useful tools of all? A big-ass black Sharpie pen and a little digital camera. I carried three Sharpies in a pouch right above my magazine. Once we got a house cleared, I took a count of all the people and all the material we found. Instead of writing on paper or writing on my wrist with a grease pencil like some officers did, I'd write on the wall or the floor of the house, every piece of information I needed to report from the raid. Everyone's name, the broken door, the money on the counter, any documents lying around, whatever it was. Then I'd take a photo and when I got back, make it part of my permanent report.

WE WERE ON our way in from a night op when we got word that Mark had been killed. He had been responding as part of a quick-reaction force to fellow SEALs who needed help in a gunfight. Mark was a member of Task Unit BRAVO. But everyone at SEAL Team Three called the task unit TU BRUISER. TU BRUISER experienced the heaviest, most sustained combat of any SEAL Team Three Task Unit. Their base of operations was down the road from us in Ramadi.

Our unit had been out for fifty hours straight. These grinding marathons weren't as long as Hell Week, but they were tough. It was almost 9 a.m. when we were finally pulling our gun trucks back onto base and heard some disturbing radio chatter from higher headquarters. Word was that there'd been a gunfight and Mark was killed.

A memorial was being held that morning in Ramadi, about twenty miles away.

Mark was a warrior, one of the best, and a good friend of ours. When we heard the news, all the guys were smoked and tired and just done. But no way were we skipping Mark's memorial. We stopped quickly at the base. We fueled up the trucks. We reloaded the guns.

"Let's go," I said.

We hauled ass to Ramadi as fast as we could.

That took us along one of the worst IED roads in Iraq, and it was light outside as we began the drive. You'd rather do this drive at night-time. Barreling along in the morning, you could see a lot of suspect people wandering around.

Half a mile out of Ramadi at a sharp bend in the road, someone had dumped a pile of garbage. This was a common trap. You swerve to miss the garbage and drive across an IED. *Ka-boom!* The front of your vehicle is suddenly pointing skyward.

We knew enough not to fall for that one. Plus, we had our jammers going full blast. Those high-powered electronic signal-blockers had been protecting us on the roads pretty well, interrupting the enemy's ability to signal their remote-controlled bombs. We plowed right over the trash. What we didn't account for in all our cleverness were the two young gunmen, one fat and one skinny, both with beards, waiting for us behind a concrete barrier at the top of the bend. Their weapons were already up as we came through the curve. They both unloaded with AK-47s. But the shots weren't perfect and missed our vehicles. Thankfully, one of our turret gunners was in our lead truck in a perfect position to respond. He engaged the shooters, hitting the heavier one in the chest with a burst from the .50-cal. The fat kid disintegrated. His gun went bouncing to the road. I couldn't see what happened to the thinner shooter, but I can't imagine it was good. The firing stopped, and we rolled on. We got to Ramadi without further incident and made the service.

The battlefield teams always wanted to pay their respects before their teammates' bodies were flown back home. One of the things SEALs do—and thankfully, not too often—is sending off our fallen comrades right. We have our own special ways of honoring the ultimate sacrifice.

Mark's service was held in a small planning space that was turned into a makeshift chapel. On a small platform at the front of the room was an empty pair of boots, a set of body armor, an upside-down rifle with a helmet balanced on the buttstock, and a table holding a picture of Mark.

His closest buddies from Task Unit BRUISER stood up front. We stayed in the back along with some friends of Mark's from a couple of BRUISER's sister units. Other American and Iraqi soldiers filled in the rows. Anyone who knew the guys from BRUISER wanted to be there.

The BRUISER commander spoke movingly about the warrior and friend Mark had been to so many people in the room. How he was always eager to be helpful. How he never backed down, not once. How selfless and loyal he was to his warrior friends.

Mark's death must have been a special burden for the commander. Every action of Task Unit BRUISER was his ultimate responsibility. Standing in the back and listening to him perform this solemn duty, I couldn't help but think what I'd say if I had to do that for one of my immediate guys.

When the commander was finished, a senior Army officer and a military chaplain both spoke. Then every single SEAL in the room, in pairs of swim buddies, walked up to the shrine and to Mark's picture and said a short, quiet good-bye. When the service was done, everyone formed into a long procession and escorted Mark's casket onto an aircraft for the long flight home.

After all that was finished, we sat together for chow, Mark's closest friends from ALPHA and BRUISER, before our dicey daytime ride back to our base camp.

One of the members of BRUISER asked to have a quiet word with me.

"We're going to get some payback," he said.

"Payback?" I asked.

"We're going to get some payback. You guys in?"

I love the fight. I love getting into gun battles. I'd been in dozens already in my time in Iraq. It becomes exciting and addictive, both at once. You start to crave the action when you are over there.

But I don't believe that revenge is the best motivation for a gun-fight. It is corrupt fuel. The people who killed Mark might have been savages. They certainly caused a lot of pain. I understand how any member of TU BRUISER might feel they had a right to vengeance. The people who did this were evil and would do far worse if given the opportunity. Mark was a friend, and someone had pulled the trigger to kill him. But to me, the idea of general payback driven by such immediate emotion wasn't right. It wasn't the ethos of the brotherhood. "We've been going for two days straight," I told him. "Our guys don't have the sustained juice to stay here, build that plan, and go out again."

"What are you talking about?" he asked.

"I think we'll take a pass," I said.

He let it hang. But I don't think he was too happy about my answer. We shook hands, and my team drove straight back to Habbaniyah.

I am confident that, in the end, TU BRUISER made the right decision and returned to the battlefield appropriately. That fight wasn't for us.

11

MOMENTUM SHIFT

No bastard ever won a war by dying for
his country. He won it by making the other
poor dumb bastard die for his country.
—GEORGE PATTON

Our gun trucks were like Humvee tanks. Armored doors. Plated glass. Reinforced undercarriages. Run-flat tires. As long as you were in the vehicle, you were actually pretty safe.

Safe and sealed off.

That's unless you were the turret gunner. The turret gunner was neither of those.

When you were up in the turret, you could feel the heat, the wind, the dust—everything. You had a perfect, 360-degree view. You were the only unprotected guy in the truck and were also by far the most exposed. But your hands were on the biggest gun in the truck. You were the only one who could respond directly to any kind of aggression.

I was in Vehicle Two. Our trail vehicle—Vehicle Four with the turret gunner and the .50-cal—was forty yards behind. I heard what sounded like a concussion grenade or an IED. I couldn't see any-thing.

Before I even asked, my trail turret gunner was on the radio: "Give me a second, LT, I'm working some things out."

Then, "We had a suspicious vehicle coming up on us," he said. "I cut the front end off it. He won't be an issue any longer."

I loved riding in the turret every rare chance I got, which meant every time my guys let me. As an officer, my job was to lead. But when I got the opportunity, I was a pit bull in a steakhouse.

"Why don't you get down into the truck, sir," one of the gunners would tell me eventually. I knew if he was calling me "sir," he was messing with me.

"Leave it to the pros, will you?" he'd say. "I got it from here."

The intel sounded solid. Some financiers, some bomb makers, maybe a couple of sniper cells were safe-harboring north of our operating base in the northeast section of Habbaniyah. A small unit of Marines had already gone in there, hoping to disrupt the cozy operation. They confronted the insurgents they expected, but the operation didn't go as planned. The second time the Marines went in, a roadside bomb severely injured four of them and destroyed some of their equipment. Doubling down, the SEALs got the call: "Take your shot."

We were heading into dangerous territory, although that was be-coming a given in western Iraq. As far as we knew, no SEAL team had made its presence felt in that part of Anbar, no special-ops guys from any unit. There was no way to drive in. Not with such narrow roads and easy overlooks, perfect ambush perches. Even with the signal jammers in our vehicles, we'd be an easy target for the RPGs and IEDs. So we made our way in on foot—ten SEALs, fourteen Iraqi Scouts—not that walking provided much protection.

This was only June. But the midday temperatures were already topping out between 100 and 125. By early afternoon, the whole region was a sauna with desert mantises and sand flies. All the combat gear and body armor didn't make walking any cooler. We had our weapons, bullets, food, and water—and that was about it. We weren't taking anything to stay. Top of the list: confronting the enemy explosives team that had banged up those Marines. We didn't know when or where we might find them. But whenever and wherever we did, we knew they would have the home-field advantage.

Iraq before the Tribal Awakening was a dangerous, out-of-control place. Safety and success could never be guaranteed. I had bouncing in my head something one of my dad's law partners, a Vietnam vet with two Silver Stars and a Bronze Star, once said. My dad had been telling him how great I thought SEAL training was. "True," he answered, "but it still doesn't make 'em bulletproof." Damn right. None of us was bulletproof. What we were was better prepared than anyone else on that battlefield. And that meant a lot.

"Ready to move, Lou?" I asked my point man, one of the great all-time SEALs to have on a patrol as dicey as this one.

"Roger," Lou said.

In this heat with this gear, I knew we needed to move efficiently. "Navigate the route," I told him.

It was always daunting—exciting and nerve-racking at once—to be stepping off a path and into the wilds of Anbar Province. You just knew: Sometime on that patrol, chances were you'd come into contact with armed insurgents. You knew on this day, today, that would likely happen, and that was a shot of instant energy for all of us. It was like walking onto the field for a sudden-death playoff game—only sudden-death wasn't just a figure of speech. As we began our patrol, we couldn't wait for the fire to start. We wanted the enemy to show himself as soon as humanly possible, and then we'd see who was made of what.

A SEAL unit, any SEAL unit, knows how to walk with care across different terrains. Rural areas, urban areas, wherever it is, over dirt, concrete, sand, or snow. If we don't want people knowing we've been there, they won't have an easy time finding out. All of us are trained, in BUD/S and later, not to leave tracks or traces or anything else behind. Hostile forces have to pay awfully close attention to know when we've been passing through.

It wasn't direct confrontation we were trying to avoid. On this mission, direct confrontation was the whole point. It was surreptitious detection I was concerned about, especially anything that allowed the enemy to spot us first and predict where we might be heading—then lie in wait for our arrival. That could get ugly. We much preferred the element of surprise on *our* side. But this particular mission, like most, wasn't SEALs-only. The Iraqi Scouts were patrolling with us. We knew without a doubt that the Scouts didn't have our level of field craft. Actually, that's being kind. They were learning, but sometimes they had a way of doing some undisciplined things.

"What the hell are you thinking?" I wanted to yell more than once after some especially bone-headed maneuver. "We'd all like to get out of here alive."

When the bullets began to fly in one of our first firefights together, instead of seeking immediate cover and firing back, several Scouts shot in the wrong direction and began laughing nervously. When their heavy machine gunner tripped and fell on his back, he kept firing into the sky on full automatic. I had to kick the gun out of his hand.

But for better or worse, these were our Iraqi partners. Together, we had important business to conduct.

As we began walking down the road, I had a feeling right away that someone might be watching us. It was just a gut feeling, as far as I could tell. No one was in a posture to engage us yet.

About an hour and a half in, we came up to a canal with a small bridge across it. Three roads converged on the other side of that bridge. I knew immediately that was a dangerous location, a choke point that left us vulnerable as we pressed toward our planned turnaround location, a small cluster of homes. But as far as we could tell, that little bridge was the only way across the canal.

Our patrol line was about one hundred yards long. I was halfway down it with SEALs and Iraqi Scouts behind and in front of me. Just as we reached that choke point, the Scouts decided to stop for a food-and-water break. I thought to myself, This is not good business.

I got on the radio immediately with Chief Frank: "We're at a vulnerable location. Let's keep the stop brief. Don't let them break out all their food. Five minutes, I want to be patrolling again."

The chief was already on it. In four minutes, we were moving.

As we walked on, I noticed a handful of brightly colored M&Ms on the ground. I didn't think much of it at first. But I could say one thing with utter certainty: No SEAL accidentally dropped M&Ms on the ground. Impossible. Would never happen in a million years. Our Iraqi Scouts must have snuck a quick snack at the rest stop and dropped a few candies before they left.

I was happy when all of us were through that dangerous spot. We kept going and didn't stop until we reached the little village we were aiming for. We searched a couple of occupied houses and some outlying structures. We entered aggressively, like we always did. We made our presence felt.

That day, it didn't look like we'd be getting any real action. Just another stroll through the three-digit heat and a few busted doors. We turned around and began to make our way back, following the route we'd come in on.

As we neared the bridge from the other direction, something caught Lou's eye. Maybe it was a problem. Maybe not. "Sir," Lou said, "I just saw a suspicious individual, who was pacing and looking over his shoulder, walk away from our position. He didn't look armed. But he got into a vehicle and drove away from the spot you were concerned about earlier."

"Okay, got it," I said. "Keep moving—cautiously."

There was no chance to engage anyone. Whoever that character was, he was gone now, and the area was mostly quiet. In the distance, a woman was walking home from the store. A couple of kids had biked off the other way. There was hardly any other activity in sight.

At moments like these, the hair on the back of my neck always stands straight up. I was paying laser attention. My senses were almost tingling. I felt like I was somewhere back in the animal world, tapping into some survival skill. Fifty yards from the intersection, Lou halted the patrol. This time, his voice sounded more urgent.

"Hold," he said into the radio.

I moved up to the front with him.

"What's going on?" I asked.

"I don't know," he said. "The area doesn't look right. Let's find a different route over the canal."

That wouldn't be easy. If the patrol had been SEALs-only, we could have just swum across. But none of the Scouts could swim.

Ten minutes later, Lou had a way we could bypass the little bridge that had us so concerned. He found a culvert that stretched across the canal. "We'll tightrope everyone across the culvert," he said.

Soon enough, all twenty-four SEALs and Iraqis were stepping gingerly along that pipe. The balance wasn't easy with our weapons and sweat-soaked body armor. After we got to the other side, we paralleled down the bank, which was thick with high willows and canal grass. Lou and I, joined by a couple of our snipers, decided to get a closer look.

You can't ever discount the highly intuitive nature of well-trained SEALs. Right where I'd seen the M&Ms, five young insurgents were hunched over together, looking at something, I couldn't tell what. Concealed by grass, they couldn't see us. One of them, Lou said, was the character from the car. A couple of others had machine guns and all of them were wearing ammo chest racks. One of them was holding what looked like an 80mm artillery round, just perfect for crafting into an easily concealable IED. I couldn't see if our names were written on the device or not, but they might as well have been.

Without waiting another moment, our snipers lifted their weapons and opened fire across the canal. Two of the insurgents went running at the first shot. The three others hit the dirt and tried firing back. They didn't get off too many before our bullets ripped them apart.

Even from across the canal, we could see their bodies twitch with each new volley, jerkily inching a few feet to the left. Our guys shoot better than anybody. In any fair gunfight—and most unfair ones—we'll come out on top. This exchange didn't last more than twenty seconds, and now our attention turned immediately to that IED.

We kept our distance for a moment.

The three on the ground would never move again, but one of the other two—or some yet-unseen person—could easily have been off in the distance, ready to hit a remote detonator the moment we strolled up.

"Don't even bother touching that device," I told my EOD chief. "Set a charge nearby on a timer and give us a chance to get out."

We were a good two hundred yards away, moving through an open field, when we heard a huge explosion, enough to ring all of our ears, more than enough to destroy the IED.

I don't know if those M&Ms gave us away or not. But I don't think that IED was a coincidence. And I know it was extremely similar to the one that took out those Marines. If we hadn't heeded our gut feeling, we would have marched into an equally bloody fate.

This was a win that built confidence in the whole leadership team, and it made us eager to keep returning to northeast Habbaniyah until that whole part of Anbar could be tamed.

NOT ALL OUR MISSIONS involved seeking out the insurgents. Not directly. Ever since we'd started engaging the mortar boys, more and more insurgents were seeking us out. We were asked to spend four or five days providing security for a Marine construction crew. The Marines were building a new combat outpost deep in Indian Country. We set up several overwatch positions for our snipers to head off any threats. And we sent patrols around the area, day and night.

I made a point of joining most of the tougher patrols and assaults. That's what a leader does. He doesn't send his guys out on onerous duty he wouldn't perform. No feet up on the desk in AC'd offices. That gets noticed in a hurry, even if you don't think anyone is paying attention. Nothing undermines a leader's authority like being considered a shirker by his troops.

After one patrol in the stifling afternoon, we were walking back to the construction site when a small skirmish broke out. Not a sustained exchange, but it reminded all of us we had to be on our game. We got back to the building we were using as our overwatch position. Lope and I took our body armor off and, even though we'd seen a small bit of action out there, we thought we might slip up to the roof for a short, shady nap. But things just didn't feel right when we got there.

"Let's take another look," I said as we put our body armor back on and started climbing down the stairs.

Just as we reached the second floor, two mortar rounds—a 60 mm and an 80 mm—landed above and below us. The smaller one struck the roof. The larger one hit the ground right where a group of Marines and Iraqi Scouts happened to be standing. Together, those two mortars instantly killed two of the Iraqis and wounded three Marines. Lope and I rushed downstairs into a room that looked like a scene from a chain-saw movie. Bodies were everywhere. Two Marines were grinding through their pain stoically. One Iraqi was moaning with a missing arm. The entire room was covered in blood. A Marine was certain he had a sucking chest wound, which can cause the lungs to collapse. Corpsman Mike was all over him.

Sucking chest wounds are actually quite rare, but they can be catastrophic if they aren't treated correctly and quickly. The whole experience is panic-inducing. Mike applied an Asherman chest seal, a piece of medical gear invented by a former SEAL. It's a large patch with a valve that is slapped over the wound and instantly balances the pressure in the lungs.

One thing I noticed that day and not for the first time: The people screaming the loudest were those hurt the least. And it was causing pandemonium in that room. It reminded me of something I'd heard in SEAL training when a young officer was flipping out over some trivial mishap. A senior chief told him: "Sir, you're freaking out and it's making everyone else freak out. Let me pass on an important piece of advice: 'Calm. Is. Contagious.'"

I had two of my biggest squad members drag the loudest, wailing, noninjured Iraqis out of the room so our combat medics could get to work. Quickly, they got several Marines onto helicopters for medical treatment.

That is how it was in Iraq. Some of the people we worked with were absolutely superb. Some were worse than incompetent.

A couple of days later, I was on a roof with one of my snipers when I heard an AK-47 go off. I liked being on rooftops. It's a good shooting position, and you can see a lot of bad guys from up there.

"What the hell was that?" I barked over the radio.

"You won't believe this," Red said. "You better get down here."

On the first floor, an Iraqi Scout was wailing. He was sitting in a chair holding his left foot. An Iraqi lieutenant and an interpreter were standing with him, and one of our corpsmen was examining the Iraqi Scout's foot.

We'd been taking the Scouts with us almost everywhere. SEAL Team One had boosted the Scouts' basic competence as soldiers, but some of them had clearly benefited more than others. It was a wild mix we had. Some had been in Saddam's military, not loyal to him but professional soldiers. Some were unmotivated conscripts. A few of them couldn't wait to leave.

"What's going on?" I asked.

"He says he had an AD," an accidental discharge of his weapon, the corpsman said. "But I'm not buying it. I think he shot himself in the foot to get out of here."

"So what's the damage?" I asked.

"Well, to be honest, it's a perfect through-and-through. It entered the top of the foot, exited the bottom. I can't speak to nerve damage. But there is very little bleeding. I think the area is still shocked from the flash round being so close to his foot."

The interpreter was repeating our conversation to the Iraqi lieutenant, who was quickly growing agitated. "He must be flown out immediately," the lieutenant said. "We cannot wait. We have to medevac him right now."

The way the Iraqi officer was talking, it felt like a setup to me. I had the strong sense that they hatched the plan to get out of there. I remembered that when we had briefed this particular mission, the Scouts adamantly did not want to go. The area was too dangerous, they said. Too many insurgents.

"How critical is it to get him definitive care?" I asked my corpsman.

He shot me a look as if he knew what I was thinking. "He will survive for days," the corpsman said. "He ain't gonna be happy. He won't be running anywhere. But he can sit right here for as long as we need to be in this building."

This was early morning on the first day of a two-day operation.

"Sounds good," I said. Turning to the interpreter, I said: "He doesn't require any treatment that my medic can't provide. We will extract from this target as planned forty-eight hours from now."

"And one more thing," I added. "Tell him if he wants to give himself an injury to get out of his job, he's gonna have to do better than that."

With any team, you have to establish yourself as leader, as the alpha prepared to make decisions and stick with them. If the Scout had been in any jeopardy, we'd have pulled him out of there. But I wasn't having a quitter with a minor foot wound put an end to our day.

For every faker we were cursed with, we were blessed with a real pro. Sam was the best interpreter our unit ever had. He was a southern Lebanese Christian who had fought in wars before and had the scars to prove it. He was a real Gunga Din. He always knew how to find cold water and extra food in the field. We trusted Sam to carry a rifle, a pistol, and a full combat load out. He was constantly urging me to come back and visit him in Lebanon for the world's best French Middle Eastern cuisine.

Our platoon was hitting a bunch of targets, doing house raids off the daily intel and getting bad guys every night. Then, all of a sudden, we started getting dry holes. We were doing the raids as usual, but at every house, the targets we were looking for turned out not to be there.

The intelligence reports still smelled reliable. Everything else was similar. I couldn't figure out what was going on.

I pulled Sam aside one day when he wasn't in the rotation. I had an idea. I asked him to dress in full SEAL gear, including faceguard, and join us on the next raid. "No matter what you see, no matter what you hear, say nothing until we're back," I told him. "Pay attention to everything the interpreters say."

Sam kept his mouth shut during the raid. But when we got back, he was fuming.

"You were telling the interpreter, 'Put pressure on.' And the interpreter was saying, 'This is the name of the person they're looking for. Don't admit to being that person and they'll let you go.'"

We got rid of the corrupt interpreter immediately. I don't think he knew Sam ratted him out. But all of a sudden we were back on our former pace again. And the progress kept building on itself. While the insurgents weren't sending up any white flags, the support they were receiving from local civilians seemed to narrow a little more each week. The zealous anti-Americans were just as committed. But even their numbers did gradually seem to shrink.

That was what we were there for, changing momentum in the country by changing momentum on the battlefield.

WHEN I THINK about my time in Iraq, no incident defines the experience more eloquently than the death of our friend Mikey. That was the single most painful loss we suffered and the most inspiring example of courage, sacrifice, and brotherhood I have ever experienced. And most telling of all, Mikey didn't act after long, drawn-out deliberation. He wasn't nudged, pushed, or pressured. He was one man acting in the flash of a moment, reflecting a value system built over years in our brotherhood, epitomizing everything that we stand for.

Even today, I can't talk about Mikey without getting emotional.

A talented machine gunner and a fun, loose guy, he arrived in April 2006, about a month after I did. A member of Task Unit BRUISER in Ramadi operating about twenty miles to our west, he spent his days and nights patrolling Indian Country and preparing Iraqi soldiers for the inevitable day the Americans would leave. Almost immediately, he showed what he was made of and the kind of teammate he was. He'd been in-country just a few weeks when another SEAL was shot in the leg during a chaotic urban patrol. The bullets were still kicking up dirt. The wounded SEAL lay vulnerable and exposed in the street. Mikey ran out to rescue him, dragging his wounded brother back to safety. He got a Silver Star for that, and his tour had only begun.

He seemed to be at the front of every firefight. When the duty was toughest, he was among the quickest to volunteer. He had only one speed, and that was fast-forward. He was ready for anything.

One terrible Friday, his platoon had just engaged four insurgents in a firefight, wounding one and killing another. Expecting further attacks, Mikey and three SEAL snipers, along with three Iraqi Scouts, took up a rooftop position as a mob blocked off the street below. A nearby mosque broadcast an urgent announcement, calling faithful warriors to fight the American and Iraqi soldiers. The crowd in the street looked up at the roof and opened fire with automatic weapons and rocket-propelled grenades, or RPGs. A grenade smacked Mikey in the chest, pounding off and landing near his feet.

"Grenade!" Mikey yelled to the two SEALs closest to him, about fifteen feet away.

But there was nowhere for them to go. Standing closest to the stairway, Mikey was the only one who could have rolled down the stairs or leaped to safety. He did exactly the opposite. He threw his body on the live grenade. A couple of seconds later, the grenade went off in a loud, concussive explosion. Mikey's two teammates were injured. But he absorbed the majority of the blast. Though evacuated immediately, in thirty minutes Mikey was dead.

I don't pretend to know exactly what was going through Mikey's head when he was thumped by the hurled grenade and saw it land on the rooftop in front of him. But I know the man he was, how he was trained, and the kind of teammate he had always been. He didn't think of his safety first. He decided instead: "I'm gonna eat that thing and take care of my buddies," who didn't even realize what danger they were in. He easily could have saved his own life. Mikey was the only person on the roof, American or Iraqi, to die that day. That's a place no one can force anyone to go. That's the kind of warrior Mikey was. That's the kind of warrior we're looking for. Mikey got all the honors the U.S. military can give including, posthumously, the Medal of Honor. He was only the second Navy SEAL, and the fourth U.S. service member, to earn the military's highest commendation since the War on Terror began. His parents accepted the medal for him at the White House from President George W. Bush. Soon afterward, Donald Winter, secretary of the Navy, announced that the second ship in the Zumwalt class of destroyers would be named the USS *Michael Monsoor*. The U.S. Department of Veterans Affairs honored Mikey with a new name for one of the streets at San Diego's Miramar National Cemetery: Monsoor Avenue.

Those are all rare tributes. But I think the one Mikey would have most appreciated was what his brother SEALs did after his funeral in San Diego.

As the pallbearers carried his coffin from the hearse, the SEALs lined up in a long column of twos, all the way to the grave site in Fort Rosecrans National Cemetery. As he was reverently passed down the center of that long line, each SEAL slapped down a gold Trident he had removed from his own uniform and pressed the medal hard into the wooden coffin. Step by deliberate step, the slaps rang out across the cemetery. They could be heard by everyone who was there, including President Bush. "The procession went on nearly half an hour," the president said later, still obviously moved. "When it was all over, the simple wooden coffin had become a gold-plated memorial to a hero who will never be forgotten."

12

SEVEN MONTHS

The dance of battle is always played
in the same impatient rhythm.
What begins in a surge of violent motion
is always reduced to the perfectly still.
—SUN TZU

If I came back from a gunfight without leftover ammo, I was doing something wrong.

I carried a heavy load any time we left Camp Habbaniyah. That meant seven, thirty-round magazines for my primary battle rifle, the M4, six of them in a chest rack on my body armor. Plus, I had one magazine already loaded and a round in the chamber ready to go. And I wasn't scared to open up. But if you are the officer in charge of a gunfight and you're constantly on your gun, you are no longer running the gunfight.

There is an elemental connection between a shooter and his weapon. Shooting is the fun part. There is no denying that. But it doesn't leave room for much else. When I am in that moment— looking down my sights, assessing my target, breathing calmly, squeezing smoothly, deciding whether I need to reengage—for that time at least, no one is running the shooters. No one is asking, "What would be a better position to fire from? Where am I moving the squad next? Is anybody hurt? Am I passing appropriate information back to higher authority? Do I have good verbal and radio communication with my squad? How long have we been in this fight? Is it time to break contact and move on? Do I need to toss some ammo to anyone? I've got extra." That's how you run a gunfight.

This can be a difficult lesson for junior officers to learn. These are aggressive, hard-charging young men. They want to be shooters and gunfighters. But in my platoon, pretty much everyone had more kills than I had. I took tremendous satisfaction in that. I ran the gunfights where they got those kills. Every mission success meant I had done my job right. Their success was my success. We were a team.

Before I climbed into the gun truck for a mission, I liked to go back to my room. Very deliberately, I put on my gun belt and then the rest of my gear. Then my body armor. I checked my pistol—was it cleaned? Was it oiled? I did a press check to be sure a round was loaded and ready. Then I closed my eyes and touched every piece of gear in my kit. I tried to think if I was forgetting anything: I threw a smoke grenade last night. I need a new one . . . Are all my magazines topped off? . . . Do I have fresh batteries in my GPS?

I never put my helmet on until I was inside the truck. And right before I went outside, I read my letter of the day.

Before I left for Iraq, Tracy wrote me fifty letters. Then she collected letters from my family and friends. Letters of encouragement. Letters of love and support. From college friends, high school friends, distant relatives, all kinds of people I knew.

If I opened one a day, I decided, I would have enough letters to last me almost my entire deployment.

People wrote regular stuff. Things they remembered we did together. Restaurants I should definitely go to when I got back. Movies I had to see. "We're thinking about you," they wrote. "Please let us know if you need anything. We are so proud of what you are doing." Those letters always brought me back to a normal place in my life.

But then Mark and Mikey got killed. And I had a friend from college pass away back home. I looked at that big box of letters, and I started to think, What a shame if I don't come back from some mission. I wouldn't get to read them all.

I had never peeked at the letters in advance before. I had stuck to one a day. I liked the surprise of that. But now I had this terrible quandary. Would it be a total breach of my own plan to read the letters early? I'd feel really guilty if something went wrong, if someone had taken the time to write a letter and I never even opened it.

So midway through the deployment, I started reading two or three letters a day. I still kept them in order. I still read each one carefully.

Then I walked out to the gun truck and put my helmet on.

WE HAVE AN EXPRESSION in combat units. "The biggest gun in any platoon is the green radio." An Mk 48 machine gun is a powerful weapon. But a 105 mm howitzer round from an AC-130 gunship can take out a building.

That's why all SEALs learn the language of aviators. A little air support can turn a challenging gunfight into a hands-down triumph.

So when we want rockets, bombs, and missiles raining down on our enemy, we have to communicate clearly with the warriors in the sky.

We have our own system for calling in close-air support. Most units make a nine-line call, providing nine specific data points to the pilot. We abbreviate that to a five-line, including the unit's location, the enemy's location, details of the target, some visual signal, and a description of the impact after the strike. It's not quite as thorough, but it gets the action started that much faster.

And to be helpful, an experienced pilot doesn't even need weapons.

One day in early fall, my teammates and I were conducting a scout mission, finding the right spot for a new combat outpost. As we patrolled close to the Euphrates, we started taking fire from a known enemy hot spot. You couldn't really call it a gunfight. We couldn't quite tell where the bad guys were firing from. We knew the general direction, but it's hard to hit a target you can't see or locate.

My radioman went onto the shared frequency, calling to any friendly aircraft nearby.

One pilot answered immediately from the cockpit of an F/A-18 Super Hornet, a workhorse fighter jet.

"I'm three minutes out," he said. "But I'm Winchester. No bombs, no missiles. I got nothing left. Would a buzz help?"

My guys and I glanced at each other.

"Couldn't hurt," I said. And it wasn't like we had many other options. We were shooting blindly, one round at a time.

"Whatever you can do," the radioman told the F-18 pilot. "Just flying by would be a help."

That Super Hornet is one sinister-looking aircraft. It's also loud enough to shake the trees.

"I got flares left," the pilot said. "Let me see what I can do."

Four minutes later, he was banking past our location, launching his countermeasure flares, burning-hot phosphorous canisters designed to ward off inbound enemy rockets by disrupting their heat-seeking mechanisms.

It was pure shock and awe. Screeching up the river. Screaming down the bank. Shrieking over the hillside where the shots came from.

The daredevil Blue Angels had nothing on this guy. He flew so close to the river, I thought the water was going to erupt. It was an impressive presentation. I can't say for sure what the shooters made of all that empty drama. But it must have scared the hell out of them. Their assault on us ceased immediately.

THE PACE WE KEPT was just ferocious. No days off. No real breaks. Nothing. Day missions, night missions. We never slowed down. A raid to take down a house, a five-hour operation, and we might do two or three of them a night. We'd get the intel. We'd take down the house. We'd bring the prisoners to the holding facility. Then the guys would go back to the base, clean the gear, make sure the trucks were ready to go out again. With my two junior officers and a couple of key platoon mates, I'd go to the TOC, the Tactical Operations Center, to write up the operational summary. Some nights, we didn't get done until 4 a.m. Collapse. Then we were up again by 8 a.m., planning or launching another operation. From the second we started until the second we dropped, it was always scorching outside. We were wearing body armor. We were walking down streets and inside houses and up on roofs. On those roofs, the tar was more like a swimming pool. Up and down, in and out, sometimes getting into gunfights, sometimes not—but never slowing down.

As our deployment wore on, I noticed something disturbing. We were still getting the job done, but little things were going wrong. A tire was flat. Someone forgot a radio. Two guns that weren't working had to be fixed. Somebody screwed up the navigation computer and we had to turn back. No one got hurt as these things were happening. But we were causing messes for ourselves. We seemed a little more clumsy, a little less nimble.

It seemed to me like we were losing our edge. It wasn't dangerous yet. But it was a noticeable contrast to how smoothly things had been running before.

What the hell is going on here? I thought to myself.

I discussed it with the task unit commander, my boss and good friend who was overall in charge of Task Unit ALPHA.

"Rob," I said, "I think we're riding for a fall here. I don't know if we're pushing it too hard or we've been at it too long or what exactly the reason is. Maybe a combination. But something's gonna go wrong. I don't know how the leadership feels, but I say these guys could use a break. How 'bout if we take a couple of days and let them all relax."

I wasn't sure if I'd get pushback from Rob. I didn't. "You got your pulse on the guys," he said. "If you think they need a break, break 'em. None of the missions we have in our deck won't be here two days from now."

So that's what we did. We took a little break.

We had a mission already set for that night. As usual, the team was all jacked up and ready to go. I went in to brief the mission like I always did. I think the teammates were all surprised by what they heard.

"Hey," I said, "I feel like we're in a bad spot right now. Everybody's tired. We're making mistakes, the type we can't afford. We're not gonna make it with everyone running on empty like this. So the mission's off tonight. We're not going out. Keep your gear on. Load up in the trucks. We'll have some good food. I think everyone's ready for decent chow. Everybody will get a big block of sleep. When we get up in the morning, let's relax and have some fun for a change. You guys figure out what that's gonna be."

We drove to the main mess hall on the other side of the base for pizza, ice cream, and an array of other high-calorie, high-taste, low-nutrition food. That dinner was one of the best meals I ever had.

On the way out, someone stole some pizza dough from the dining room. A SEAL from our predecessors at Team One had built an ingenious, wood-burning pizza oven from a fifty-five-gallon drum. SEALs can be resourceful, even beyond the battlefield.

The next morning, the guys broke up into teams for a reverse-hand softball game. The righties played left, the lefties played right. Playing backward like that, these guys were some of the worst athletes in history. But everyone had fun. We had a highly competitive water-balloon fight with the Marines, using a surgical-tubing launcher as our support-by-fire weapon. SEALs don't know how to abandon their aggressive tactics even in a water-balloon fight. Eating, smoking some cigars, we had nothing but fun for the next two days.

We found some inflatable Zodiac boats in a storage facility near Lake Habbaniyah, and one of our guys showed up with a wakeboard—where did he get that?—and spent a couple of hours pulling SEALs around the lake. As I stood on a ridge looking down, watching my guys briefly unplugged from all the tension of war, I felt like I'd stepped into that scene from *Apocalypse Now*, where Robert Duvall asks the new guys from California in his air-cavalry unit to surf the point break, even though bombs were coming in. That may not be a standard operating procedure in any combat zone, but I knew for a fact it was what we needed at the time. When we got back into the battle, we were fresher, sharper, and more energized. We had the steam we needed to get us to the end.

SEVEN MONTHS is not long in the course of a lifetime. I have seven-month stretches in my life that I can barely remember. But the members of BRAVO Platoon packed so much life and death into that mad seven-month deployment in western Iraq, I wasn't sure how much more I could ask of them. Like our exhausted boat-mate Coop during Hell Week, our whole platoon had really given everything they had. A new platoon was arriving. Our stay was coming to an end.

We had a responsibility to turn over our region to the incoming team. Their senior leadership arrived a month early. They started joining us in planning missions and coming out on patrol. When the rest of the new team showed up, everyone got a taste of the battle space.

It's never easy, turning over to another team all that you've been fighting for. I'm sure it was hard for SEAL Team One, who turned the region over to us. No matter how you explain it or what you show them, the new team doesn't fully understand the whys and hows of what you've done. You're trying to jam an intense seven months of combat experience into a short two-week turnover window. But life goes on, and so does the fighting. War by its nature is always a team sport. We'd had our chance. If, as SEALs say, "All our lessons are written in blood," we had to share them willingly with the new guys. And we did. We pushed it to the end. The week we were scheduled to leave Iraq, we were still conducting missions.

That last week, on the Wednesday, I was out on yet another op. It went well. We were home by 2 a.m. I knew our turn was almost over. I wrote up my last after-action report and at about 3 a.m., I was ready for bed.

"No more missions for you, huh?" Rob, my task unit commander, asked me. "That's it?"

"Not for me," I said. "Nick's going out in the morning." Nick was one of our assistant officers in charge, a smart young leader with good things ahead. He was taking a patrol on another dangerous route to the northeast. This time, I wasn't on the force list.

Rob slapped me on the back and said, "Good night."

I got back to my barracks room and got cleaned up. I was putting my gun down, straightening up my gear and getting ready for bed, when a thought occurred to me: Unless they shoot our plane down, I'm gonna make it home.

I had looked at Nick's plan already. He knew what he was doing. He was taking armed Humvees then going out on foot patrol with the usual mix of SEALs and Scouts. I figured I'd stop by for a word with him before I hit the rack and encourage him for the morning.

The light was on, and he was still poring over details when I stopped by. "Plan looks good," I told him. "Everything looks fine." We'd done that a hundred times already.

"You want me to come, Nick?" I asked him.

"No," he said. "You don't have to, LT. We're good."

But as I stood there, ready to say good night, something in the back of my brain was nagging me.

I couldn't shake the feeling that if something went wrong out there and one of our guys got hurt, if the mission went south in any way at all, I would never forgive myself for staying in bed and missing the last mission of my deployment in Iraq. It didn't matter what Nick said.

"I'll join you," I told him.

After a couple of hours' sleep, I was back up again. I threw my gear on. I got outside just as they were loading the trucks.

Although I'd read Nick's plan, I hadn't even been in the mission brief. So going along really wasn't such a good idea. As I climbed into the truck, I smiled as I thought to myself, Man, if I lose it on this mission, won't that be the bitch.

I knew it was overkill, being out there. Thankfully, the patrol that morning was totally routine. We exchanged a few rounds of fire with some roving bad guys. We took no casualties, and as far as I could tell neither did they. But just being out there this one last time gave me a real feeling of confidence. The SEALs who were replacing us seemed to know exactly what they were doing. This shouldn't have come as a surprise, I know. They were trained the same way we were, but it sure was nice being with them and seeing with my own eyes. Working with their leaders, Nick had integrated the new team seamlessly into our battle plan, and I knew our efforts would be continued. The gains we had made would be held and expanded on. The new guys would move the ball another ten yards down the field.

The way theater airlifts worked, we couldn't all fly home together. A few of my teammates went home before I did. Some stayed a few days later. But everyone was back in San Diego within two weeks of each other. Only then did I allow myself to feel anything like relief.

We had our close calls. A sniper bullet came through an open door but only a fragment hit one of my guys. I still believe that bullet was fired from a mosque. Cams was on a roof with a few other boys when a grenade went off. Some of the fragments caught him in the upper body and face. He earned a Purple Heart for that one. When I saw him, he was, no exaggeration, covered in blood.

Truly, it was amazing how lucky we were. Ro was the turret gunner when a huge IED went off, knocking everybody out. They all woke up together and alive in the Humvee. They staggered a little. But they all returned to base.

I've been to funerals, too many. But I never had to go to a funeral for one of my platoon mates. As an officer in charge of a SEAL platoon, you don't make every call. So much is happening fast and on the go. A lot of calls my team members make on their own. That's a special thing. People are making complex decisions all the time. But I also knew that the ultimate responsibility for BRAVO Platoon of Task Unit ALPHA was mine.

That is the very definition of the burden of command. It's the weight of knowing you have in your hands the lives of your closest teammates, your very best friends, the future of their families and loved ones.

All of these men said at the start they wanted to be there. All of them were happy they had come. And they all felt hugely grateful they were going home. They knew the horrors and hardships of war and knew what could happen on the battlefield. Every teammate of mine recognized and accepted that the worst could happen until the moment they were home.

There's a different understanding of fate on the battlefield. If you are a devout person, that may provide some comfort or some explanation. Religion is something people can fall back on. You may believe your every move in life is guided by a greater power. That may explain who lives and who dies.

If the worst happened, as it had to Mark and Mikey, we'd hold a little ceremony in the theater at the base. Then that teammate's body would be escorted back to Dover Air Force Base in Delaware. And even before that happened, a teammate in uniform and a chaplain would be walking up a stairway or onto a family's front porch. They'd deliver the worst news the family would ever hear.

It would be right for the officer in charge of a fallen teammate to deliver that news to his family. Any one of us would do it if we could. I'd met all those families, the mothers and fathers, the wives and children. We'd spent time at barbecues and beach parties and bonfires. I'd gotten to know many of them. Delivering that news would have been one of the most gut-wrenching moments of my life. But that is not how it happened, and that is one of the experiences of war I am grateful to have missed.

We'd had this most active and violent deployment. An amazing group of warriors had done a phenomenal job. The momentum had started shifting in Anbar Province. Fewer snipers, fewer mortar attacks, a genuine reduction in support for al Qaeda. We'd had a measurable impact on the region.

And everyone I brought to war, I brought back home.

It's a point of pride and satisfaction and gratitude for me.

13

KILLING SCHOOL

And now the youth
was to enter the line of battle with his lord,
his first time to be tested as a fighter.
His spirit did not break and the ancestral blade
would keep its edge, as the dragon discovered
as soon as they came together in the combat.

—BEOWULF

The house is not always the right one. Our intelligence may be mistaken. Maybe it's not a bomb factory or a safe house. Maybe it's a husband, a wife, and six children who just happen to live in a dangerous neighborhood. When we're wrong, we do what we can to make amends. We pay reparations to fix the door. We get whatever intel we can. And we move on.

But still.

I can only imagine how scary it is to be in a house in Iraq or Afghanistan when the SEALs come blowing through the door. These are people living in another era. They hardly have electricity at night. And all of a sudden fifteen or twenty-five of what must look like Terminators are flooding the house. We are physically bigger than they are. We have large weapons and body armor. With the eerie green glow of night vision, we appear almost otherworldly. It must be terrifying and maddening at once.

I know how I'd feel if foreign troops came busting through the door of my house in San Diego. I'd be worried about the safety of my wife and daughters. I wouldn't want invaders stomping around where we live. I'm sure I'd feel something precious was being violated, whatever their business was.

I know I'd want to respond, and it wouldn't be politely.

Nevertheless, house raids were something we had to do in the battle zone. The thought of it didn't keep me up at night. It didn't mean I couldn't go out again tomorrow. But as many houses as we raided, I never forgot that feeling. And neither, I'm sure, did the Iraqis who lived there.

I can't say for certain when I first killed someone. It was in Iraq. I know that much. It was in Indian Country with my guys. It may have been in a gunfire exchange across the Euphrates River. It might have been the morning we narrowly dodged an ambush on the road to Fallujah and then doubled back to pop the insurgents from behind. It could have been in any one of many firefights with mobile mortar boys. But that's all just conjecture.

Gunfights are a lot murkier in real life than most people realize. Because of movies and TV, people expect a gunfight to be decisive and clear. Onscreen, we get the benefit of a director's trained eye and such great camera angles, we see everything vividly. We see the gunfight from the bad guy's perspective and the good guy's perspective—the far angle, the close angle, every little detail. And no one ever dies without falling to the ground in front of a camera. Even if the scene's wildly chaotic, the whole purpose of movie and TV gunfighting is to let the audience know who just killed whom. In *Tombstone*, the hapless Thomas Haden Church doesn't have a chance against Val Kilmer's deadeye Doc Holliday. In *Taxi Driver*, there's no doubt that Robert De Niro's Travis Bickle blows away the Times Square pimps. The carnage is right there on the screen. Even when no one dies, there is rarely ambiguity in a movie shoot-out. In *Terminator 2*, Arnold's under strict orders from John Connor to harm no human beings. So Arnold demolishes the police cruisers with his mini-gun until panicked cops all run in terror.

But the sight lines don't always cooperate in real battlefield gunfights. No one's keeping score in a live-fire war zone, and often, the results can't be easily verified. When I'd be out with my platoon in Iraq, we'd get shot at from a tree line or a palm grove or a building across the river. We'd usually return the fire. Sometimes we could see the bad guys—exactly who was shooting from what window or from behind which tree. Sometimes we could only tell that someone was shooting and we were the target.

A sniper usually knows. He's on a scope. His shot can be confirmed in the moment. He selects the target, pulls the trigger, and, more often than not, can see if the shot connects and how. But for most of us in active combat, rolling right, rolling left, shooting at moving targets, it was often hard to tell if we were fighting one or fighting twenty guys. And often we didn't know exactly how many, if any, we had hit.

Then, one day it happened right in front of me.

. . . .

WHEN I MEET PEOPLE and they hear what I do, they sometimes say to me, "You're a killer." Yes, I am. I do not shy away from that at all. To me, that is in no way an insult. Warriors exist and train for that eventuality. That's the business I have chosen. It's an important one. My duty is to be guided by just principles and to do it well.

Like so much else in the lives of SEALs, my preparation as a killer built up gradually over the years. And it started back at BUD/S, where the firearms training was as realistic as it could possibly be. We began with paper targets—but not just any paper targets. Every one of them featured a real-looking bad guy with a gun, a rocket, a grenade, or a knife. No circular bull's-eyes in SEAL training. That may seem like a tiny detail, but it gets you thinking from the start about who is on the other end of our firepower and what flying lead can do to them.

We had a recruit quit right before he became a SEAL. This was when I was running all three phases of BUD/S. He was sizing up one of those targets. The target was a teenage boy with a gun. We face child soldiers on the battlefield, and some of our practice targets resemble teenagers with guns. As he stared at the kid in the target, a pained look settled across his face.

"I can't do this," he said.

"What do you mean?" I asked him.

"That target looks like my little brother with a gun," he said. "This isn't for me."

I tried to ease his concern. "Based on the enemies we've been fighting lately," I told him, "I don't think we'll be facing anyone who looks much like your brother."

"Yeah," he said. "But it'll be someone else's brother."

It will be.

And that's an emotional issue all of us need to come to terms with. This job involves killing people—for good purposes, yes, but killing people nonetheless. What the recruit said to me that day was honest and, I'm sure, difficult to admit, surrounded as he was by SEAL recruits on their way to doing exactly that job, working as hard as they possibly could to sharpen their precision and expertise. What he said— and how he followed through by leaving—made me respect him as much as anyone I've worked with. Despite the level of training he'd received, he recognized this wasn't for him.

Those SEALs who get through the training and become members of a team have an emotional maturity and balance about this part of our job. In our unit we don't spend much time talking about killing people. We just don't. Our guys have come to terms with killing or they wouldn't be here. When required, we will bring lethal force to an identified threat. From the range to the field to eerily authentic combat re-creations, SEALs learn to choose our targets carefully before the trigger is pulled. We must accurately discriminate between armed combatants and innocent bystanders, between people we want to engage and those we need to protect. Slowly, repeatedly, with firm direction from expert trainers in marksmanship—that's how SEAL recruits prepare themselves for this central activity of the job.

The fact of the matter is that by the time any SEAL gets on the battlefield, he has so often gone through the physical and mental processes that lead to taking another person's life, killing becomes in part mechanical.

WE WERE PATROLLING in the middle of the daytime, a dangerous area deep in Indian Country, a very active battle space. Few American forces had been through there before. We came out from behind a palm grove near an irrigation ditch. There was an intersection a short bit ahead. It was another choke point. There were lots of those in western Iraq. I instinctively didn't like the idea of all of us being in this one at once.

So I split the team in two. I told half the guys to keep patrolling. "Just continue up the road," I said. I wanted anyone watching us to see them leaving the area and think we'd all moved along.

My explosives tech, my communicator, my heavy-gunner, my point man, and myself—the five of us stayed back and waited, hidden in a stand of swamp grass, as the rest of the team walked off. I didn't want them to get too far in case we needed to call them back into the fight—but far enough that anyone watching would believe they were gone.

"Just keep busy over there," I told them. "Don't come into sight unless you hear from us on the radio."

Slowly, quietly, the five of us who held back slipped out of the swamp grass and continued toward the intersection in a low crouch. As we were about to step into the open, we could hear voices, urgent voices, not twenty feet away. My heart was pounding. There were only five of us. I couldn't see anyone yet. But they were close enough that I almost could have poked them with a stick.

My EOD tech broke cover before my point man did. I have no idea why he did that. He probably doesn't, either. But he stepped out of position and yelled at the top of his lungs, "HALT. STOP. DON'T DO THAT."

There were four of them altogether, three with AK-47s, one holding a belt-fed machine gun like our Mk 48. After my EOD tech's outburst, they could see all five of us, I'm sure, and the fight was on.

I felt no hatred for them, any more than a hunter hates his prey. I always respected my enemy and what they were capable of.

We were up and blazing. So were they. I don't how long the whole encounter took. I never do at times like that. My mind gets so acutely focused when the bullets are flying, the action in a battlefield shoot-out almost slows to a crawl. I feel like an elite quarterback who's totally in the zone. The receivers are running their routes. A defender is circling from the left. The rushers are being held at the line. There's the target. I'm executing a play practiced ten thousand times. Everything's in slow motion. I'm moving on muscle memory.

Up came my weapon. I truly felt calm as I shouldered it. I put my sight on the center mass of one insurgent with an AK-47. I let go two rounds. It was as if I'd hand-delivered each of those bullets, like I could see them inching through the air. Every detail was unfolding methodically. I felt like I had all the time in the world. This was obviously a bad guy, hell-bent on doing bad things to us.

I saw that the rounds I was putting downrange were hitting the target they were intended for. Even as it was happening, I knew this was the first time I'd be killing someone in such an up-close and personal way.

Him and me. Face-to-face.

I saw him recoil. I saw him hit the ground. I heard what sounded like a small yowl. He balled up on his side, not moving. And he just stayed there. He was no longer in the fight, this gunman I had beaten to the trigger. And my guys had taken care of his friends.

After the bullets stopped flying, the speed of the action returned to normal. My adrenaline was still ferociously high, but gradually it eased down. I don't know whether I was breathing hard or I wasn't breathing at all. I just know that through the whole encounter, I was on some kind of warrior's autopilot, and thankfully I'd landed safely.

We surveyed the area to make sure the danger had passed, that no cohorts or backups were lingering in the nearby grass. Within a minute or two, the other half of our group returned. Then I took one deep breath and exhaled.

"Nicely done," one of my teammates said.

That first time didn't feel traumatic at all. It didn't even feel like the first time. I had shot so many weapons. I had aimed at so many targets. I had spent so long perfecting my technique. I had probably killed people in battle before, even though I couldn't precisely identify them. Crossing that line was not such a giant leap for me.

When it finally happened and the results were clear, I felt something almost like relief. I had finally done something I'd trained for. I did it well. We won the fight. Everyone on my team returned home safely. We'd removed some dangerous characters from the battlefield. We'd been looking for that crew or some of their associates for a long time. This was definitely going in the win column. Winning beats losing every time.

That night, after we completed the after-action report and the follow-up operational summary, we cleaned our weapons and made sure our bags were packed and ready to go again the next morning. I had something to eat. I showered. I got into bed. Then I took a moment in my mind to acknowledge the fact that there now was one fewer question I had to ask myself: Could I do it?

I had confirmed what I believed was the case, that I was capable of executing the most intense exchange between two human beings, the attempted taking of one another's lives, a deadly force connection. And that I was the one who'd come out alive.

I was now in a new category of warrior. I was a "meat eater" now. That's the expression SEALs use for someone who has killed on the battlefield. When I entered the category of those who had done that, it was a special distinction to me.

Because of our training and our temperament, SEALs are attuned to a more primitive version of what men were once required to be—and still are—when our special skills are called for.

This is nothing to be embarrassed about. People, good people, go to dark places from time to time, whether they want to or not. There is something in the human psyche that just sends us there. At some time or another, almost everyone has said or thought, "I wish I could kill that person." Most people never act on those feelings, and rightfully so.

It's a real thing, taking somebody's life. We operate under the U.S. Forces Rules of Engagement. We take those rules seriously. In their most basic terms, they require us never to target noncombatants. But we have the right and the duty to defend ourselves or our unit from attack or threat of attack. And we may use deadly force against hostile combatants to further the legitimate aims of the war.

Nevertheless, I am cognizant of the fact that the people we took off the battlefield had families, too. I know that I have changed a family, that this is a son, a brother, a father, or a husband whose life is now over while mine continues. It is not something I dwell on. Nor is it something I can deny. But I feel like I've been lucky. I didn't see anyone we shot at who wasn't prepared to shoot at us—or wasn't already shooting. I've never shot at a target or an individual I didn't believe was absolutely the enemy. I have never had a moment where I wondered, Was that a good shot or not? A lot of guys have experienced that. For any decent person, that's a real challenge.

I can't speak for women on this. Maybe it isn't as much a part of the female psyche. But most men and boys today, at some point in their lives, have lingered in bed or stood in the shower or stared at the mirror and thought to themselves:

What would I do if I were confronted with a deadly-force encounter? If I were in a pizza joint and a man came in with a shotgun, if someone on the street flashed a big knife and demanded my wallet, if someone I loved was threatened somehow—what would I do?

At some point or another, almost every man wonders: How would I perform in mortal combat? Could I kill before I was killed? Who would I kill for? Who deserves to die?

For some of us, just thinking and wondering is not enough. There is a breed of man with something inside him that pushes him to find out.

My wife always notices things about me I don't notice about myself, like the way I can't ever seem to sit still. My body can't do that. I move and adjust and reposition constantly. I don't feel like I'm uncomfortable. I don't feel like I need a new La-Z-Boy in the living room. I don't even realize I'm doing it. But after we'd been together for years, Tracy said one day: "You are unbelievable. You can't sit still for three minutes on a couch." And she's right.

Over the years, she has asked me, "What did you dream last night?" She would feel me moving in my sleep or hear me saying something. I would tell her what I'd been dreaming. I didn't think too much about it except, Well, Tracy must be interested in dreams.

One day, she told me something else I hadn't realized. "Every single dream you ever told me about involves some kind of deadly conflict encounter," she said.

Someone was chasing me. Someone was threatening me. I was trying to save someone in harm's way. Every dream had something to do with adventure and conflict—most of the time mortal combat. I can't say for sure if becoming a SEAL satisfied a subconscious desire to enter mortal combat. But it was certainly connected to something fundamental in my makeup.

When I first got home from Iraq, Tracy asked me a little about the deployment and how it had unfolded. I told her it had been an extremely violent experience. We'd been in a lot of fights. I didn't talk about the details. It wasn't that I didn't want to share. She didn't ask me for too many details, and I didn't offer them on my own.

Then five years later, we were out at dinner one night and she said: "You've never told me if you killed anyone, what specifically happened or how often that happened."

It was a profound moment for us. For the first time, I shared with her a lot of details from that deployment. I don't know if I'd been worried she might be horrified. Sitting across from her in the restaurant, I watched her face. But she didn't seem to be. I could see in her eyes what looked to me like a great deal of almost relief that I had been able to test myself that way. She knew me so well. She knew how it would have weighed on me if I'd been through all that training, if I'd built up all that experience, if I had such a violent deployment in a truly historic war—and I hadn't been tested in the ultimate way.

She was right.

By then, I was back in San Diego, working my way up the training hierarchy, taking a larger and larger role in the development of the next generation of SEALs. That meant building on the power of my own experience. It also meant a chance to be home as Tracy and I planned the next adventure in our lives as a couple and eventually as parents. If I still had that hanging out there, if I hadn't had that opportunity to be the warrior I knew I could, I know deep inside me how unsettled I would have felt. I would have been itching for the next adventure.

And now I know. The potential and ability to perform the ultimate act of a warrior lives inside of me. I know because I have let it out. And that's given me a higher sense of responsibility and a stronger appreciation for all that life offers. Those who have fought in combat units in any way know what I am talking about. When you have fought for your life, that life means more to you.

Food tastes better. Moments with family feel closer. Hobbies give more pleasure than they used to. Your senses are actually heightened. You don't sweat the small things like you used to. You have pushed the human experience about as far as it can go.

At the same time, I feel like I have been part of a needed organization. I know there was evil pitted against me. I know there were bad guys in Indian Country who wanted to take my life as much as I wanted to take theirs. I confronted them in the most intimate way imaginable. And I'm still here.

I have spent my entire adult life in the company of SEALs. It is only when I'm away from my brother SEALs with old friends or new ones, that I notice. People look at me strangely. I can tell they are thinking, I bet that dude killed some people.

I'm not going to pretend I don't like being looked at as special in that way. It wasn't my motivation for joining. It wasn't what kept me in. But it is part of who I am forever.

14

FAMILY TIME

I never feared the day
That death comes take my hand.
I fear the cries of my family
So I'll live as long as I can.
— NATE DENVER

I have attended too many warrior funerals.

All of them are overwhelmingly sad. But there's not a single funeral I've been to where the rest of us haven't felt the tiniest bit of envy that we weren't that guy. I know most people can't imagine feeling like that. But a fellow warrior understands the draw of going out that way. Shoulder to shoulder with your brothers. Fighting the bad guys in a savage land. That's dying with your boots on. That's a gunfighter's life.

Whether it was Mark or Mikey, Nate or Mike, or any of the other brothers our community has lost, I felt grief-stricken. Everybody did. But I was still convinced that dying in war would be a hell of a way to go, an honorable way to end this life and move on.

When I first enlisted and sought a commission in the Navy, I had never given much thought to what military service would mean for my family. I had heard people say, "Your family serves right along with you." But I had no idea in practical terms what that might mean. It's hard to know going in. Gradually—and especially when I began deploying to war zones—I began to feel the weight of what I was asking of my mom, my dad, my brother, and, when I met and married Tracy, especially my wife. I was the one who had decided to walk this warrior path. Without their ever agreeing, I made it their path as well.

With my long and constant absences.

With all the emotional pressures that this life entails.

With the genuine possibility that I might not come home.

As I was heading to Iraq on what I knew would be a highly aggressive SEAL team deployment, I started thinking about what my death might mean to my father. He loved me. I knew that. He'd miss me. But for my father, my dying would bookend his life in a hugely potent way. My dad's dad was killed in World War II. To have his son die, too, in a war zone while serving his country—that was more than anyone should ever have to bear.

My mom has always known I was an aggressive person who constantly liked to push himself. I don't think she was surprised when I joined an elite military unit. But my mother, like most moms, is an emotional person, and she worries about me. Even today. When I learned I was headed to Iraq, I had a talk with my brother, Nate. I told him I really did feel at ease going into that violent war zone. Whatever happened would happen. I had chosen this life.

"But I've been thinking about Mom," I said. "If something happens, don't let her descend into hate or anger. I don't want her feeling bitter at the country that sent me to war or at our leadership. Remind her I chose this. I'm doing what I want to be doing with guys I want to be doing it with."

I was already a SEAL when I met Tracy.

She folded immediately into the life and banter and culture of BRAVO platoon. It was an alpha-male world. Sonny, Irish, Face Man, and the others were a wild group of guys. Most of the platoon members were still single then. They were going out and running hard and having crazy romances. Almost all the girlfriends got nicknames—not all of them flattering. But the whole platoon treated Tracy differently. They called her "K-Wonder," the Kentucky wonder. It took a woman like that, they decided, to lock down Diesel, to pull him off the market.

And Tracy really connected with the team. Yes, they had their raw side. But they seemed like a cool throwback to her. "It's like they're from another era," she marveled. They would hold the door for her. They'd stand when she walked up to the table. They'd give her a hug and kiss when she came into the room. She knew if someone had ever said something disrespectful to her, any one of the BRAVO boys would gladly have flattened him—or worse.

And then there was me. You can't say Tracy didn't know she was marrying a warrior. If anything, that was part of what drew her to me. I always believed she was attracted to me because of who I am, this job I hold, this culture I am part of. She understood it from the start, including the stresses and the absences and the notion of me not coming home. She wanted to be with someone who believed in the things that I believed in, who was passionate about something to the point of being willing to die for it. A huge burden goes with that. But together, we had to figure out how to make it work. We've never found the perfect answer. But we always found a way.

One issue was phone calls. Whenever I was away, Tracy and I spoke on Sundays. That was our day. If I was on a mission or somewhere I couldn't get to a phone on Sunday, we would skip the call. I wouldn't call on Monday or Tuesday. We would roll it to the following week. That way, she wasn't sitting by the phone every day, wondering, Is today the day he's going to call? It takes a strong woman with a lot of faith not to be overwhelmed by fear, to wait an entire week to find out why I couldn't call. That might not be right for everyone. But that's what worked for us.

I had junior team members who called their wives or girlfriends every night. They'd Skype. Or use a mobile phone. Or at the very least, they'd email. That seemed to me like a terrible idea. I told them: "You know, we're gonna get called up to do things. You won't be able to call home for three or four nights in a row. If you set a rhythm of talking every night and then you break it, people are going to start flipping out."

And that happened. Frequently. We'd come in from a mission. Guys would be bolting for the computer or the phone. They'd established that pattern. Their women were having meltdowns. Even one night away was a problem for them.

Tracy and I didn't have children yet. That would have made being away from home even tougher. I have monumental respect for all those warrior families with children. Whatever the latest communications techniques, none of them is remotely the equal of cheering at a Little League game, attending a school play, or tucking the little ones into bed at night. No one's figured out yet how to Skype a hug.

The absences for SEAL families go on and on. There are months and years of training, and most of it can't be done in your own backyard. You're running off to Stennis, Mississippi, for Jungle Warfare Training or to Fort Knox, Kentucky, for Land Warfare Training or to San Clemente, California, for Maritime Training or up to Kodiak Island, Alaska, for Winter Warfare Training. Even at home, the calls are relentless: "Can you come back in?" which is never really a request. It is an order. And once you're in a tactical unit—well, my deployments were eleven months, eight months, six months, numbers like that. They add up to a whole lot of neglected family, however diligent you try to be.

When I was heading off on a deployment, Tracy and I never said good-bye to each other with the other families at the airport or the pier. We did it at home, just the two of us. Saying good-bye that way felt more personal. Tracy wanted to keep it together as I was leaving. Once the door closed, that's when she would lose it.

She would cry as much as she wanted to. She would feel whatever she felt. But I never saw that.

Every couple and every family has its own rituals. They give little gifts to each other. They share a special meal. They have some magic words or special phrases that they exchange. They have some routine that for them makes the leaving just a little easier. What Tracy and I found was that saying good-bye was so intense, we didn't want to make that experience last one second longer.

When I was being deployed to the Mediterranean, it looked at the last minute like our departure might be delayed a day or two. Tracy and I had already said our good-byes, and I'd checked in at the ship. I decided immediately I wasn't going back home. I would stay on board and say nothing. I would see Tracy when I returned. I couldn't imagine doing our good-byes all over again. They are that difficult. When I told her about that later, she said: "Absolutely. That was totally the right call."

When I came home from any extended time away, we had our rituals for that as well. All the families would be waiting in the airport terminal or at the pier, waving signs and flags. They'd be hugging and kissing and welcoming their SEAL men home. It's a beautiful scene. But it wasn't for us. Tracy would stay at the house and wait for me there. That reunion was just for us. We wanted to preserve some separation for ourselves. Our welcome-home reunions were our special time.

As hard as the separation was for both of us, we loved those amazing little honeymoons. She'd make the same welcome-home meal: chicken cacciatore, broccoli-and-cheese casserole, and an amazing pecan pie. We'd spend some quiet time together.

The wives of SEALs have a powerful outreach network. Most of the wives are part of that. They share family outings, offer emotional support, and lend a hand with child care. No SEAL wife ever needs to be alone. But there are also disadvantages to being so plugged in.

When Mark was killed, word of his death spread immediately among the SEAL wives, days before it was officially confirmed. The same with Mikey when he jumped on the grenade. But the reports spread haltingly, before all the details were confirmed. Forty wives from SEAL Team Three knew that a SEAL team husband had been killed in western Iraq that week. Agonizingly, they waited days to find out who.

The worst example was the "lone survivor" attack, which Marcus survived. Word got passed back home that a bunch of SEALs had been killed. None of the names came back immediately, and the early rumors said everyone was dead. Marcus's family thought he'd been killed. Then word came that he might be alive, but no one could say with any certainty. Finally, the good news arrived. Marcus had been the lone survivor of this horrific attack. But there was still bad news for some families and a real roller-coaster ride for others.

Maintaining operational secrecy is tough today when communication is so instant and accessible. But a family shouldn't ever learn from the wives' network that their loved one isn't coming home, any more than they should learn it from Fox, MSNBC, or CNN.

I'm lucky that Tracy is so strong. I always say, "The toughest person in our house isn't the SEAL."

She's physically tough. One time when we were snowboarding, she fell and her wrist snapped.

All I saw was her fall. I went rushing over. She looked okay.

"I think I just broke my wrist," she said with absolute calm.

"You broke your wrist?" I asked.

She wasn't screaming or crying. A wrist break is excruciatingly painful. I was pretty sure she hadn't broken her wrist. But when we got to the emergency room, the doctor ordered X-rays.

"Yeah," he told her, "you broke your wrist clear through."

Still, she hadn't shed a tear.

She delivered both our children with no drugs, no doctors, just a midwife, her, and me. I helped deliver our second one. Being able to do that meant something to her. Generations of powerful women have brought children into the world without medical intervention. She wanted the experience.

Much in the same way I sought out the extremes of male warrior interaction, Tracy's personality was just as strong. She wanted the absolute most extreme female experience of childbirth, doing it the way it was meant to be done. And she got it.

But the thing that really displays Tracy's toughness is how she deals with the emotional demands of this warrior life. She accepts that I need to go off and do these things for the country, for the team, and for our family. She's allowed me to do that without the burden of wondering if the house is taken care of or the lingering concern that she is emotionally spent. There are, I'm sure, hundreds of things I don't know about that she suffered and dealt with on her own. It's a gift I don't know I'll ever be able to fully thank her for.

I love her attitude. I love her independence. I think she is a complete and utter knockout. I love her walk. She has a walk that drives me crazy. It is so effortless, unintentional, and just off-the-charts sexy. I might be the only one who sees that. Isn't that great? It taps into some very deep part of who I am.

Once we had children, we had a new scenario to consider. If I died,

I wouldn't be leaving just Tracy. I'd be leaving two young daughters behind. Our time together had barely started. There was so much yet to do. We had only begun to guide the girls through life.

Some soldiers write death letters to those they love, putting down on paper as clearly as they can the feelings held most deeply in their hearts. They ask a trusted buddy to hold that letter in confidence, then pass it along to the parents or the wife or the children should the worst ever occur.

I had never written a death letter.

I felt almost superstitious about the whole idea, that writing with my premature demise in mind could somehow become a self-fulfilling prophecy. And frankly, I never felt the need.

My family leaves almost nothing unsaid. I tell my brother I love him every time we're about to get off the phone. My mom, my dad— I say the same to both of them. We share our hopes. We share our problems. Deep emotional repression just isn't the Denver way.

And when I got married, it was the same thing. Tracy and I don't keep many secrets. But now that I have small children, I think I'll write that letter if I ever go to war again. If I died, I'd still want to guide them. If I couldn't talk to them, maybe my words still could. There's so much I want to tell them that they aren't yet old enough to hear. There are so many things I might not have the chance to pass along.

I know Tracy would do a lot of that on my behalf. She knows me so well, she would know so much of what I considered important and share that with the girls. But some things I'd still want to say directly to them, things large and small that their warrior-father has learned over the years.

Laugh a lot.

If you want to live a life free of pain, think of others first.

Crunchy peanut better is better than smooth. That is a fact.

Read. You can always talk with another reader.

Tell the truth. You won't regret it. The truth saves an awful lot of time.

Push yourself. Get uncomfortable. Do things that challenge you. That's where the growth is.

Search out mentors. Cultivate as many as you can. They will open your eyes to new ideas. They will challenge your thinking.

When you get a blister on your foot, slap a big dollop of Vaseline on it. Pull your sock and shoe back on. Keep doing what you're doing. Pa taught me that one. It is gold.

Seek good company and friends. There is no discomfort too harsh that good friends can't ease and make almost enjoyable. There is no great moment that can't be ruined in the company of fools.

Take time to create balance in your life. Recognize what is important. Have lofty goals and ambitions but not at the expense of your friends, your loved ones, and your enjoyment of life.

Find what you are passionate about, no matter where that leads. Don't be bound by what others expect of you. Your passions are your own.

Stuff newspaper into wet shoes or boots if you need them dry by the morning.

Treat everyone with kindness and equality until they give you a reason not to.

Recognize in others the difference between errors in judgment and errors in character. You can suffer and forgive the first. Keep well clear of the second.

If you ever find a water fountain with strong pressure and cold water, mark its location. That is one of life's simple pleasures.

Own your mistakes. Do not run from them. Accountability is a dying concept today. Hold yourself to standards especially when you err.

Don't ever settle in love. The great man you deserve is out there. He will be the lucky one. Make sure he is willing to fight for you.

Family is everything. Always keep faith with your family. I hope you will maintain that and pass it along, keeping it strong and true for future generations.

As sisters, take care of each other. You will not find a better friend in the world. I am so much stronger because my brother is in my life. Take care of that. It's a gift that will last forever.

When you turn eighteen, have your mom get you a pair of shoes with red soles. Tell her Papa said so. I don't know what they're called. But every woman on earth does. And you'll want a pair.

A great love affair began the day you were born. There are photos that prove it—the midwife handing over our firstborn to your mother, me handing over our second. Find those pictures. Look at your mother's face. You will see what I mean.

I could go on for hours. I have so much to say. Once I got started, I wouldn't know where to stop.

But when I finally got to the end, I would quote from one of my very favorite poems. It is written by Chief Tecumseh of the Shawnee Nation. He was one of the most impressive warriors to ever walk this land. His words have helped to guide me.

"Live your life," Tecumseh said, "that the fear of death can never enter your heart. Trouble no one about their religion. Respect others in their view, and demand that they respect yours. Love your life, perfect your life, beautify all things in your life. Seek to make your life long and its purpose in the service of your people. . . . Show respect to all people and grovel to none. . . . When it comes your time to die, be not like those whose hearts are filled with the fear of death, so that when their time comes they weep and pray for a little more time to live their lives over again in a different way. Sing your death song and die like a hero going home."

I hope that death is a long way off for all of us.

But we'll be ready. I know we will.

15

TWO OPS

I wish to have no connection with any ship that
does not sail fast for I intend to go in harm's way.
—John Paul Jones

Of all the mission profiles SEALs are capable of, nothing quite matches the magic of a rescue. Convoys, overwatches, foot patrols, raids. They have their special challenges and rewards. But extracting a civilian from the clutches of hostage-takers or extracting a cornered comrade from a firefight—the urgent call of commando duty gets no purer than that.

We can all imagine ourselves needing to be rescued. Everyone knows how tragically those dramas can end. Often, the assault team is someone's last, best hope for survival. And if the SEALs can also capture or kill the bad guys, that's a double win.

Don't believe the movies and television. Assault team rescue missions are exceedingly rare. But when the call comes, it always comes in desperation. The stakes are almost always life-or-death. There isn't a SEAL on any team anywhere who doesn't dream of missions like that.

How strong is the draw? A veteran master chief in one of the teams put it to me like this:

"Here's the scenario," he said. "I have a rescue mission, two helicopters, and not enough room on board for all the guys. We all know for certain that one of those helicopters will crash on the way in."

And?

"I'd be worried that I wouldn't have enough SEALs for the mission—after the brawl they fought with each other for a chance to volunteer."

Now this was teamwork: three SEAL snipers, lying on the swaying fantail of the USS *Bainbridge*, looking through the scopes of long-barreled SR-25 Mk 11 Mod 0 semiautomatics, waiting for three Somali pirates to step into view at once.

"Green . . . green . . . red," the snipers said in rapid succession.

"Green . . . red . . . green."

Each shooter had an individual target. The armed pirates and their hostage, an American cargo ship captain, were inside the cabin of a five-ton covered lifeboat being towed behind the U.S. Navy warship. The sight lines were ridiculous. A bouncing lifeboat. A moving ship. A long towrope between them. From the stern of the *Bainbridge*, there was no telling how long it might take for all three pirates to line up perfectly.

"Red . . . red . . . green."

As the SEAL snipers waited to shoot, the whole world was transfixed by this life-or-death drama at sea. A new American president was still finding his international footing. President Obama hadn't been tested in a crisis like this. If the snipers got it done, the SEALs would earn a whole new level of credibility and acclaim and pave the way to even bigger missions in the future. If the snipers shot the captain or missed the pirates or botched the mission in some other way, the result would be human tragedy and international embarrassment. Either way, everyone would know. A whole lot was riding on a few swift shots.

This was just the kind of high-pressure, technically complex mission that their SEAL training had prepared these men for. From the team-building small-boat races in Hell Week to the moving-target shooting courses in Kentucky to the whole refuse-to-fail mentality of the SEAL brotherhood—they were ready.

Calmly distinguish between the good guys and the bad guys.

Don't rush the shot.

Stay in total synch with your fellow operators.

This could have been the final test at the Trident boards.

They were 240 miles off the Horn of Africa. The Indian Ocean was choppy. The wind was picking up. Armed thugs had attacked six vessels in a week, demanding tens of millions of dollars in ransom. Four days earlier, four pirates had stormed aboard the MV *Maersk Alabama*, the first successful seizure of an American-flagged cargo ship since the nineteenth century. But after failing to gain engine control, the pirates forced Captain Richard Phillips onto a lifeboat and motored away.

With guidance from the FBI, *Bainbridge* Commander Frank Castellano had been trying to negotiate for the *Maersk* captain's release. At one point, the pirates agreed to be towed by the *Bainbridge*. But as the talks ground on and the weather deteriorated, the Navy commander was given the authority to do more than talk. If the captain's life was in imminent danger, the orders from the White House said, Castellano could green-light a more aggressive approach.

He called in a SEAL assault team.

In the normal course of business, violent, personal assaults really aren't Big Navy's specialty. Navy ships do not have assault teams and snipers aboard. The ship's regular crew would surely include some aggressive seamen and perhaps a sailor or two who was a pretty good shot. But aggressive seamen and a pretty good shot wouldn't get this job done. Some Navy ships have a VBSS team, a visit-board-search-and-seizure team. They get basic tactical training in how to board a vessel, usually in a compliant situation, and take some measure of control. But when it comes to sniper operations and commando assaults, that is what the SEALs do.

There are other units in the U.S. military that have capable assault forces that can operate effectively at sea. But the SEALs are the maritime component of the U.S. Special Operations Command. No one else conducts hostile missions at sea with the training and intensity that we do. That unique combination—violent assault, maritime environment—is in our DNA. It *is* our DNA. No SEAL would ever say we have mastered the oceans, but we are far more capable there than anybody else.

Eight years into sustained combat in arid Iraq and Afghanistan, we hadn't been called for too many waterborne assaults and rescues. We weren't taking down oil rigs or chasing pirates every day. Very few terrorists had nukes on private yachts. The most notable combat deployments post-9/11 have been on hot, dry land.

When the call came from the *Bainbridge*, the SEALs were ready to go. Our teams are up and running in no time, even if we haven't been using those skill sets in theater, even if we have to pull the mission plan off a shelf somewhere. We can still make a complex profile work.

There are so many things that could go wrong on a hostage rescue at sea. The wrong person could get shot. We could lose one of our team members in a botched assault. The enemy could fire back and get lucky. We are in harm's way every time we go out there. We can't be overconfident. Every top military unit makes mistakes. That's just the nature of this business we are in, even though our SEAL success rate has lately left the public expecting something close to perfection. We can never forget how quickly one bad shot leads to disaster.

But taking those shots wasn't the only big challenge here. Before the SEAL snipers ever had a chance to show what kind of marksmen they were, they had to get to the ship. And that was a huge undertaking in itself, a crucial part of this hostage-rescue story. Many things had to go right for those SEAL snipers to get their chance to squeeze those triggers. Their journey is worth retracing in some detail.

When the first call came, the SEAL team was nowhere near the Horn of Africa. The SEALs had to be flown in from Norfolk, Virginia, eighteen hours by air. But no one wasted any time getting ready. SEALs are always ready. Our gear is always prepped. Our bags are always packed.

The easiest way to get aboard a Navy ship at sea is by helicopter, but the team couldn't be flown onto the deck of the *Bainbridge*. That could easily have raised the pirates' suspicion about a coming assault. Instead, the full SEAL contingent—snipers, corpsmen, breachers, communicators, plus the senior enlisted leaders and a couple of frontline officers—flew on a Boeing C-17 military transport plane, specially outfitted to carry a stack of high-speed assault boats. The assault craft were equipped with high-performance engines and loaded with everything the SEALs might need for their mission—weapons, ammo, and enough gear for an extended stay if that was required. All of it was strapped in snugly.

The boats were rigged with static-line parachutes, set to open automatically the instant the boats cleared the aircraft. The drop spot had to be within a mile or two of the *Bainbridge* or one of its sister ships but not so close that the pirates on the lifeboat would catch a glimpse of what was about to occur.

"Ready to drop," the SEAL jumpmaster told the crew chief as the aircraft moved into the zone.

With a sharp, mechanical slap, the boats were released above the ocean. You never want be standing too close when SEAL boats are skidding out of an aircraft. You could just as easily be dragged along for an unexpected ride. The second the boats cleared the bird, their chutes unfurled automatically and the boats began their float toward the Indian Ocean.

The SEALs jumped out right behind the boats with their own parachutes.

That maneuver left little room for error: jumping out of an aircraft into an open ocean, chasing a boat with all your gear, hoping that when you climb out of the water and pull yourselves aboard, the radio and navigation equipment will all be operational so you can find your way to the ship. And you'd better pray the engine starts.

When they hit the water in their parachutes and climbed aboard their assault boats, the SEALs didn't go directly to the *Bainbridge*. They made their initial rendezvous with the nearby USS *Halyburton*, then transferred to the *Bainbridge*. Every step of the way in an operation like this, there are subtleties to manage and unknowns to confront. Critical command decisions always have to be made on the scene, frequently with uncertain or inadequate facts. Even after the SEALs arrived, there was no clear understanding yet of exactly what they were there for and what approach made the most sense—a waterborne assault, a combat-swimmer mission, a sniper operation, some combination of those, or nothing at all.

Often, in cases like this one, large personalities will have to be managed as well. A junior SEAL officer has to coordinate with a senior Navy commander. The SEALs will be exercising significant operational autonomy aboard his ship. That's no small thing to swallow for a man who has command at sea, submitting his craft and his crew to even the partial direction of outsiders, even if we are all part of the same U.S. Navy.

Thankfully, Commander Castellano was engaged, supportive, and highly knowledgeable.

As he continued negotiating with the pirates, the SEAL assault team quickly assessed the options at hand, coordinating every step of the way with the commander. Before any aggressive action was taken, all options had to be carefully explored.

The SEALs could attack and board the lifeboat from other boats in the water. They could almost certainly overwhelm the pirates, easily outgunning and outmanning them. But at what cost? The pirates would most likely see the SEALs coming, and the captain would be dead or dying before the first SEAL got on board.

The SEALs could swim up to the lifeboat like Toro and I did on that combat-swimmer exercise back at Roosey Roads. But even that option, it was determined, carried too much risk of detection on the way in.

The best but most technically complex option: put SEAL snipers in a position to engage.

The SEALs scouted for the right location to shoot from. Some spot with clear sight lines. Somewhere the snipers could lie side by side. The fantail of the *Bainbridge*, jutting off the stern of the ship, looked ideal.

The snipers carefully monitored the movement on the lifeboat. The pirates and their hostage weren't lounging on an open deck. That would have been fish-in-a-barrel. Any weekend warrior could have landed that shot. But the pirates and their hostage were sheltered inside the lifeboat's enclosed cabin, leaving anything but a steady, unobstructed shot.

The assault team leader remained in close, direct conversation with Commander Castellano in the ship's combat control center. The commander had all the authority he needed. The snipers were in place. All they were waiting for now was the order to proceed.

The order came from Castellano to the assault team leader to the SEALs on the fantail:

"SEALs are cleared to engage."

They held their position, peering through their scopes, waiting for their moment to arrive. What no one could control was where the pirates and their hostage would be when the timing was right.

"Green . . . red . . . green."

"Red . . . red . . . red."

"Red . . . green . . . green."

Then the moment arrived.

Inside the door of the cabin, Captain Phillips stepped within view. One pirate was standing behind him, pointing an AK-47 at the captain's head. The head and shoulders of the other two pirates were visible as well.

"Green, green, green."

Three triggers were squeezed at almost exactly the same instant. Three shots were fired, the tiniest millisecond apart. Three pirates fell instantly to the lifeboat floor.

Looking stunned, the captain was completely unharmed.

And three SEAL snipers breathed a huge sigh of relief.

In an instant, a couple of boats were off the side of the *Bainbridge* and in the choppy water to collect Captain Phillips. The boarding party checked to be sure none of the pirates was moving. Quickly, they hustled the captain into a boat, which took him back to the ship. He was flown by helicopter to the USS *Boxer* for medical evaluation to confirm he was all right.

The SEALs had done their job.

I wish I'd been there when senior military officials walked the new president through the details of exactly how the mission had gone down, saying, "Yes, this is how we did it."

I know this much: Senior officials in Washington and across the military were saying to each other and to themselves, "My God, who are these guys? It's good to know they're on our side."

What began as a leap of faith by an untested president—a well-earned and well-briefed leap but a leap nonetheless—ended with a new level of trust in the talent and competence of the SEALs. The mission's success became a turning point for the teams. The confidence that mission built would not be forgotten when the ultimate test arrived two years later and the world was watching even more closely.

A SHIPBORNE HOSTAGE RESCUE will always to some extent be a case of when-we-get-there-we'll-figure-out-what-to-do. The Somali pirate mission showed the SEALs' remarkable ability to improvise. Getting Osama bin Laden, by contrast, demonstrated the opposite talent, our ability to plan and plan and plan some more, down to the very last detail.

With precision fire in a third-floor bedroom, a SEAL assault team achieved what no one else had been able to in ten frustrating years, taking the terror mastermind off the battlefield he helped to define. SEALs stormed the walled compound in Abbottabad, Pakistan, where bin Laden was holed up, and a lingering piece of national business was taken care of.

At last.

That mission more than any other has become the teams' signature.

May 2, 2011, wasn't just the day bin Laden was killed. It was also the day that millions of people around the world absorbed the happy news and asked themselves in wonder: What *can't* these SEALs do?

I wasn't on that op, as I hadn't been on the pirate rescue. I wish I had been at both. Every SEAL wishes he was. Hell, every special operator wishes he was on either mission. But here's what surprises nearly everyone about the historic and gratifying bin Laden raid: As SEAL missions go, the assault on bin Laden's compound near the Pak-Afghan border wasn't all that hard for our guys. As a planning and technical matter, it was far less difficult than the Somali-pirate hostage rescue.

Locating bin Laden was a challenge. It took almost ten years. America owes a huge debt to the CIA agents, NSA analysts, military-wide intelligence pros, and others who tirelessly pursued this most-wanted man. But for the SEAL assault team that pulled that high-profile duty, the mission was like walking out to the porch and picking up the morning paper. Everyone involved had followed this routine a thousand times before. Trained during and after BUD/S. Practiced in the field. Gamed out repeatedly in advance of the bin Laden raid. Every man knew what he was doing that night.

Like all missions, this one had risks and surprises, one of them nearly a tragedy. But the actual mission, the X's and O's on the chalkboard, the execution on the ground—this is what we trained for. Most of us have executed far more challenging missions with far less preparation. Even the glitches would have to be called routine.

I'm not minimizing the effort involved. Obviously, there were logistical difficulties. There always are. Everyone had to be secretive. The assault occurred in a denied battle space. The United States had no permission from the government of Pakistan to be there. But this was a known location, a walled compound nearly identical to the one the team had used in training. The assaulters had detailed satellite imagery and known enemy strength. The bad guys didn't know we were coming. The area was self-contained. The target was well past his prime fighting years.

I guarantee you there was an actual and specific discussion of what would happen if one helicopter went down. How about if two helos went down? The team had already thought out the implications and devised a clear adjust plan. On a mission so important and high profile, we doomsday every possible scenario.

Everyone knew what a disaster failure would mean. Embarrassment at home. Outrage across the world. A newly emboldened al Qaeda. If the mission had gone wrong, we'd have been drowning in gleeful bin Laden tapes that mocked the evil and incompetence of the great Satan, America. And who knows what his henchmen would have been planning next.

There were no rookies on any of the helicopters that came out of Afghanistan, across the border and into Pakistan. This was the SEALs' varsity team, the best shooters, the best spec-ops pilots, the best intel leveraged for the mission's success. And we had total support up the chain of command. The president and his top advisors were even watching a live video feed in the War Room at the White House.

Far more difficult is what these extraordinary warriors have been doing day and night in Afghanistan and Iraq in the years since bin Laden's vicious attack on America. All of us, including the operators on the bin Laden mission, have raided houses on the darkest of nights in the most lawless quarters of those challenging battle zones with a force of only seven SEALs and sixteen Iraqi conscripts, hunting for a target who could be almost anywhere. That's more the norm than the exception.

It's those experiences that help the highest-profile missions succeed. Blast inside a quiet house and you don't know what you'll find there. Two old men could be asleep on the couch. Forty armed insurgents could be opening fire. No air cover. No on-scene ground support. No Rangers sealing the block and backing you up. No intel that is remotely reliable.

You don't know the language. The culture is impossible to crack. The good guys and the bad guys are hard to tell apart. That's the warrior business, day in and day out. As the officer on the team, you need to be a warrior. You need to be a diplomat. You need to be a lawyer. You need to be a priest and a parent.

Compared to those unnoticed missions, the bin Laden raid met relatively little resistance. What made the mission so sexy and spectacular and profoundly important was the identity of the target. Since the start of the Age of Terror, no target was bigger than this.

About that glitch: On that night, one of the helicopters did go down just as the SEALs reached the compound. But even that didn't slow the mission. In fact, as the bird quickly lost lift, the operators aboard were able to get out and meet up with the rest of the team.

The SEALs flew bin Laden's body out of the compound so it could be officially identified and the White House could be absolutely certain the SEALs got the man they had come for.

The bin Laden assault team earned that mission. It was so long in coming, so crucial to the nation's War on Terror, so important to show all the world's terrorists and the nations that enable them that America will not allow them to win. Those extra-important missions need total support: "What do you boys need to get it done?"

Once confirmation was in, the president made an unforgettable announcement in a special Sunday night address to the nation.

"Tonight," he said, "I can report to the American people and the world that the United States has conducted an operation that killed Osama bin Laden."

All across America, from college campuses to downtown retail strips to the park across from the White House, people gathered and began to chant:

"U-S-A! U-S-A! U-S-A!"

But here's what's also telling about the SEALs.

The guys on that mission weren't doing any chanting. I promise you that. Neither was anyone else in the SEAL brotherhood. We weren't pounding our chests or bellowing into the night.

We reacted with more of an internal, metabolized satisfaction, the chance finally to say, "Mission complete."

PART THREE

Passing It On

16

MAKE MORE SEALS

*Ten soldiers wisely led will beat
a hundred without a head.*
—EURIPIDES

There are famous missions that get all over the media. There are momentum-shifting operations that the historians of war will look back on. "That one," they'll say. "That's when the tribal leaders came to see what thugs those al Qaeda insurgents were." Or "That's when the Afghan Taliban really went running." Or "That's when America showed the world those SEAL snipers really can shoot."

But this brotherhood of ours isn't about ego. We don't care if most of our missions are never known by anyone outside our own circle.

The time we captured that sniper who had killed a Marine.

The time a teammate got his eye shot out then walked off the battlefield to the helicopter on his own two feet.

The time our EOD guys saw a booby trap that everyone else had missed, saving at least half a dozen teammates' lives.

The time we caught a fish with a hand line in a canal off the Euphrates.

The time I stepped into what I thought was an irrigation ditch but was really a sewer trench and then spent the rest of the mission with Iraqi toilet waste oozing through my toes. I can still smell that now.

These are the missions the guys are BS'ing about over Slamburgers at Danny's Palm Bar in Coronado. Herculean efforts were made. Nothing went wrong. The critical goal, whatever it was, was achieved flawlessly. These are the missions celebrated with a slap on the back and an extra beer on me and, "We all know what happened out there."

As a SEAL, that's something you get to take with you down the road forever. It's the feeling that danger, adrenaline, and success always bring, a feeling you never lose.

I f 2,500 SEALs can achieve this much, imagine what 5,000 SEALs could do. Or 50,000. Or 500,000. The way some people have been talking lately, they're ready to turn the whole U.S. military into one super-sized SEAL platoon and tell the Army, Big Navy, Air Force, and Marines to call it a day.

Good luck.

That talk is flattering to the SEALs, I guess, even in its less exaggerated versions. If our missions kept failing, no one would want more of them or more of us. With all our high-profile triumphs since 9/11, politicians, pundits, and the public all keep asking for more. More SEALs. More missions. More whatever-it-is-the-SEALs-bring-to-the-battle-space.

But more isn't always better. These calls for dramatic expansion are often misguided in a couple of fundamental ways: They ignore how much we depend on other parts of the U.S. military, and they misunderstand what makes our special operators so special in the first place. It would be a hugely damaging miscalculation if we got more—but worse and less effective—SEALs.

The debate has been raging inside the White House, at the highest levels of the Pentagon, and across the SEAL community. And every time the arguments have erupted, I have been an active participant—often a vocal and passionate one. Running basic and advanced training, I had to be.

I found myself navigating between two powerful constituencies. On one side was the top SEAL leadership, who were under intense pressure to expand the head count. On the other were the frontline SEAL instructors, who viewed themselves as defenders of our standards and quality but, frankly, sometimes do go a little too far.

We have to get this complicated balance right. I don't believe we always have. We can't expand in ways that lower our standards or let the wrong people in. At the same time, we shouldn't be driving potentially great SEALs away in some misguided attempt to prove how tough we are. How this debate is resolved—how we strike the right balance between exclusivity and size—will have a major impact on the future of the SEALs and other special-operations forces. And it will also go a long way in determining how the U.S. military meets its fundamental responsibility—keeping America safe in the years to come.

To understand what's at stake and where this inside fight is heading, you really need a little history first. Some of it predates the start of my SEAL career, although all of it affects my generation and the ones to come. For the SEALs, the glow of Vietnam lasted a good long while. That's where the early SEALs made their name. Those guys were legendary, and still are, for using the guerrillas' own techniques against them.

But as the 1980s arrived and then the 1990s, some of that special-operations mystique had definitely begun to fade—and not just for the SEALs. The Vietnam guys were getting older. The public had lost its taste for almost anything connected to Vietnam. Like a yellowing Marcinko paperback, those early swashbuckling exploits and jungle derring-do were slipping further into the past. Some people around the Pentagon were even beginning to wonder if the U.S. military needed these quasi-independent special operators anymore.

The Army's 1980 hostage-rescue fiasco on the way to the U.S. embassy in Iran came to symbolize America's ill-equipped and dispirited special operators. Those clumsy SEAL missions in Panama and Grenada didn't help, either. And it wasn't just the SEALs whose prestige was getting battered. All the special-operations forces got lumped together in this period of poorly conceived and executed missions. I'd argue we maintained our standards and esprit de corps better than most of our fellow special operators. The SEALs were training and staying fit, remaining ready for whatever might come next. But not much did. And in the eyes of Washington and the world, despite our own bravado, some of that legendary edge and focus, made famous in Vietnam, was undeniably gone. In the committees of Congress, even among the top Pentagon brass, special operations was increasingly seen as an unruly backwater of the U.S. military—a mishmash of disconnected units, spread among the various branches with an ill-defined role and uncertain competence. In those dreary days, hardly anyone was demanding more SEALs.

Two things changed that, one of them gradually, one like a slap in the face.

The U.S. Special Operations Command was established in 1987 by President Reagan. Headquartered at MacDill Air Force Base in Tampa, Florida, SOCOM was designed to improve coordination among the various special-operations forces and to get them more money, better equipment, and whatever else they needed to do their jobs. Special operators are by nature fiercely independent. All the units were instinctively suspicious of coordination efforts from above. But gradually, this plan worked. The SEALs, the Rangers, and the others maintained their unique identities. We weren't all mushed together into one big "Special Operations Branch." And over the next few years, SOCOM really did help to improve special-ops focus and readiness.

Then 9/11 came, and the real action began.

Suddenly the world was looking a whole lot more dangerous and complicated than it had before. Suddenly what America needed most was what we did best.

Special-operations forces led the invasion of Afghanistan, with SEALs and Green Berets at the front of the pack. The same was true in Iraq, in fact, even more so. The special operators finally got the chance to show what they could do. We were fighting in multiple theaters in different countries against different types of enemies. Pretty soon we were getting far more than our share of the action.

So much about these wars was going wrong—the fruitless hunt for the weapons of mass destruction, the dwindling public appetite for drawn-out conflicts. What we were doing was going right. Battlefield commanders and Pentagon planners seemed to agree, and the public understood: The best return on the battlefield was coming from the special-ops guys, very much including the SEALs.

I don't believe the Army saw this coming. I think the Army figured they would own the top tier of the operational battle space forever. But post-9/11, the special-operations forces truly achieved the premier spot in the stack of U.S. military. Bang for the buck, we were the best use of the taxpayer money around. And once Osama bin Laden was added to the mix, there was no stopping us. From civilian and military leaders, from Democrats and Republicans, the call was the same:

Get more special operators.

Lots more.

Now.

Donald Rumsfeld, George W. Bush's secretary of defense from 2001 to 2006, was among the first to sound the expansion call, as he and the Joint Chiefs of Staff tried to envision a U.S. military better suited to the twenty-first-century War on Terror.

"The global nature of the war, the nature of the enemy and the need for fast, efficient operations in hunting down and rooting out terrorist networks around the world have all contributed to the need for an expanded role for the special operations forces," Rumsfeld said at a Pentagon briefing in early 2003 as he began pushing to expand our numbers and our budgets, the true sign of Washington love. That push continued through the Bush administration, and President Obama has been just as staunch a supporter of special ops, especially the SEALs. Those around the president say his confidence was built by the Somali-pirate mission and then sealed by the bin Laden raid.

"So much of what you do will never be known by the citizens we serve," Hillary Clinton, Obama's secretary of state, told an International Special Operations Forces Week conference in Tampa in 2012. "But I know what you do and so do others, who marvel and appreciate what it means for you to serve." Then, as the latest round of troop reductions and budget cuts became a pressing reality across the Pentagon, the Special Operations Forces were mostly spared.

"There are no sacred cows," Admiral William McRaven, commander of U.S. Special Operations, said as the budget fights heated up. That being said, he added, the Special Operations Command "is in a particularly good position as our collective capabilities offer the nation comparative advantages against many of today's threats and those that may potentially emerge."

That was Washington-speak for "Don't worry, you'll get what you need."

In an unclassified blueprint he circulated at the Pentagon, McRaven laid out the special-ops logic quite forcefully. "We are in a generational struggle," he wrote. "For the foreseeable future, the United States will have to deal with various manifestations of inflamed violent extremism. In order to conduct sustained operations around the globe, our special operations forces must adapt."

Special-operations forces "are an exceedingly cost-effective and combat-effective investment," McRaven said.

WHILE ALL THIS was playing out above, those of us in the SEAL community were so busy we could barely stop to think. Afghanistan was roaring. Iraq was in flames. Things rarely got quiet in the post-9/11 world. In our entire SEAL history, we'd never been this busy before. But our future was also on the line. It was that question from high school algebra all over again. If x was good, wouldn't $2x$ be better? And what about $10x$?

To many in Washington, the answer was obvious: make more SEALs.

It wasn't exactly an order, the way it came down from the Joint Chiefs of Staff through the Special Operations Command to the senior SEAL leadership to those of us in command positions on the ground. It wasn't "Hey, get this done, consequences be damned." It was more along the lines of "We need to increase the head count. Tell us what your requirements are. We'll get you the clearance or the funding or the facilities or whatever it is you need."

By the barked-order standard of the U.S. military, the tone of the directive was downright polite. And it wasn't aimed only at the SEALs. All Special Operations Forces were urged to beef up. The message as it was delivered from General Bryan "Doug" Brown, SOCOM's commander, was simple: "You guys need to make 'em grow."

Then an interesting thing happened.

The special-operations forces of the Army, Air Force, and Marines each produced projections of how their units could expand. Those units all expanded as promised. Class sizes were increased at Ranger School, at the Special Forces Qualification Course, and at the other special-operator selection programs. They all put out more graduates. And the flow of new operators promptly increased, enhancing the numbers all around.

There was one notable exception: the SEAL teams.

For almost a year, the SEALs acted as if nothing at all had changed. We went along pretty much as we always had. New classes arrived for BUD/S, same as always. These classes were filled with eager recruits, the vast majority of whom DOR'd before or during Hell Week. And the numbers of newly minted SEALs hardly changed at all. It was up a few, down a few, about like it always was.

It didn't take long, less than a year, for a fresh directive to find its way to the junior and senior SEAL leadership, this one considerably firmer in tone.

"That wasn't a suggestion," was the way we heard it on the ground. "We want more SEALs. You will get us more SEALs." There was also an addendum to that, unstated but still perfectly clear: "And if you won't, we will find new leaders who will."

That spurred one of the greatest silent and under-the-radar wars in our community's history. On one side were the senior commanders who were charged with creating more SEALs. Their superiors wanted it. So did the politicians in Washington. On the other side was, basically, the rest of the force junior to them. Without question, all the instructors were dead set against lowering the standards in any way that would get more guys to graduate.

Their attitude: "You can send as many people as you want to. If they don't meet our standards, they aren't getting through. We are the guardians of the SEAL community."

It wasn't that there was anything wrong with the idea of having more SEALs. We'd have no trouble finding operations to send them on. I for one just believed that bigger wasn't necessarily better and that being small, creative, and nimble was what got the SEALs this far.

When we discussed the issue among ourselves, we all agreed the way to create more SEALs was not to ease the entry requirements, not to change BUD/S, not to lower the training demands, not to reduce the talent pool in any way that could have serious ramifications for what happened on the battlefield. The solution, we believed, was to attract an even higher quality of candidate—and not just from the usual places SEALs have always come. The initial concept was sound. If we could get a better product in the front door, maybe a higher percentage would make it through.

That's the right way to make more SEALs.

But making that happen was far more difficult than it sounded. The whole idea of active recruiting was brand-new territory to the SEALs. We didn't go looking for people. They found us. To men who thought they might have what it takes to be SEALs, we provided an opportunity to see if they did. That was our idea of recruiting.

What I believed and what a lot of the operators believed is that there just aren't that many people in the world who are built to succeed in our training regime and as part of our tactical units. If that assumption was correct, it would be almost impossible to find many more of them and bring them in.

I was sitting at a senior meeting one day in Coronado. The topic of "targeted recruiting" came up, how we could expand our numbers by convincing guys from a variety of different backgrounds to come join us. A lot of very smart men, senior leaders, were giving their opinions and arguing back and forth. The discussion grew tense at times. In two and a half hours, no one left the room. I didn't say anything until right near the end, when the officer running the meeting said: "In one sentence, I want one idea from everyone on where we stand on this whole recruiting issue."

The captains and commanders weighed in first. "Send SEAL recruiters to college wrestling tournaments," one of the officers said. "Reach out to rookies who are cut from the NFL," said another. Then it was my turn. I was a lieutenant at the time, but not a shy one. "With a show of hands," I asked, "who in this room was recruited?"

Not a single hand went up.

"Nor was I," I said. "I read Winston Churchill, and here I am. I'm sure every one of you has some story about how you became aware of the SEAL teams or some moment that convinced you that this was the right place for you. In every single case, I bet, the SEALs did not find you. You found the SEALs. You found a place you truly wanted to be. You laid it on the line. You gave your best to this community, and here you are."

In addition to trying to increase the number of people who applied, the senior leaders became increasingly focused on trying to predict in advance who would make it through BUD/S. They held more meetings. They hired outside consultants. You've never seen more mechanics under the hood of a car that was running perfectly well. These learned outsiders were all brought in to come up with the absolute, definitive answer to what it is that gets someone through this course of instruction. The old business of predicting wasn't proving any easier this time.

The best attempt, as often happens, came from inside the brotherhood. Credit Commander Eric Potterat, the first active-duty psychologist at the Naval Special Warfare Center, a rare non-SEAL who is held in the highest regard by senior leaders and junior operators alike. He and three colleagues devised a one-hour Computerized Special Operations Resilience Test, which measures attributes like goal-setting, stress tolerance, emotional control, vigilance, self-talk, and leadership orientation. The test doesn't predict BUD/S success. Nothing seems to do that. But when coupled with the candidates' physical performance scores, it can say with 97 percent accuracy who is certain to DOR by Hell Week.

Three years in, that resilience test is still proving valuable. Right at the start, we can identify the bottom quadrant of applicants, the ones who have absolutely no chance of making it, and quit wasting our time and theirs. But still, no one has figured out the reverse. No one can say in advance: "These are the precise qualities that get someone through."

Suddenly the instructors were being asked to make extra efforts—what felt like extra allowances—to help the struggling candidates get through. There was undeniable pressure from above. I felt it. No one in senior leadership ever said explicitly to me: "You will do this. You are gonna graduate more guys." Everyone always said, "We're not asking you to compromise on quality." But there was definitely trickle-down guidance from above that added up to much the same thing: "Figure out how to take more risk and get more guys to graduation day."

You can imagine how well that went over with the suspicious instructor corps.

Everyone on the ground kept resisting the ease-up.

But top leaders kept intervening, greasing the path to graduation. An awful lot of do-overs became routine. When I went through SEAL training, you got four chances to pass drown-proofing, the fifty-meter underwater swim and the pool competency test. After a couple of tries, they might roll you back to another class for remedial help. But when I was running the Academic Review Boards and I was reviewing students' performance, some of them were getting ten, eleven, and twelve opportunities to pass their tests.

In the past, when the cadre would recommend up the chain of command that a candidate be dropped, nearly 100 percent of the time that person would be dropped. That changed, too. A disturbing number of times, students would be reinstated and sent back into the pipeline for another opportunity. This started to undermine the instructors' authority—and their ability to make the students believe that failing the next knot-tying exercise really matters. And if one class of recruits was feeling that, the impression would trickle into the next class as well.

It became a divisive and toxic time in our history. The SEAL instructors could barely contain themselves. Some threatened to quit. They said some questionable students were getting chance after chance to get through.

The instructors kept none of this to themselves. Very quickly, they shared their complaints with their operator buddies at the SEAL teams. These guys were all close. They were either just leaving tactical units to be instructors or going the other way. There aren't too many secrets inside the SEAL community.

"Stand by for some of the guys coming to the teams," the instructors said. "They have gotten way too many tries getting through this place."

I had an argument one day with a capable officer who went on to command one of the teams. At the time, he was a training director. I was saying that these multiple opportunities to pass were undermining the quality of SEAL training. This guy is fantastic with numbers and metrics and percentages and statistics. He pulled out a spreadsheet.

"Look at how much risk we're really taking," he said. "This is only going to generate somewhere between seventeen to thirty additional graduates a year. If those guys graduate, that will cover our quota in a couple of years. Honestly, it's seventeen to thirty guys. That is basically one platoon or one task unit. Don't you think we can absorb that? One platoon. It's not that many guys."

My response was instinctive, not political.

"Not a platoon I want to be in charge of," I said. "A group of guys who need five tries to get through the course of instruction—who'd want to be in charge of that platoon?"

To me, the calculation is simple. Growing the force is a nice goal. Some growth is probably a good thing. I take seriously the complexities of the world today and the valuable role the SEALs can play. With more SEALs, we could conduct more missions and do more good.

I just don't want to see what makes us great get watered down. Quality has to come first. That's what makes the SEALs the SEALs. America already has the best conventional forces on the planet. When large numbers are needed, they're the ones with the troop strength.

We almost never go on our missions alone. Someone has flown us there or shipped us there. Someone has collected the intelligence we're acting on. Someone is providing medical backup, technical support, or combat support. We love and need these guys. And generally speaking, we don't hang around for years or decades. We execute high-paced, short-duration targeted missions. We are small, nimble, and quick.

Elite organizations can't be mass-produced. Something gets lost in the multiplication.

Harvard is a great university. They have something special there. But I don't see the Harvard deans suggesting new Harvard branches in malls across America. In elite organizations, quality trumps quantity every time.

That said, the instructors can sometimes go overboard. As they kept being nudged to ease up, I'd sum up their reaction like this: *Let's see about that.* They proceeded to make BUD/S even harder, and it was already damn hard.

Constant improvement is one of the hallmarks of being a SEAL. That is what we do. For a sniper in a SEAL platoon, that means finding a way to alter his stance, to adjust his weapon, to apply some new change no one ever tried before. In ways small and large, that's how a SEAL sniper becomes a better sniper.

Something similar happens with SEAL instructors. They are always pushing the students harder, increasing the demands, making BUD/S better, which inevitably means making it a tougher experience. Pushing the curriculum, that's the absolute nature of a SEAL instructor's personality.

Over the years, SEAL training has gotten tougher as a result.

BUD/S instructors are always convinced they know exactly how to use the curriculum to push the students to precisely the right breaking point, which will soon enough reveal who are the right guys to get through. I believe it should still be hard. But I also believe there comes a point where BUD/S is hard enough to achieve what it is supposed to—to help us identify the right new guys for our brotherhood.

Anything beyond that is at least counterproductive and at worst dangerous.

I do believe that, without our even realizing it, the toughness was escalating. We used to do log PT for a couple of hours. It's a brutally punishing event. We would lunge with logs at a chest carry, standing in one spot. One of the first times I came to an event, my instructors were lunging the students with these logs all the way around the obstacle course—they wouldn't admit it but basically they were going to keep it going until someone or something broke. They wouldn't stop, not until someone was injured. They had pushed that class as hard as you could possibly push them. No one was quitting voluntarily. Everyone who was left had utterly proven himself. And the instructors kept pushing them.

I or my master chief, a highly responsible and disciplined and intense guy, had to pull the instructors aside and say, "Stop. We have to move to another evolution."

I felt very torn on that battleground. I really believed in the instructors, and I believed our job was to be the guardians of the brotherhood and see that the right candidates were getting through. But I could see there were a few instructors who had drifted off the reservation on how hard to be pushing students. And despite our legendary independence, we are a military organization. We do ultimately have to answer to people above.

Finally, I knew I had to address the entire instructor cadre. This whole issue of balance had turned into a war.

"You guys live this job passionately," I said. "That is the right thing to do. But I think you are about to lose the fight. I think you will be replaced if you don't find a way to balance the playing field a little. Then the floodgates will open. You won't be able to protect the brotherhood. All that we worked for will be in other people's hands. I don't even want to think what that might mean."

In terms of SEAL training, this was our Cuban Missile Crisis. Very few people know how close we came to disaster in October 1962. The same thing was happening here. There was an alarming chance that SEAL training would be put in the hands of civilians or retired SEALs or conventional Navy instructors. Someone would follow orders and they'd get more people through some lighter version of SEAL training, regardless of the quality that produced.

"I'm not saying cancel BUD/S or make it Diet BUD/S or BUD/S Light," I told the cadre. "But this is as bad as it's ever been. I think we've begun to lose sight of what we're doing here. We're not here to destroy people. We are here to select the right guys.

"We're gonna lose a lot of guys in the first three days of Hell Week," I said. "By about day four, no one's gonna quit. Someone might get hurt. But by Wednesday night, most of the guys who are here are staying here. You need to recognize that and you need to throttle back a bit. We're not gonna change water temperature. We're not gonna keep them dry. We're not gonna give them warm towels and tell them to put their feet up. But by then, we have the core of the guys who are going to get through Hell Week and get through training and join this brotherhood."

"They are the future," I wanted them to understand. "We should be proud that our program has identified them."

"If it's four or if it's eighty, I don't care," I said. "There is always going to be a worst guy in a class of any size. And if you get the class down to one, he'll be the worst and the best guy."

How was all this resolved? It hasn't been.

Through trial and error and much grinding debate, I believe we have managed to find a balance that is close to right. The cadre and the top leadership both seem to get what we are doing here.

The instructors seem to have found a level everyone can live with. BUD/S is still extraordinarily difficult, far tougher than when I went through, tougher than when I returned to Coronado as a training officer after my Iraq deployment. And yet in the past three years we have graduated some of the largest classes the training center has ever seen.

Both sides have gotten much of what they needed.

Instructors still grumble sometimes about pressure from above, just as the leadership still grumbles about uncooperative instructors. That tension is probably inevitable, maybe even healthy. In the end, we still need a better understanding of what all that toughness is for. It's not to torture. It's not to injure. It's not to drive away. It's certainly not to meet some politician's or some general's quota of how big the force should be.

We're making SEAL warriors here, and the world has never needed them more than at this moment in history. That has to mean something. We're creating a challenge that will help the community discover—and help the candidates discover—who the right new guys should be.

another round of beers or Scotch whisky—or an especially difficult fight.

"To all those who have been downrange, to us and to those like us. Damn few." That was the modern-warfare version Dave came up with.

I liked that. It felt like us on the beach, a special group of warriors heading into battle together, not an ounce of hesitation among the whole lot of us.

---

hen they asked if we'd like to be in a movie, all of us answered exactly the same way.

"No."

Dave, Sonny, Ajay, all of us—immediately, emphatically, unequivocally, "No."

A bunch of active-duty SEALs teaming up with a couple of independent Hollywood directors to appear in a big-screen feature film—I don't think so. We weren't actors. We were SEALs, secret warriors, the quiet professionals of the battlefield, famously suspicious of outside attention, shrouded in decades of mystery and intrigue.

We'd had that old refrain drummed into our heads for years: Do your job—and keep your mouth shut.

So of course I was wary—more than wary—when Mike "Mouse" McCoy and Scott Waugh showed up in Coronado in the summer of 2008, saying they wanted to make a movie about the SEALs. The Bandito Brothers, Mouse and Scott called their production company, weren't total strangers to our community. Two years earlier, they'd been hired by the Naval Special Warfare Command to make an online recruiting video about the Special Warfare Combatant-

17

OUT OF THE SHADOWS

*Take time to deliberate, but when the time
for action comes, stop thinking and go in.*
—Napoleon Bonaparte

We had already shot the bonfire scene. Like all the scenes in *Act of Valor,* it came right out of the SEALs' experiences at war. Scott, one of the directors, had asked me what I would say to the guys as we were heading out on deployment. Did I give a little speech to get them motivated? I told him they didn't need to be motivated. They couldn't wait to get to war. I told him that before a deployment I liked to talk to the guys about balance. Without balance in life, a warrior will have problems on the battlefield. I said it while the cameras were rolling just like I'd said it plenty of times before.

When we were finished filming that part of the scene, Scott asked, "Does someone have a toast or something?"

I didn't have a toast. But Chief Dave came up with one. He said he'd heard it a couple of times from other SEALs. It came originally from something people used to say in Scotland, Dave told us. It was a short poem or incantation that might be uttered on the way to craft Crewmen who operate and maintain our high-performance boats. That video, which was shot during a couple of training exercises, came out great. The footage was dramatic. That video gave an unusually vivid overview of how important and special the boat teams are.

Even ordering a recruiting video was a little unusual for the SEALs. We always thought that slick recruitment promos were for branches of the service that had trouble attracting manpower.

But this was a unique period in our history—and our nation's. America was fighting two wars at once, in Iraq and Afghanistan. The SEAL leadership was reluctantly open to the idea of creating a higher public profile, as long as it could be done *our* way.

Now Mouse and Scott were back with a truly ambitious plan. No little video this time. They had been green-lighted by the most senior SEAL leadership to make a full-length, high-impact, theater-release, military-action movie about the SEAL brotherhood. Not just a gunfight movie. Not just another blood-and-guts war film. Something that looked great on the screen but also represented us in a way that was authentic.

Just meeting those two, you could tell they weren't your typical Hollywood hotshots. Before they'd ever gotten behind a camera, both had built careers as movie and TV stuntmen. They'd been jumping off rooftops, falling through windows, and taking punches from Vin Diesel and Sylvester Stallone and two full generations of major action stars. Mouse was also a champion off-road motorcycle racer who'd won the grueling Baja 500 and Baja 1000. Scott was the son of the original "Spiderman," Fred Waugh. With his dad, he'd developed the 35 mm helmet-cam and an innovative handheld camera called the Pogo Cam, which brought higher levels of intensity and realism to fast-paced onscreen action. They were scrappy, focused, and eager to prove themselves on the toughest possible terrain. Calling their little company the SEALs of Hollywood wouldn't be entirely wrong.

"We want to do this right," Scott said the first day he and Mouse returned to Coronado. They repeated that intention over and over again.

But if they were going to make a SEAL movie that was anywhere close to the truth, they had to interview some SEALs.

About twenty-five of us were invited—more like ordered—by the Navy public-affairs office to report to the beach one morning and speak with the movie directors. The half-hour interviews would be videotaped. But they wouldn't be released. This was backstory information, research that might help the filmmakers figure out what to put in their film.

I didn't make any special preparations. I showed up in my regular blue instructor T-shirt. The questions Mouse and Scott asked were basic conversational stuff. Where are you from? What made you join the SEALs? What about the SEAL teams appealed to you? What was training like? What jobs have you had?

I think Mouse and Scott were impressed by the SEALs' diversity, that we weren't all giant storm troopers with a one-dimensional focus on war. The guys they interviewed were a typical SEAL cross section of backgrounds and types, and most of us had families who meant a lot to us. We spoke about our time on the battlefield and our role as trained warriors. But several of the guys also shared their personal motivations, their commitment to service, their deep desire to protect their families, their country, and their brother SEALs.

If Mouse and Scott were surprised to be hearing this, I think some of the SEALs were just as surprised to be saying it so directly. That certainly applied to me.

I got choked up when I talked about Mikey jumping on the grenade in Iraq. I never discussed that with anyone. I wasn't on the rooftop when that happened. But it was such a powerful thing in our mythology, serving with a guy who was willing to do that without hesitation.

A couple of weeks later, I got a call from the captain who was the Navy's project leader for the film. "I'd like to show you a video compilation they put together from those interviews," he said. "Would it be okay if I stopped by your house?"

He arrived the next day.

It was just a short montage, not even five minutes long. But I couldn't believe how powerful those edited interviews were. Hearing Dave and Sonny and me talking about our SEAL experiences and our lives. Clearly, the Banditos knew how to tell a story. I didn't even remember saying half the things I said.

When we finished watching the video, the captain said to me: "The directors would like to meet with you and your wife. They are interested in casting you and Dave in the lead roles in what will become a theatrical-release movie."

No one had mentioned the idea of us being *in* the movie. I told the captain it didn't sound like something I'd be interested in. Maybe I could offer them some guidance on their story or be a sounding board. But I didn't see myself doing something like that.

"SEAL, not actor," I whispered to Tracy as the captain walked to his car.

Scott and Mouse didn't waste any time getting back to San Diego. Those crafty little bastards showed up at my house with a really beautiful bouquet of flowers for Tracy. We'd barely sat down in the living room when they had me opening up again. We talked about my grandfather, who was killed in World War II as a member of a B-24 Liberator aircraft fighting squadron. They asked me why Churchill meant so much to me. Then they presented their case for me being in this movie.

They'd gotten into the editing room, Scott and Mouse said, and they were moved at what they saw and heard. Powerful stories. Gripping stories. Humble stories from real-life warriors who rarely if ever spoke like that and, frankly, didn't seem to realize how inspiring their experiences were. When he and Scott were watching the raw footage, Mouse said, the idea hit them like a rifle butt. "If we're gonna do this right," he said, "we have to cast the real guys."

No professional actors could tell this story as effectively. Only real SEALs could do justice to the role of SEALs. These roles required a genuine understanding of the human dimension of these characters, plus, for the battle scenes, an extraordinary level of special-operations training and skill.

"Here's how I can explain it," Mouse said. "It would be way easier to teach Navy SEALs how to act than to teach actors how to be Navy SEALs."

The real-SEALs idea was not well received in Hollywood. The industry experts and shrewd investors seemed skeptical as well. You can't cast a bunch of no-name military guys in a big action movie and expect to put a lot of butts in the cineplex seats. Active-duty SEALs might be wonderful warriors, but they aren't trained actors. And no one's ever heard of them. Put Colin Farrell, the Rock, or Chris Hemsworth in the movie, said the people who supposedly knew.

But Scott and Mouse wouldn't budge. They'd raise their own money, they decided, and take their chances with us.

"You and Dave are the right guys for the leads," Mouse said before they left the house that night. "We believe we can make something very special here. We believe we can represent your community authentically like it has never been done before." If we agreed to participate, he said, we would get full veto over the story to ensure they didn't screw it up or reveal anything they shouldn't. "If it doesn't happen on the battlefield or in your lives," he said, "we don't want it in the film. We will expect you to keep us honest here."

I nodded as he spoke. Then I told him what I'd told him before.

"No."

And I meant it.

"We don't do that," I told Mouse and Scott before they left. "Nobody's gonna do that."

Over the next few weeks, though, I started thinking about what the directors had been saying and the kind of movie they wanted to make. I reflected on our responsibility as America's preeminent special operators, our power to inspire and our need for public understanding and support. I considered the reality that in this super-saturated media world of ours, if you don't tell your own story, someone else will tell it—and not necessarily the way you'd like.

We'd been shrouded in secrecy so long and for good reason. But maybe there were also some benefits to a little more openness. The Navy leadership, the SEAL command, my teammates—everyone would have to be behind it. But the world really could use a truer understanding of this brotherhood of ours—what motivated us and what we were capable of. And I had a good feeling about Mouse and Scott and their integrity.

Tracy and I discussed it. She had my back either way. "Your experience in the SEAL teams and what you want to reveal is more important to you than to me," she said. "What I do know is you can represent the brotherhood in ways few SEAL leaders could."

Dave and I met for coffee. We discussed the pros and cons. He and I were working at First Phase together, where he was one of my chiefs. We had run a shift of Hell Week together for five or six classes. We trusted each other fully.

It occurred to both of us that eventually somebody was going to say yes. We didn't want it to be the wrong guys—self-promoting "lethal killers" who'd never earned the respect of the SEAL community.

"Well," Dave finally said, "if you're doing it, I'm interested."

I said, "I'll do it if you're interested."

At that point, it just felt right. We knew we could have input into the story. We knew we could protect the secrets. We knew we could have some influence over who the other guys in the film would be.

The final group selected for the film was absolutely first-rate: Sonny, Weimy, Ray, Ajay, Mike, and interrogator Van O, along with the captain, Dave, and me. We were placed on official Navy orders to support the project. Our leadership was on board.

Word spread quickly through the community. There was going to be a no-kidding movie—not a documentary—featuring active-duty Navy SEALs. I wouldn't say everyone was instantly supportive. But the overwhelming reaction was very positive. "If somebody's gonna do it," people said, "I'm glad it's you guys, some of the real meat-eaters."

The screenwriter was Kurt Johnstad, who'd written the screenplay for *300*, about King Leonidas and the force of three hundred men who fought the Persians at Thermopylae in 480 BC. Working from interviews with all of us, Kurt wove together a plot from our community's recent history. The guidance he got from Scott and Mouse was, "We want you to write a script that has a geopolitically current-threat scenario, woven around five 'acts of valor.'" Relying heavily on real stories, that's exactly what the writer did.

Several of the plot points involved battlefield moments from our era of warfare plus a couple of scenes ripped right from my life. A SEAL with his eye shot out keeps on fighting. Another SEAL jumps on a grenade to save his teammates' lives. An operator is shot twenty-five times and still walks to a helicopter that takes him to the hospital.

Act of Valor, the movie would be called.

It took almost four years to get the film made. Much of the principal photography occurred during preplanned SEAL training exercises—with live ammunition and real explosives going off. No one has ever made a war movie that was any more real than this. The weapons were real. The aircraft and boats were real. What looks in the movie like an armed nuclear-powered submarine really was an armed nuclear-powered submarine, the first time the Navy ever made one of those available for a movie shoot. "You've got forty-five minutes" to be at a certain lat-long, the filmmakers were told. "The boat is going to surface there. Then we're going back under. You'll get your footage, and you can leave when the boat surfaces again."

This could only have happened with the full support of Big Navy and the Department of Defense.

With their stunt backgrounds and quick-action minds, Scott and Mouse knew how to safely choreograph violent action scenes the Hollywood way. But they had some things to learn about the SEAL way. More than once as they were blocking out a raid or rescue, we stopped the action prematurely. "No, no, no," one of us said. "If we did it like you're suggesting, we'd all get killed."

We were filming a jungle scene at the John C. Stennis Space Center in southern Mississippi, where the SEALs often conduct immediate-action drills. The filmmakers had preplanned how they would shoot us rushing a waterside compound.

"Wait," Chief Dave said halfway into the walk-through. "If this were a real mission, that isn't how we would do it. That's not the door we'd use. That's not the order we would go in."

Scott and Mouse and their cameramen clearly were not used to having actors choreograph their own scenes. But the crew listened to everything we said. I think that turned out to be a real aha moment for them.

"Why don't we sketch it out for you," I said.

Thirty seconds later, half a dozen SEALs were crouched on the ground with a large piece of butcher paper and a black Sharpie pen, diagramming a complex raid. It didn't look so different from a football coach's X's, O's, lines, and arrows. We'd done this hundreds of times in training and in war. In less than ten minutes, we had a basic mission brief.

The camera operators shifted their position and we did the raid the real SEAL way.

Things really started humming at that point. We wore helmet-cams. We gave the directors a fast-paced inside view. We showed them how to stand just an inch or two outside the live fire. And they were fearless. They climbed into the water with us. They stomped around with us in the muck and the mud with the snakes and the alligators. They weren't even spooked by the tracer fire.

The directors told us that no one had shot a movie like that since the 1930s, when blanks replaced live bullets in Hollywood. But the Bandito crew loved the live-fire sound, even if they did end up sacrificing a couple of cameras. The experience gave one or two cameramen nightmares, but we didn't kill anyone.

You could have a few tiny quibbles with what ended up on the screen. Some things were inserted for the sake of storytelling or drama. On a real op, SEALs might not dog-paddle across a bayou in full combat gear—not before searching for a nearby bridge. There's a scene aboard a C-130 transport plane. After the ramp has been lowered for a free-fall rescue mission, Chief Dave and I are talking without our oxygen masks. The dialogue is easier to hear that way, but we'd have had real trouble breathing.

IN MY YEARS as a SEAL assault team member, I've found myself in more than my share of dangerous situations, encounters I thought I might never get out of alive. But none of those was quite the equal of kissing a beautiful actress while my wife watched my every move on a live video feed, my wife who had just delivered our first baby four days before.

The directors of *Act of Valor* had asked Tracy to play a character based largely on her, the wife of a SEAL lieutenant whose husband keeps rushing off to war.

No way.

Tracy always looks gorgeous. And I'm probably not the only husband who found his wife especially beautiful immediately after childbirth. And Tracy, I'll bet, isn't the only woman who, when asked to appear on film for worldwide release just after delivering a baby, would respond with something to the effect of "Are you totally nuts?"

The actress who was cast, Ailsa Marshall, was a pro. She and Tracy had a great conversation before we shot the good-bye make-out scene. Tracy explained how she reacted when I was leaving on a deployment.

A few minutes before the cameras rolled, Ailsa and I finally had a chance to talk. She was nice and businesslike. She didn't seem at all uncomfortable about kissing me—or, to be honest, especially excited at the chance.

"Are these the kind of roles you usually get, the wife and mother?" I asked her.

"No," she laughed. "I'm usually cast as the slut or the bitch."

She played the scene perfectly, I thought, holding her bubbling emotion right below the surface as our characters hugged and kissed and said good-bye, then erupting in tears and collapsing on the floor as soon as I shut the door behind me.

We probably shot that scene forty times. Ten takes from one angle. Ten takes from another. Twenty takes from a third. My lips were almost chapped by the time we were done. And for every last take, Tracy was watching the live feed. I was kissing this beautiful young woman, who is theoretically her but isn't her. In the world of dicey operations, this one definitely merited at least an "Oh, boy!"

I'd say I got off easy.

"Rough day at work, huh?" was all Tracy said when we were finally finished.

"Doing what I gotta do for God and country," I said with a smile.

I love *Platoon, Apocalypse Now, Saving Private Ryan,* and HBO's *Band of Brothers* series. But to me, *Act of Valor* stands alone, blending professional moviemaking with real-life operators who actually know what they're doing out there. And when it was done, the Banditos ended up with a $13 million film that looked like $200 million on the screen, an amazingly true-to-life military-adventure film made for not much more than Tom Cruise's catering bill.

Not everyone appreciated this greater openness. Some of the old-timers especially had trouble getting used to it. Just as *Act of Valor* was coming out, retired Lieutenant General James Vaught personally assailed Admiral William McRaven, commander of the U.S. Special Operations Command, for drawing too much attention to the bin Laden raid, the rescue of aid workers in Somalia, and other recent SEAL successes.

"Back when my special operators extracted Saddam from the hole, we didn't say one damn word about it," the retired general said. "We turned him over to the local commander and told him to claim that his forces drug him out of the hole, and he did so. And we just faded away and kept our mouth shut."

With all the recent attention SEALs have been getting, the general said, "the other guy's going to be there ready for you, and you're going to fly in and he's going to shoot down every damn helicopter and kill every one of your SEALs. Now, watch it happen. Mark my words. Get the hell out of the media. Your comment?"

McRaven didn't get personal or say anything rude. In fact, the admiral started out quite warmly.

"I'm not sure how I follow that up," said McRaven, who'd risen through the SEAL officer ranks before assuming command of all U.S. special forces.

"One of the reasons I became a Navy SEAL," he said, "was my sister was dating a Green Beret. It's a little-known secret. And the Green Beret actually convinced me to become a Navy SEAL. But the reason I was so infatuated was I had seen this movie starring John Wayne called *The Green Berets*."

I'd never heard that story from the admiral before, and I don't think too many other people had.

"So the fact of the matter is, there have always been portrayals of SOF out in the mainstream media," Admiral McRaven said. "We are in an environment today where we can't get away from it. It is not something that we actively pursue, as I think a number of the journalists here in the audience will confirm. But the fact of the matter is, with the social media being what it is today, with the press and the twenty-four-hour news cycle, it's very difficult to get away from it."

McRaven wasn't done.

"But not only does the media focus on our successes," he noted. "We have had a few failures. And I think having those failures exposed in the media also kind of helps focus our attention, helps us do a better job. So sometimes the criticism, the critique, the spotlight on us actually makes us better."

After that exchange, some of the sniping about the movie seemed to die down. Partly, I think, that was because a handful of early screenings were held for military officials. Some of the early critics got to see what was actually in the film. They realized their apprehension was wildly overblown. We were extolling the heroism of

SEALs and our sister services, shining a light on the brotherhood, sharing SEAL values with the broader world—but never once compromising any operational secrets.

To bring attention to the film, most of the SEALs in the movie flew to three red-carpet *Act of Valor* premieres. We didn't go in the usual Hollywood luxury. We flew coach, had government-rate rooms at modest hotels, and got no red-carpet swag. We were on government orders, the same as on any official trip. But it seemed like everyone wanted to meet the "real SEALs who were in the movie." Weimy couldn't make it. He was deployed in Afghanistan. We wore our dress uniforms, not something we got to do very often. Lots of people came up and said, "Thank you"—more for our service, I think, than our screen time. We answered questions from the media about being SEALs and playing SEALs. "The hardest part was saying the lines," Ajay told one reporter. "Running around and shooting guns and moving and communicating—that's commonplace. That's nothing."

I don't have much experience with red-carpet movie premieres, but I'll bet not too many of them have been like ours. In Nashville, the guests included country music stars Keith Urban, Wynonna Judd, Trace Adkins, and Jake Owen, all of whom had contributed songs to the *Act of Valor* soundtrack. In New York, we did a special screening at the Intrepid Sea, Air and Space Museum, a retired World War II aircraft carrier docked in the Hudson River off the west side of Manhattan. In the audience that night were hundreds of first responders, New York cops, firefighters, and paramedics, many of whom had rushed to the World Trade Center on September 11, 2001. They stood and cheered as the credits rolled. Quite a few of them wept openly. It was an honor to meet those men and women.

The Hollywood premiere got most of the flash. As Arnold Schwarzenegger, Tim Tebow, and other celebs mingled in front of the Arc-Light cinema on Sunset Boulevard, six Navy SEALs dropped from the California night sky, parachuting right onto the red carpet. It was quite a dramatic drop-in.

Tracy, who'd been to about as many Hollywood premieres over the years as I had—zero—came to the event. She'd had some concern about what to wear. But Mouse said he could help with that. His wife, Carm, came down to San Diego, rented a hotel suite, had it filled with designer dresses and shoes, and let Tracy take her pick. Don't ask me who designed the dress she wore. All I know is she looked fabulous.

Amid all this, *Act of Valor* got excellent pre-opening buzz. As the trailers began to play in the theaters across the country and ads appeared on network TV—three in the Super Bowl between the New York Giants and the New England Patriots—people were saying the action scenes were amazingly true to life.

I hadn't told many of my college and back-home friends that I was in a movie. When those Super Bowl ads hit, my cell phone exploded with shocked calls.

The story sounded uplifting. People were intrigued by the idea of Navy SEALs playing Navy SEALs. And when the film finally opened, it opened huge. That first week, *Act of Valor* was the number-one box-office draw in America, making back the film's production costs in just a few days. I can only imagine the frantic backpedaling by those experts in Hollywood.

I didn't read the reviews, although my mom told me some of the critics, while praising the authentic action, complained that the SEALs were not trained, professional actors. Guilty as charged. To those who thought the SEALs didn't come across the way that SEALs were supposed to, Mouse had the perfect comeback: "They *are* SEALs. What you see on the screen is exactly who SEALs are and what SEALs do. These guys are as real as moviemaking gets."

18

GLOBAL PURSUIT

*Two qualities are indispensable: first, an intellect
that even in the darkest hour retains some glimmerings of
the inner light which leads to truth and second,
the courage to follow this faint light wherever it may lead.*
—CARL VON CLAUSEWITZ

I'd been back in San Diego a good while when a text came in saying twenty-three SEALs were killed in a helicopter crash coming to the aid of Army Rangers in Afghanistan. The names hadn't been released yet, but I had a lot of good friends on that team.

I was at Sea World with Tracy and the girls when I got the news. The dolphin show was getting ready to start. The music was coming up. The cast members were stepping out. And I was sitting there with my family.

It hit me all at once. I was glad I was wearing sunglasses because I began to tear up. Tracy could tell. "What's going on?" she asked.

I'm not sure if it was the number—or the fact that the SEALs were rushing to help another unit in distress. I had known plenty of SEALs killed in action. But this one just seemed so close.

I needed a minute or two. "Families just like ours," I said to Tracy, "their kids won't be able to go to Sea World with their dads anymore. I get to go with you three because buddies of mine are dying in a helicopter in Afghanistan."

Twenty-plus families were about to walk into a nightmare that every family prays they will never experience. And here I was, sitting in the stands, surrounded by hundreds of good people who were just living their lives, and none of them had any idea what had just occurred on the other side of the world.

A bunch of absolute professionals who had committed their entire lives to chasing the nation's enemies had just paid the ultimate price on behalf of all of us.

As the war in Afghanistan trudged on and on, I found myself increasingly wondering: What are we still doing there? I think a lot of people were wondering the same thing, even some of the SEALs who'd been fighting so valiantly in what had become America's longest-running military conflict.

Most well-read, educated people—academics, students of history—would have said early on: "When it comes to Afghanistan, invade if you need to, but do not plan on staying for long. Just don't. Afghanistan is the graveyard of empires." The British discovered that the hard way. The Russians certainly did. So did occupying powers going back to Alexander the Great. The terrain, the warlords, the corruption, the weather, and the fiercely independent tribesmen—they all conspire against foreign powers in Afghanistan. I'm a sports guy. I know how to read a box score. In Afghanistan, the visiting team is currently 0 and 42.

Someone overlooked that history lesson, and I don't mean the U.S. and British special operators who led the invasion or the hundreds of thousands of conventional troops who followed them in. Under highly trying circumstances, they did everything they were asked to and more. The problem was an outmoded strategy. On a twenty-first-century battlefield, America decided to prosecute a twentieth-century war. The mistake wasn't that we went in so aggressively. The mistake was hanging around so long. Afghanistan should have been conceived from the start as a limited-duration special-operations campaign. That would have achieved what we needed to and allowed us all to move on.

U.S. troops, along with a handful of allies and fighters from the Afghan Northern Alliance, launched Operation Enduring Freedom on October 7, 2001—and for good reason. Less than a month earlier, al Qaeda terrorists had committed the worst mass murder in U.S. history. The evidence was clear: The terror network had been using Afghanistan as a training base with the full agreement of the country's Taliban government.

The initial action unfolded in a series of violent, aggressive special-ops assaults led by the Navy SEALs, Green Berets, the Army Rangers, the British SAS, and other elite commandos. Almost all of that went our way. The U.S. air support, from drones and manned aircraft, was overwhelming. The Taliban fighters were simply no match for our special-ops teams or for the conventional U.S. Marine and Army units who backed us up. The results were swift and dramatic. The Taliban regime was ousted in a few short weeks. Most of the senior Taliban leaders fled to neighboring Pakistan. Our handpicked choice, Hamid Karzai, was installed as Afghanistan's interim president three days before Christmas.

And that, right then, would have been an excellent time to leave.

By then, we had killed or chased off—rough estimate—60 to 80

percent of the active Taliban mujahideen and almost all of their protected al Qaeda buddies. We had degraded the enemy's fighting capacity by similar amounts. Very quickly, we'd achieved most of what
we came for, delivering an appropriate response to 9/11. It was time to
go. But before we departed, we should have left a note on the ground
in Mullah Mohammed Omar's stronghold, reminding the Taliban
chief and his fundamentalist followers what would surely happen if
they ever decided to harbor al Qaeda again:

"Do not make us return. It will be worse next time."

Instead, like so many powers before us, the United States got
bogged down in a deadly and expensive occupation and nation-building
campaign that has proven almost impossible to extract ourselves from.
As a culture, those Afghan tribal warriors are tougher than we are.
That's just a fact. They hold blood feuds with each other for generations. They truly respect killing. They seem almost admiring when
their enemies put up a good fight. Whether it was Alexander, Genghis Khan, Timur, or the Mughal Empire, the people of Afghanistan
have had ample experience tangling with powerful invaders, sometimes overwhelmingly powerful ones. What sends the Afghanis into a
blood-boiling frenzy, what makes them crazy, is being occupied. Their
independence matters to them more than almost anything. Being under the control of a foreign power goes totally against their most basic
tenets in life. No matter how much they hate their own government
or how much they hate the tribe one mountain pass away—they cannot abide occupation.

We should have approached Afghanistan like a sudden punch in
the face—hard, quick, and done. That's what's most effective with
these terror-age enemies.

I understand the argument on the other side. It has some merit. A
decade of war got us Osama bin Laden. The pressure we applied, the
intelligence we gathered—that long and rocky path through the

Hindu Kush led eventually to Abbottabad. But no one can say that wouldn't have happened anyway.

Iraq presented similar issues. It's all a matter of using our military power in the most effective ways. I'm not suggesting that the SEALs didn't contribute during those long occupations in Iraq and Afghanistan. They contributed mightily. Every unit did. The SEALs and special-ops commandos remained deployed and highly active the entire time the U.S. military was present, making momentum-shifting contributions to both fights.

We're still the best. We have the absolute top-shelf guys. But the truth of the matter is that in both countries many of the missions we were involved in could have been handled by conventional Army and Marine units.

Iraq and Afghanistan have provided the conventional forces a tremendous chance to hone their own deadly expertise. Nothing builds battle prowess like going into battle, and since 9/11, our entire military has had nearly endless opportunities for that. Experience counts in war, and they've been getting lots of it. So the gap between conventional and special ops has been narrowing. They're getting awfully good at this stuff. And with every raid they go on and each roadside firefight, they're narrowing that gap some more. There will soon come a time, if it isn't here already, that conventional Army and Marine units can handle many of the aggressive battlefield encounters that we performed so effectively.

It's great to see those Army and Marine conventionals develop beyond their traditional roles and grow into more comfortable and cohesive units.

I'm not saying we should change the SEALs' objective entirely. I can never envision the day when SEALs don't conduct assault missions and commando raids. These really are at the core of our warfighting skills. And even in the video-game era of high-tech drone wars, there will always be times to suit up for action and get the job done. Plus, let's admit the obvious. Those adrenaline-pumping missions are really, really fun.

But if the others can do some of what we've been doing, maybe it's time for us to find some new and exciting challenges. It's about recognizing which important tasks the SEALs are uniquely qualified for. There won't be just one thing, of course. We have never been a one-hit wonder.

We have a real opportunity here, coming off bin Laden and the pirates and some of our less publicized but even dicier missions. We've proven ourselves quite dramatically in that realm. We are lethal. We are patient. We know how to leverage intelligence and local assets. And around the world, the message has been clearly received by our enemies and potential enemies: "Even if it takes us a decade, we will get you."

I see a new direction for the SEALs, one we are perfectly suited for. As we look forward, we should be out roaming the earth in Global Pursuit Teams to capture or kill the worst of the worst of the worst. It's an idea I've been interested in for a while now. Its time has very much come.

We could take our inspiration from the FBI's Ten Most Wanted List, the one that used to hang at the local post office, and create a new Global Pursuit Ten Most Wanted List. Yesterday's domestic bad guys with their scrunched-up faces, distinguishing marks, and creepy nicknames fired the imaginations of a million future cops, prosecutors, and federal agents—and recruited the American public into J. Edgar Hoover's nationwide law-and-order dragnet. It was great PR for the bureau. Whenever they nabbed someone, the special agents would hold press conferences and trade attaboys while thanking the local authorities for being so cooperative. Not infrequently, some ruthless killer, kidnapper, or bank robber from the list would inspire a full episode of the popular ABC television series *The F.B.I.* Sometimes, at the end of the hour, Efrem Zimbalist Jr. would come on with an update on a real-life Ten Most Wanted case.

Today's international bad guys are far worse than the criminals Inspector Erskine and Special Agent Colby used to nab. Terror is just another tool for today's Most Wanted. They are frequently aligned with violent guerrilla movements and protected by corrupt governments. Their motives often go beyond personal passion or monetary gain. The havoc they inflict knows no bounds.

I like the idea of personalizing the hunt. We can say: "This is who I'm assigning in the Special Operations Command to hunt you down. That will be their job. This team won't be building bridges. They won't be performing medical support operations. They won't be engaged in nation-building partnerships with other foreign nationals. The only thing they'll be doing is globally pursuing you. Yes, you. Wherever you are, this special team will be hunting for you."

I think it would be great if the president said, "The entire special-operations budget is now devoted to chasing bad guys. We'll put individual spec-op country teams in Chad or Yemen or Indonesia" and wherever else makes sense. "You will grow beards and blend in with the local populations. You will partner with other U.S. three-letter agencies and share intelligence. You'll make connections and figure out who's bad and who's good. You'll develop those networks and those alliances."

Then a phone call would go back to SOCOM. The assault force would head back into action. We would just start knocking characters off the list.

Let's go get 'em, I say.

Moving across borders like that brings up all kinds of international issues, but they are not unsolvable. It may mean negotiating a deal with the government in Country X. We'd call the president of

Country X and say, "Here's the deal. We have actual intelligence, and this is a one-shot opportunity. We know he is at this grid location in your country. We can hit him alone. You can hit him alone. You can hit him with us. Or you can do nothing. We're giving you those four options. It's the only time we're giving you this information, and it's the only time we'll ask permission to come do it. We believe vital American and world interests are met by taking this character out."

If that country says, "We'll get him," we'll see if they do. If they do, "Great. Job done. We appreciate it. Aid continues to flow into your country." If they say, "We'll partner with you—let's do it together"—sweet. We'll put local guys in the helicopter. Together, we'll get the target. If they say, "Come get him," you know we will. If they say, "No," we'll say, "Fine. No more aid comes to your country. Done. Not a dime gets sent from American funds to your nation until we get him. You have chosen to harbor this international outlaw." Then we leave.

And if we decide to go in anyway—well, I think we've proven we know how to slip in and out of challenging places and take care of some serious business while we're there. Just ask Osama bin Laden.

Regardless of which approach we follow, we'll announce it: "Okay. Got him. He's off the Global Pursuit Ten Most Wanted List. Who's moving up?' "

Just announcing these Global Pursuit teams and their Top Ten mission would be a psychological nightmare for any of those targets. "Son of a bitch," they'd be thinking to themselves. "Ten years, and they found bin Laden, barely living, hiding in a damn house. The SEALs got him."

I don't mind the world's worst characters glancing over their shoulders, constantly concerned about when the SEALs will arrive. Worrying when Big D's breacher charge will bust open the door to their hideaway, when Sonny and Josh will appear with their heavy machine guns, when Lope will be standing outside with his big green radio calling in air support, when our snipers have eyes on and the end is near.

THE CHOICE TO SERVE is the best decision I have made in my life, short of marrying Tracy. As most of my friends went out to make a living, I was discovering what I was made of and how I could give some part of that back.

Every minute of this SEAL experience has been clean for me. I joined for the same reasons most of my brothers did—because it meant something special for each of us. The fact that the journey was exceptionally difficult was a big part of what made it so appealing to me. It has been an incredible honor to be part of a community that believes in taking on great challenges and does what it takes to meet them.

That mind-set is hugely potent. It applies to many things in life.

I am not certain what is next for me. When you've been through the things that we have, everything that follows is a gift. Your perspective is forever changed. You don't worry about things that a lot of people worry about. You know you can withstand the daily inconveniences. You know you can meet the most hideous challenges. As you look forward, you know that you can always find a way to do things right.

I know for a fact I will continue to serve.

I have a commitment in my head. I plan to carry it with me. My sword has been and will forever remain in the service of the nation. But it turns out that the values that SEALs live by, the values that SEALs measure themselves by, apply far more broadly.

Be excellent.

It pays to be a winner.

The only easy day was yesterday.

Don't ever let your teammates down.

Carry your full measure of the load.

Don't disrespect the game by not preparing fully or playing it as well as you possibly can. Be present always.

That's really what it's all about, wherever we find our battlefields. All of us are carrying our own piece of the load and carrying someone else's if we're needed.

I will do my best to follow the inspiration of Tecumseh, a message so pure and powerful, I'll be passing it on to my girls.

"Live your life," the Shawnee chief said, "that the fear of death can never enter your heart."

I have, and it won't.

THE WARRIOR'S BOOKSHELF

ANCIENT WAR

The Peloponnesian War, by Thucydides
You thought Iraq and Afghanistan dragged on long? This brilliantly crafted account of ancient warfare explores the earliest attempts at democracy. Written by a true historical and philosophical genius.

Scipio Africanus: Greater than Napoleon, by B. H. Liddell Hart
Timeless lessons from one of history's few undefeated warriors. An insightful read for leaders and military strategists.

The Art of War, by Sun Tzu
The definitive work of military strategy and tactics, attributed to a high-ranking Chinese general of the late 400s BC. Everything you need to know to wage war.

Gates of Fire, by Steven Pressfield
Intensely dramatic, perfectly nuanced, this meticulous novel has achieved mythic status among modern warriors. The gold standard of warrior-brotherhood fiction, our culture at its most extreme.

MODERN WAR

The Personal Memoirs of Ulysses S. Grant
There is no finer memoir of a military career.

Once an Eagle, by Anton Myrer
An incredible novel about leadership, selflessness, and courage, it follows a career U.S. Army officer from the Mexican expedition to Vietnam. Great stuff.

On Combat, by Lieutenant Colonel Dave Grossman
A fascinating exploration of the physiology and psychology of deadly-force encounters, and what happens to men's bodies and minds when they go to war.

An Army at Dawn: The War in North Africa, 1942–1943, vol. 1 of the Liberation Trilogy, by Rick Atkinson
The crucial but often forgotten lessons of World War II's North Africa campaign.

Matterhorn: A Novel of the Vietnam War, by Karl Marlantes
Incredible novel of young men at war, although I may be biased. The story follows BRAVO Company. I was always a BRAVO Platoon SEAL.

Band of Brothers, by Stephen E. Ambrose
Do I really even need to go into detail?

Blood Meridian: Or the Evening Redness in the West, by Cormac McCarthy
Because writing about violence and the borderlands just doesn't get any better.

Last of the Breed, by Louis L'Amour
The great gunfighter novelist of the Wild West explores the world of U.S. Air Force test pilots. No special military leadership lessons, just a fun, gripping read.

THE IDEALS WE FIGHT FOR

Declaration of Independence
Because it is staggering in foresight and beautiful in language.

Constitution of the United States
Because you haven't read it yet.

Gettysburg Address
Because it wastes not a single word.

ACKNOWLEDGMENTS

I believe in giving thanks. Partly, this is because I have so much—and so many—to be thankful for. But the importance of expressing appreciation is also one of the greatest lessons I have learned in my years as a Navy SEAL.

We do not live in the golden age of American manners. Today, decorum is often dismissed as an outmoded formality—unnecessary and insincere. But customs and courtesies still matter in the military. Warriors uniquely understand: These rituals of kindness and respect are a rare and special thing. I have never once felt that a genuine thank-you was wasted on anyone.

The way I see it, if you are in this book, you have already made the supreme cut. Thank you again. You got me here.

To my cherished cousins, uncles, aunts, and grandparents: You have helped to make me who I am. Please accept that the intensity with which I wrote about family in this book applies as well to you. I am sincerely grateful to all of you.

To my team at Brillstein (D Mac), CAA (The Council), Ziffren Brittenham (MJ): You are my new dogs of war, and I like our chances. To Peter and the crew at Foundry: Thank you for your crucial insights in conceiving the project and patiently nurturing it to life. To Elisabeth and everyone at Hyperion: Thank you for your valuable support and advice. Your energy, focus, and resilience keep impressing me—rigid when I pushed back, bending when required: the modern literary equivalent of bamboo. A reader my entire life, I never appreciated the value of a visionary editorial team.

To Ellis: I could not have chosen a partner in the trenches better than you. You truly know how to craft and tell a story. You have the work ethic of any SEAL. You are a teammate and "swim buddy" for life.

To Gilmore, Hewitt, Wallace H., Bob K., Slugger, Desko, Neal, John, and Mary Jo: May I be half the mentor to others that you have been to me.

To Lipton, Chris G, Duane and Kathy, Bock, Brick, Shipley, Long, PK, Michelle, Pauline, Kathy H., Max, and Jacob: I have been blessed with such amazing friends.

To BAJ, Pressfield, Coes, P. McHugh, and Churchill: Across miles and years, you made me love and respect the awesome power of well-crafted words.

To those of you behind the many names that cannot even be hinted at, much less published here: You know who you are and what you've done—and I will never forget, either.

To my fellow SEALs, warriors, and patriots: This country is ours to shape. Together and forever, let us maintain that fight.